The Inside Guide To
The iPad Air 2

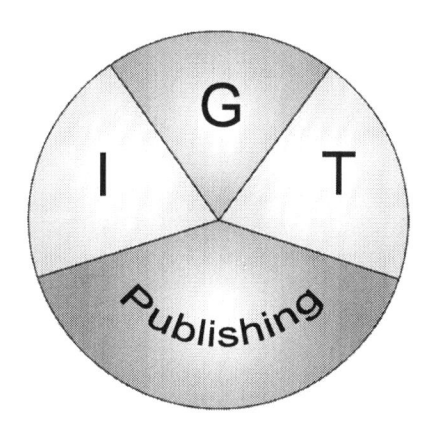

1st Edition

Covers the iPad Air 2 and the
iOS 8 operating system

The Inside Guide To The iPad Air 2

Published by IGT Publishing

Copyright © 2015 IGT Publishing

All rights reserved. No part of this book shall be reproduced, stored in a retrieval system, or transmitted by any means, electronic, mechanical, recording, photocopying, or otherwise, without the prior written permission of the publisher.

Notice of Liability

A great deal of effort has gone into ensuring that the content of this book is both accurate and up to date. However, IGT Publishing and the author will not be held liable for any loss or damage from the use of the information herein.

Trademarks

iPad® is a registered trademark of Apple Computer, Inc. All other trademarks are acknowledged as belonging to their respective companies.

ISBN-13: 978-0993266140
ISBN-10: 0993266142

Contents

Chapter 1 – Controlling Your iPad

Introduction	8
Controls	9
On/Off Switch	9
Wake/Sleep Switch	10
Volume Controls	10
Screen Rotation Lock	11
Home Button	12
Hardware Features	13
The iOS 8 Operating System	14

Chapter 2 – iPad Elements & Features

The Home Screen	16
The Touchscreen	18
Multitasking Interface	19
The Control Centre	20
Notifications & Notification Centre	22
The Lock Screen	25
Locking Your iPad	26
Spotlight Search	27
Siri	28
The Keyboard	29
Working With Text	33

Chapter 3 – Setting Up Your iPad

Setup Wizard	36
Name Your iPad	38
Screen Brightness	38
Wallpaper	39
Date & Time	41
Sounds	42
Privacy	43
Accessibility	44

Chapter 4 – Apps

What is an App?	48
Pre-installed Apps	48
The App Store	51
Browsing the App Store	51
Reviewing & Installing Apps	52
Updating Your Apps	54
Managing Your Apps	55
App Folders	55
Deleting Apps	56
Reinstalling Apps	57

Chapter 5 – Networks

Connections Overview	60
Set Up a Wi-Fi Connection	61
Set Up a Tethered Wi-Fi Connection	63
Turn Off Wi-Fi	64
Set Up a Cellular Connection	65
Wi-Fi or Cellular?	66
Managing a Cellular Connection	67
Turn Off a Cellular Connection	68
Turn Off Data Roaming	68
Bluetooth Connections	69

Chapter 6 – The Internet

Safari Web Browser	72
Opening a Web Page	73
Searching with Safari	74
Viewing & Navigating Web Pages	76
Browsing with Tabs	77
Viewing Articles with Safari Reader	79
Bookmarks & Favourites	80
Reading Lists	82
Private Browsing	83
AutoFill	84
Privacy & Security on the Internet	85
Alternative Browser Apps	86

Chapter 7 – Email

Email Accounts	88
Email Services & Protocols	88
Setting Up an Email Account	89
Syncing Email Accounts	90
Managing Email Accounts	91
Receiving Email	94
Sending Email	97
Sending Images	98
Sending Links & Attachments	99
Managing Email	101
VIPs	101
Thread Organisation	102
Emailing with Siri	103
Email Apps	104

Chapter 8 – Organisation

Creating & Editing Contacts	106
Finding & Using Contacts	108

Contacts App Settings	109
Syncing Contacts	110
Using Contacts with Siri	111
The Calendar App	112
Adding Events to a Calendar	114
Working with Multiple Calendars	115
Adding an Alert to an Event	117
The Reminders App	118
Hiding & Deleting Reminders	119
Working with Lists	120
The Notes App	121
Using Maps	123

Chapter 9 – Pictures

The iPad's Cameras	126
Taking Pictures	127
Viewing Your Pictures	129
Creating Photo Albums	131
Uploading Pictures to the iPad	132
Moving Pictures	135
Deleting Pictures	136
Sharing Pictures	137
Editing Pictures	139
Printing Pictures & Documents	141
Adding Pictures to Your Contacts	142

Chapter 10 – Video

The iPad's Video Cameras	144
Recording Video	145
Locating Your Videos	145
Playing Back Your Videos	146
Editing Video	147
Uploading Home Videos	148
Uploading Films & TV Programs	150
Video Storage Space	152
Uploading Video to Facebook	153
FaceTime Video Calls	154
Play iPad Video on a TV	155
Mirror the iPad's Screen on a TV	156

Chapter 11 – Audio

Getting Music on to the iPad	158
Playing Music	160
Playlists	161
Creating a Standard Playlist in iTunes	161
Creating a Smart Playlist in iTunes	162
Creating a Genius Playlist in iTunes	164
Using Playlists	165

Creating Playlists on the iPad ... 166
Audio Settings ... 169
Controlling Your Music with Siri ... 170

Chapter 12 – Reading With The iPad

Newspapers & Magazines ... 172
Books ... 174
Finding Books ... 176
Previewing & Downloading Books ... 177
Syncing Books ... 178
Controlling Books ... 179
Working with Text ... 180
Listen to the iPad ... 182

Chapter 13 – iCloud & Related Services

What is Cloud Computing? ... 184
iCloud Automatic Data Synchronisation ... 185
iCloud Drive ... 186
Family Sharing ... 187
iTunes Match ... 191
iCloud Keychain ... 192
iCloud Photo Sharing ... 193
iCloud Photo Library ... 194

Chapter 14 – Security

Touch ID & Passcode ... 196
Content Restriction ... 198
Backing Up Your iPad ... 199
Restoring Your iPad ... 200
Locating & Protecting a Lost iPad ... 201

Chapter 15 – Troubleshooting & Maintenance

Troubleshooting Techniques ... 204
Troubleshooting Ancillary Devices ... 206
Extending Battery Life ... 207
Updating iOS 8 ... 208
Wi-Fi Connection Issues ... 209
Managing Storage Space ... 210

Index

CHAPTER 1

Controlling Your iPad

One of the features of Apple products in general is the minimalist styling employed. The result is that their devices, of which the iPad is a classic example, have a sleek, streamlined appearance due to the sparse and unobtrusive controls.

In this opening chapter, we take a look at these controls and the hardware supplied with the device.

We also provide an overview of the device's operating system – iOS 8. This is, in no small part, one of the main reasons for the success of the iPad.

Introduction 8

Controls 9

On/Off Switch 9

Wake/Sleep Switch 10

Volume Controls 10

Screen Rotation Lock 11

Home Button 12

Hardware Features 13

The iOS 8 Operating System 14

Introduction

At its top-level, the iPad Air 2 is a relatively simple device and is thus very easy to get up-and-running.

The setup wizard that is initiated when you first switch on the device walks you through the steps needed to establish an Internet connection, send and receive email, and create an Apple ID (required for buying and downloading apps from the App Store).

For many users, these are the most important of the iPad's functions and, having set them up, they will have no need or desire to dig down into the device's settings. Others though, will want to see everything their iPad has to offer and what can be done with it.

Then there is the older generation, many of whom know little about tablets and computers because the technology involved didn't even exist in their youth. They find much of the terminology employed baffling, and thus off-putting, which is a shame as tablets are actually well suited to many of the issues that typically affect the senior citizen.

This book is intended for all these users. Accordingly, it is written in a simple and straightforward style with obscure terminology, or computer-speak, kept to the minimum.

However, while we may have kept it simple, the book is in no way superficial. All the iPad's important features and functions are covered with explanations and descriptions that are clear, concise and fully detailed.

Accordingly, there should be something here for everyone.

Controls

Your iPad initiation begins with the power button. Situated at the top-right of the device, this control actually serves two functions:

- On/Off switch
- Wake/Sleep switch

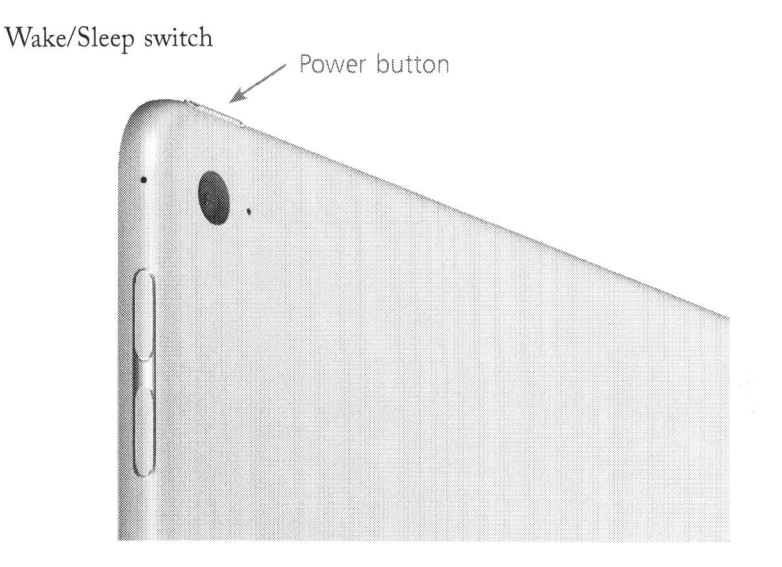

Power button

On/Off Switch

To switch your iPad on, press the button and hold it down until you see a white screen with the Apple logo. Release the button and wait for the Home screen to appear. When it does, your iPad is ready to use.

To switch your iPad off, press and hold the button down until you see the 'slide to power off' slider.

Place a finger on the slider and move it all the way to the right. A few seconds later the iPad will shut down. If you change your mind about switching off just press the Cancel button at the bottom of the screen.

Typically, you'll want to switch the device off to conserve battery power or when it won't be in use for a while. Usually though, it's left on standby.

cont'd

Wake/Sleep Switch

When the iPad is in use, it can be switched to Sleep mode (also known as Standby mode) by pressing the power button once. This cuts the power to the touchscreen thus turning it off (you'll see it go black). As a result, the power used by the device drops considerably.

Note that any apps that are running when the device is put to sleep continue to run. For example, if your email app is running, the device will still receive incoming emails. Sleep mode also prevents accidental inputs (taps) from inadvertently triggering functions on the device. This also helps to reduce power consumption.

Generally speaking then, putting your iPad to sleep whenever it is not in use is the way to go. There is, however, one exception to this rule and that is when you are abroad. Be aware that even in Sleep mode, the iPad will continually attempt to connect to any available network. If you aren't using a suitable international data plan, this can result in huge data roaming charges.

Therefore, when overseas, either make sure you have disabled 'Cellular Data' and 'Data Roaming', or power the iPad off completely when not in use. Sleep mode is not a good option in this situation.

Volume Controls

To control the volume on your iPad, the device provides the two controls shown below:

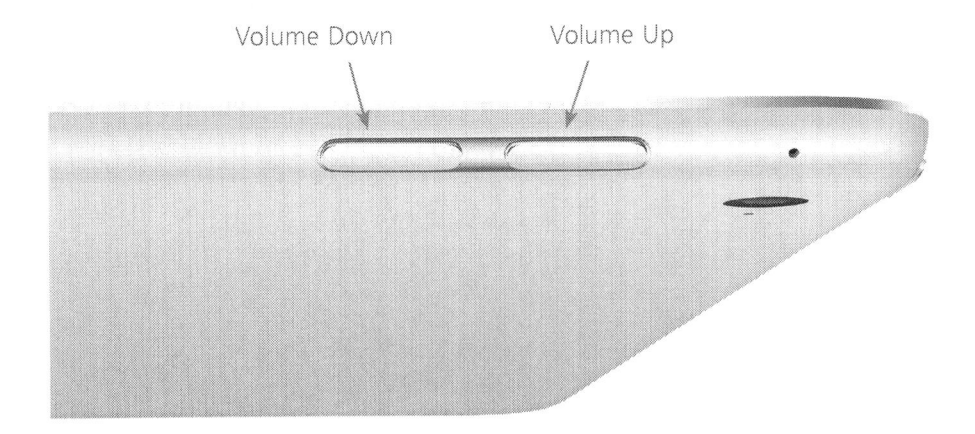

Press either of the switches and you'll see a speaker icon (shown overleaf) appear on the screen with a volume level bar at the bottom.

- Press the Volume Up switch repeatedly to increase the volume in steps

cont'd

- Hold the Volume Up switch down for maximum volume

- Press the Volume Down switch repeatedly to decrease the volume in steps

- Hold the Volume Down switch down to mute the iPad

Screen Rotation Lock

With the iPad Air 2's predecessor, the iPad Air, just above the volume controls was a small switch known as the Side switch. The purpose of this switch was to lock the iPad in either Portrait or Landscape mode to prevent it changing when the orientation of the device was altered.

With the iPad Air 2, the switch has been removed and the function is now carried out with the Control Centre (see pages 20-21) as we explain below:

1. Hold the iPad in the desired orientation – Portrait or Landscape

2. Swipe up from the bottom of the screen to open the Control Center

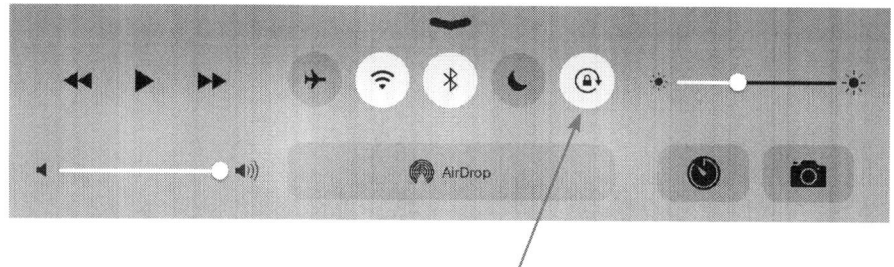

3. Tap the Orientation button to lock the iPad in the required orientation mode

Having the screen orientation locked can be useful in certain situations. Of course, there are times, such as when browsing the Internet, that having it off is also desirable. Whichever, your iPad lets you choose for yourself.

cont'd

Home Button

Now we come to one of the main features of your iPad – the Home button. This is located at the front of the device at the bottom.

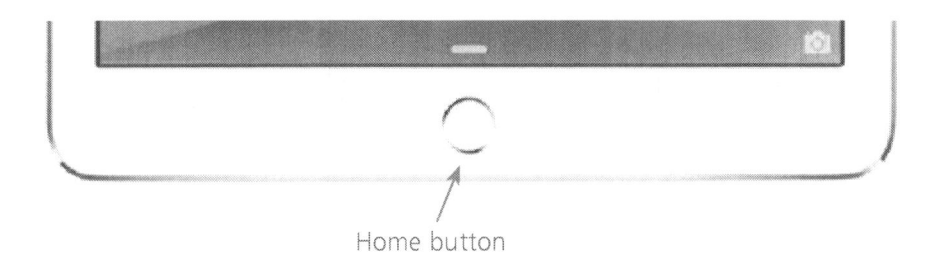

Home button

The control you'll probably use the most, the Home button provides a number of functions:

- Built-in to the button is a biometric fingerprint scanner. This recognizes your fingerprint and will automatically unlock the iPad without the need for a passcode to be entered. It can also be used to authorise purchases from the iTunes Store, the App Store, and the iBooks Store

- When your iPad is in Standby mode, pressing the Home button wakes the device and displays the Lock screen

- Wherever you are in the iPad, or whatever you are doing, pressing the Home button immediately takes you to the Home screen

- If you have several home screens and are not on the main one, you will be switched to it

- Pressing and holding the Home button down activates the iPad's voice recognition feature, Siri (assuming it has been enabled). Siri allows you to control many of the iPad's functions with voice commands. We'll see some examples of this later in the book

- If you have the touchscreen turned off while the Music app is running, pressing the Home button will bring up the music controls allowing you to pause, play, adjust the volume, etc. You won't be able to select which tracks to play in this view though

- Double-pressing the Home button gives you access to the iPad's multitasking interface (also known as the Fast App switcher). This shows all apps that are open and allows you to quickly switch between them. It also lets you shut the apps down by swiping upwards on the app in question. We'll see more on this feature later on

Hardware Features

So far we've covered your iPad's physical controls. Let's see what other hardware features it offers.

Looking at the bottom edge of the device, you'll see three things:

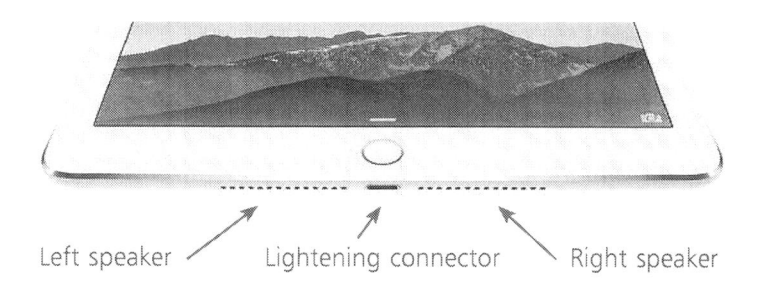

Left speaker / Lightening connector / Right speaker

At the left and right are two loudspeakers that give you a stereo effect as long as the device is held in Portrait mode.

Between the loudspeakers is a Lightning connector that you will use to charge the iPad, and also to connect it to a computer or laptop in order to use Apple's iTunes software.

Turn your attention to the top-rear of your iPad and you'll see a headphone jack, dual microphones, and a camera lens.

Microphones   Headphone jack

Camera

The 3.5mm headphone jack is where you connect a set of headphones to listen to the audio output of your iPad. Note that headphones are not supplied with the device.

The dual microphones enable your iPad to capture clear sound and help to reduce background noise during FaceTime calls.

At the top-right is the main camera – this is an 8 megapixel snapper that produces good quality pictures. At the front top-centre of the iPad is another camera – this is a lower quality 1.2 megapixel affair that is intended for making FaceTime video calls.

The iOS 8 Operating System

iOS is the name given to the operating system used on the various mobile Apple devices – the iPad, iPad Mini, iPhone and the iPod Touch. 8.3 is currently the latest version of iOS and is the one covered in this book. Note that Apple update iOS on a continuous basis so by the time you read this, it may well be different.

One of the best things about iOS is its security. The chances of getting a virus or malware when using an Apple device are much less than with devices that run Google's Android or Microsoft's Windows. Apple's 'walled garden' App Store – where applications are fully vetted before being made available to customers – has prevented widespread infection of iOS devices.

Another of its great features is the way it links, or synchronises, with other Apple devices. iOS 8 and OS X Yosemite (the latest operating system used on Apple Macs) are effectively joined at the hip with the Handoff feature that lets you pick up where you left off between devices.

For example, you can start a project or email message on an iPad or iPhone and then finish the task on a Mac. Similarly, with iCloud Drive you can store your PDFs, presentations, spreadsheets, images and any other kind of document in iCloud and access them from your iPhone, iPad, iPod Touch, Mac or PC.

iOS 8 features a new Photos app that offers an improved search function, powerful editing tools and smart albums that make organising your photos a snap. Apple's iCloud lets you view your pictures on other iOS devices.

Another greatly improved feature in iOS 8 is messaging. You can easily capture any sound, or record a message, and then send it to a friend or FaceBook. You can share video in the same way. Group conversations can be held and you can share your location with people in the conversation.

A family-friendly feature new in iOS 8 is Family Sharing. It enables up to six people to share data, as well as purchases, from the iTunes Store, the iBooks Store, and the App Store. For example, if you buy an app and download it to your iPad, family members will also be able to download the app to their devices without having to pay, i.e. the app is shared. Once Family Sharing is set up, family members get immediate access to each other's music, films, TV programmes, books and apps.

Other improvements in iOS 8 include a time-lapse option in the Camera app, predictive text when using the keyboard, a tab view in the Safari web browser, and interactive notifications.

The Spotlight search function now gives you suggestions from Wikipedia, places nearby, trending news and more. It's also smart enough to recognise context and location, and thus offer you the most relevant information.

CHAPTER 2

iPad Elements & Features

In Chapter Two, we take a look at the main elements of your iPad. These include the various screens, all of which provide a specific function plus shortcuts to other functions.

The virtual keyboard is an essential part of the iPad and we show you how to get the best out of it. This includes some useful tips and tricks that will have you typing like a pro in no time.

We also take a look at some important features, such as how to secure your iPad with Apple's Touch ID security feature, and the iPad's voice recognition system, Siri – this is a much under-used part of iOS 8.

The Home Screen 16

The Touchscreen 18

Multitasking Interface 19

The Control Centre 20

Notifications & Notification Centre 22

The Lock Screen 25

Locking Your iPad 26

Spotlight Search 27

Siri 28

The Keyboard 29

Working with Text 33

The Home Screen

Once you have completed the setup wizard (see Chapter 3), you will be taken to the Home screen as shown below. This has three sections:

- Status bar
- Main screen
- Dock bar

cont'd

The Status Bar
Situated right at the top of the screen is a very narrow bar, which is called the Status Bar. The bar itself is transparent but the information it displays is visible in white text and includes the following:

- **Airplane mode** – an airplane icon appears at the far-left of the Status bar when Airplane mode is selected

- **Network connection** – displayed at the far-left, this icon indicates that you're connected to a network – Wi-Fi for example

- **Activity** – this icon appears when a task is in progress

- **Time** – the current time is displayed right in the middle of the Status bar

- **Rotation lock** – when present, this indicates that the screen orientation is locked

- **Battery** – the battery icon shows the level of charge in the battery. You also see it in figures, e.g. 40%

The above are just some of the features and functions that use the Status bar.

The Main Screen
The main part of the screen is reserved for the iPad's apps and has room for 20. If the device has more than 20 installed apps, the extra ones are placed on a second home screen. When this screen is fully populated as well, a third home screen is created and so on.

Each home screen is represented by a small white dot above the middle of the Dock bar. To navigate between the screens, just swipe left and right. Pressing the Home button takes you to the first home screen.

The Dock Bar
The Dock bar is a section of the screen reserved for the user's favourite apps. It is present at the bottom of all the iPad's home screens and so the favourite apps are always instantly accessible.

By default, the Dock bar is populated with four apps but you can add two more to make a total of six. You can also replace the default apps with apps of your own choice as we'll see later.

Screen Orientation
You can view the Home screen in either Portrait or Landscape mode – simply rotate the iPad to switch between the two. If you want to use one mode permanently, you can set this up as we explain on page 11.

The Touchscreen

You should by now be familiar with the physical aspects of your iPad. So it's time to see what goes on inside the device and, to do this, you need to know how to operate the touchscreen.

This is a quite amazing part of the iPad and it is controlled by nothing more than your finger or, in some cases, fingers.

You can create folders, scroll through lists, zoom in and zoom out, drag and drop items, and type messages. No external hardware is required – just the following finger movements, or gestures as they are known:

- **Single-tap** – this is the one you'll use most and it opens apps, selects items in lists, opens text boxes, follows online links, activates options and enters text on the keyboard

- **Double-tap** – in web pages a double-tap zooms in – double-tapping again zooms back out. This also works with pictures

- **Two-finger tap** – when in a maps app, this gesture zooms out

- **Swipe** – dragging a finger across the screen, or up and down the screen, in a swiping motion enables you to scroll across and down the screen, scroll through lists, and drag items to different positions

- **Flick** – a quick flick on the screen will scroll faster than a swipe. The faster the flick, the faster the movement

- **Spread and pinch** – touching the screen with two fingers and spreading them apart will zoom in on a screen, while pinching them together will zoom out

- **Press and hold** – this gesture is used in apps where text can be selected, such as a web page or email. Press and hold on a word and you will bring up editing options such as Copy, Select All, etc. You can also get dictionary definitions in this way

- **Tap at the top of the screen** – tapping once at the top of the screen will quickly take you to the top of a web page, list or email message

- **Four-finger swipe** – swiping upwards with four fingers opens the multitasking interface

- **Press and drag** – press on any clear part of the screen and drag downwards to open your iPad's Spotlight search feature

Multitasking Interface

The iPad's multitasking interface allows you to do three things:

The first is to close apps completely as opposed to leaving them in a state of suspension. Open the interface by double-pressing the Home button (or using the four-finger swipe) and, in the centre of the screen, you'll see images of all the apps open on the iPad – you may need to scroll to the right to see them all. Below, you'll see smaller images of the apps.

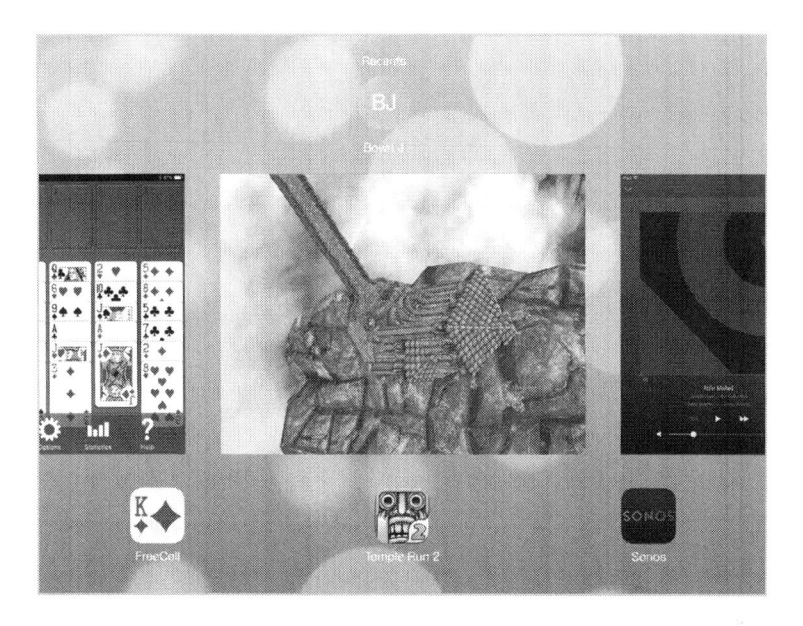

Each app can be closed by swiping the large image upwards. It will disappear from view to be replaced by the next open app.

The second is that it enables you to easily view all the open apps on the iPad and to quickly switch between them. Just tap on an app and it will open instantly. Because these apps are running, their current states, including data, are saved in the iPad's memory. So if a task you are working on requires the simultaneous use of two or more apps, you can go from one to the other without losing any of your work.

The third is to provide quick access to your most commonly used contacts. At the top of the screen, you'll see a scrolling horizontal list of the people you contact the most. This is great for quickly sending messages and starting FaceTime chats with the most important people in your life. No more digging through your contacts list anymore. Note that if you have associated an image with a contact, you will see that image rather than the contact's initial.

Just tap a contact to initiate a text message or FaceTime call.

The Control Centre

The iPad's Control Centre is a quickly accessible panel that gives the user access to a number of frequently used functions.

To open it, place your finger on the bottom edge of the screen and flick upwards – the panel will slide into view. By default, it can be opened from the Lock screen, the Home screen and from within open apps.

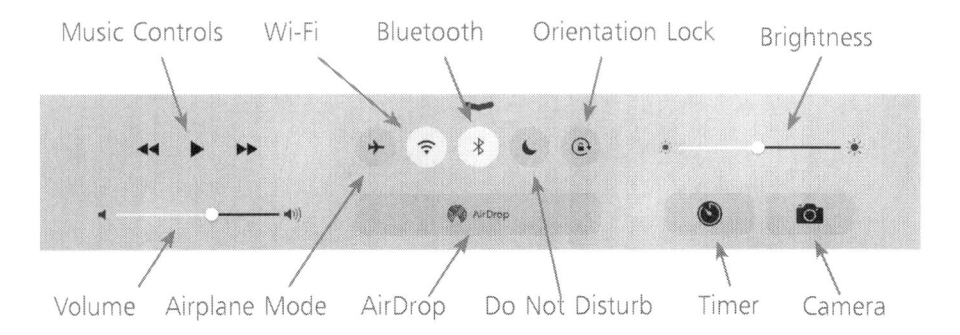

Music Controls   Wi-Fi   Bluetooth   Orientation Lock   Brightness

Volume   Airplane Mode   AirDrop   Do Not Disturb   Timer   Camera

Available controls include AirDrop file-sharing settings, screen brightness, the Camera app, the timer, system volume, and music playback. You can also enable and disable Airplane mode, Wi-Fi, Bluetooth, Do Not Disturb, Screen Orientation Lock and system mute in the Control Centre.

Some of these are self-explanatory. Others that may not be, however, are:

AirDrop – AirDrop is a method of transferring data wirelessly from one iOS device to another. It allows users to easily share pictures, video and other supported data with anyone nearby who is using a supported iOS device or Mac computer.

There are no restrictions on the size of the documents that AirDrop will transfer. AirDrop devices need to be within 10 metres of each other for the system to work. Currently, few applications support this feature.

Bluetooth – Bluetooth is a wireless network technology that creates short-range connections between suitably equipped devices at distances up to about 10 metres. A typical use is listening to music on your iPad with a set of Bluetooth wireless headphones. Note that on the iPad, Bluetooth is also required for the AirDrop feature to work.

Wi-Fi – Wi-Fi is another wireless technology that allows electronic devices to exchange data, or connect to the Internet, without the need for a physical connection. The vast majority of current computing devices, including personal computers, video-game consoles, smartphones, digital cameras, tablets, and digital audio players are equipped with Wi-Fi technology.

cont'd

Wi-Fi enables these devices to connect to a network resource such as the Internet, via a wireless network access point known as a hotspot. Typically, it has a range of about 150 feet indoors and about 300 feet outdoors.

Hotspot coverage can comprise an area as small as a single room (walls block Wi-Fi signals) or many square miles (achieved by using multiple overlapping access points).

Orientation Lock – we mentioned on page 17 that the iPad can be held in either Landscape or Portrait mode. By default, each time you swivel the device it will change from one to the other. If you would rather keep it in one particular mode, you can use this control to set it quickly.

Airplane Mode – Airplane mode disables the wireless features of your iPad in order to comply with airline regulations. When it is activated, the following wireless connections and services are turned off:

- Cellular (voice and data)
- Wi-Fi
- Bluetooth
- Global Positioning Systems (GPS)
- Location services

Note that if allowed by the aircraft operator, and applicable laws and regulations, you can enable Wi-Fi and Bluetooth while in Airplane mode.

Do Not Disturb – the Do Not Disturb control lets you silence calls, alerts, and notifications. If you open the Settings app and tap 'Do Not Disturb', you'll see various configuration options for this control. These include:

- Automatic scheduling that lets you set a specific period for which the feature will be active

- The ability to accept calls from certain people while the feature is on. Options are: Everyone, No One, or All Contacts

- The ability to accept a second FaceTime call from the same person within three minutes of the first. So if someone needs to talk to you urgently, a second call within three minutes will be accepted

- You can set Do Not Disturb to be always active or only active when the iPad is locked

Notifications & Notification Centre

Notifications
Notifications is an iOS feature that enables apps to notify you of new messages or events without you having to actually open the app – email messages being a typical example.

When a notification is generated, it will be presented on the Lock screen and also in the Notification Centre.

Notifications come in four types:

- **Sound** – a sound effect that indicates an event has occurred
- **Alert** – a message that pops up on the screen. This has to be dismissed with a tap before you can resume what you were doing
- **Banner** – a message that appears at the top of the screen and disappears automatically after a few seconds
- **Badge** – a red icon at the top-right corner of an app icon. It displays a number that can indicate various things. For example, the number of unread emails in the Mail app

Notification Centre
The iPad's Notification Centre is designed to help you make the most of the Notifications feature. It collects all the alerts and banners as they come in and displays them in one easily accessible location.

To open the Notification Centre, just swipe down from the top edge of the screen. By default, it will show you the Today view, which displays the date, a weather summary, events from the Calendar app, Reminder items, and a summary of the schedule for the following day.

cont'd

These notifications are all provided by widgets – tiny applications that carry out a specific action, and are often part of a larger application. Typical examples of widgets are weather apps and calculators.

If you want widgets other than the default ones provided with your iPad, you have to go to the App Store to get them. Note that you can't actually get widgets as such – you have to download an app that offers a widget function. A good example is the Kindle app – this offers a widget that shows the books you are currently reading, and provides a link that allows you to open them on the iPad at the current page.

Below, we see an example showing a calculator widget (PCalc Lite) that lets you calculate directly from the Notification screen:

If you scroll down to the end of the screen, you will see an Edit button (you won't see this if you open the Notification Centre from the Lock screen. Also, you must be in the Today view). Tap the button to open a screen that shows all the widgets on your iPad, both active and inactive.

Next to each widget is a red icon (active widgets) or a green icon (inactive widgets). Tap these icons to activate or deactivate the widgets. On the right of the active widgets is an icon that you can use to rearrange the order in which they are displayed on the Notification screen.

When finished, tap Done at the top-right of the screen.

cont'd

The Notification Centre also offers a second view. This is called Notifications and can be opened from the tab bar at the top of the screen. It shows notifications from other apps as we see in the image below:

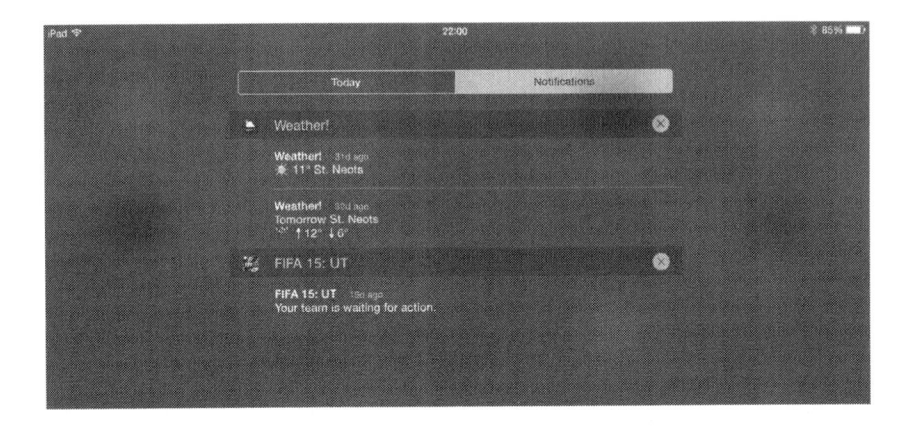

To configure which apps will show notifications on this screen, and how many, open the Settings app and tap Notifications. Here, you will see two sections, Include and Do Not Include, which together list all the notification-friendly apps on your iPad. The apps in the Include section all show notifications while those in the Do Not Include section don't.

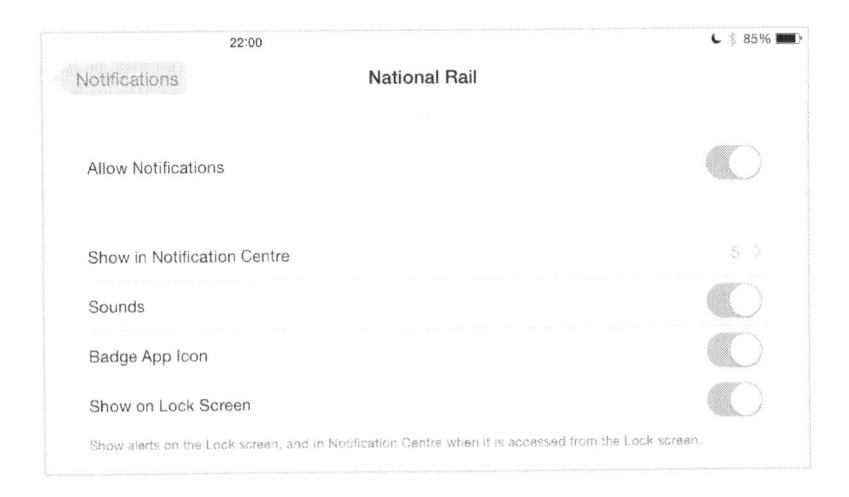

To change which apps show notifications, tap the required app (it doesn't matter which section it is in) and toggle the 'Allow Notifications' setting to on or off. You can also tap the 'Show in Notification Centre' setting and specify how many items will be shown, plus the notification's style, associated sounds, and more.

The Lock Screen

When you switch on your iPad, or the device is inactive for five minutes, it defaults to a Lock screen. This is a power-saving feature designed to save the battery, and is roughly equivalent to the Sleep option on computers. To get into the iPad, slide the button at the bottom.

You can change the default settings for the Lock screen by opening the Settings app and going to General > Auto-Lock.

Here, you will be able to specify the time before auto-lock kicks in – 2, 5, 10, or 15 minutes. You can also choose Never, which disables the Lock screen completely.

Note that you can activate the Lock screen at any time by clicking the On/Off button once.

Also, do not be mislead by the name 'Lock screen' – it does not prevent unauthorised access to your iPad. For this you need to use Touch ID or a passcode as we see on the next page.

Locking Your iPad

If you need to restrict access to your iPad for whatever reason, you have two options:

Touch ID
Introduced with the iPad Air 2, Touch ID employs a biometric fingerprint scanner that is built-in to the Home button. This takes a picture of your fingerprint when you touch the button, which is then analysed. If it matches the fingerprint taken when Touch ID was set up, the iPad is unlocked.

The feature also requires a four digit passcode to be specified during the setup procedure. This is used for backup purposes should Touch ID fail to open the iPad or need to be reconfigured.

The Touch ID setup procedure is part of the initial iPad setup wizard as we mention on pages 36-37. However, you can set it up at any time by following the instructions on page 196.

Passcode
If you don't want to use Touch ID, you can instead just use a four digit passcode to secure your iPad. To set this up:

1. Tap the Settings app on the Home screen
2. On the right-hand side, tap Passcode
3. Tap 'Turn Passcode On'
4. Enter a passcode and then tap Next
5. Re-enter the passcode and then tap Done

From this point on, the 'Slide to unlock' button at the bottom of the Lock screen will open a keypad – tap in the passcode and your iPad will be unlocked.

Spotlight Search

One of the best things about computers in general is that the search facilities provided with these devices make it so easy to locate your data.

Your iPad's Spotlight Search facility is no exception and, with it, you can find literally everything that is on the device. Whether you are looking for someone's contact information, a film, a song, an event, or a book, just type in the name and everything with that word in it will appear in the search results.

To open Spotlight Search, place your finger near the middle of the Home screen anywhere along the horizontal axis and drag downwards.

Enter your search term in the box at the top and a list of results will automatically appear – you may need to scroll down to see them all (if the keyboard is in the way, tap the Keyboard options key at the bottom-right of the keyboard – see page 29). Right at the bottom, you will see an option to also search Wikipedia.

Tap an item in the list to open it. Note that Spotlight Search can also be used to find and open apps.

Configuration options can be found by going to the Settings app > General > Spotlight Search. Here, you can choose which apps and related content are searched, and also change the search order.

Siri

What is Siri
Siri is a built-in, voice-controlled personal assistant for the iPad. It provides you with a way of interacting with your device that doesn't involve having to tap away at the touchscreen. Instead, you speak to Siri and Siri speaks back to you.

What Can Siri Do?
You can ask Siri questions and it will come up with an answer, or issue commands for it to execute on your behalf.

Siri can send messages and emails you speak into the microphone and it can read incoming messages out to you when they arrive. It can give you directions. It can listen to your questions and search not just your iPad for the answer but also the Internet.

It can set alarms and reminders, not to mention calendar events. Siri will play your music and video, and let you dictate text into documents or, indeed, any text input field.

Activating Siri
The default way to start Siri is to press and hold the Home button (if you are using a headset with a microphone button, press and hold the button). You will then see a message that says 'What can I help you with?' Wait for the next screen and you'll see a microphone at the bottom. Tap the microphone and then speak your question or command – Siri will attempt to do your bidding.

However, there is another way to activate Siri. Open the Settings app and go to General > Siri. Toggle the on/off button next to 'Allow Hey, Siri' to the On position. Now you can activate Siri from any screen by simply saying 'Hey Siri'. The only proviso to this is that the iPad must be connected to a power source – if it is not, Hey Siri will not work.

The reason for this is that the feature requires the device to be constantly listening for your voice commands, which means it would be constantly drawing power from the battery. Limiting 'Hey, Siri…' to when the iPad is receiving power means the battery won't be affected.

While in Siri's settings, you can disable the feature if you want to, set the language Siri uses, and set the gender (male or female).

You can also specify your personal details so Siri knows who you are, what your telephone numbers are, and where you are located. This lets you say things like 'Call home' or 'Give me directions to work'. Do it by tapping My Info and selecting your own contact from the All Contacts list.

The Keyboard

When it comes to entering text into your iPad you have two ways to go: The first is to use the keyboard, and the second is to dictate using Siri.

We'll take a look at the keyboard method here. While no one needs telling how to use a keyboard these days, there are quite a few tips and tricks associated with the iPad's keyboard. These can save you a lot of time and effort.

Keyboard Basics
The first thing though, is how do you access the keyboard? This is simple – all you have to do is open an app that uses text, tap in the text area and the keyboard will slide up from the bottom of the screen. For example, a web page search box or an email message window.

The iPad's keyboard is contextual – it presents keys that are related to the task in hand. For example, you will see different keys when typing an email than when typing numbers or a text message.

For those of you not familiar with keyboards, it may be helpful to highlight certain of the keys at this point.

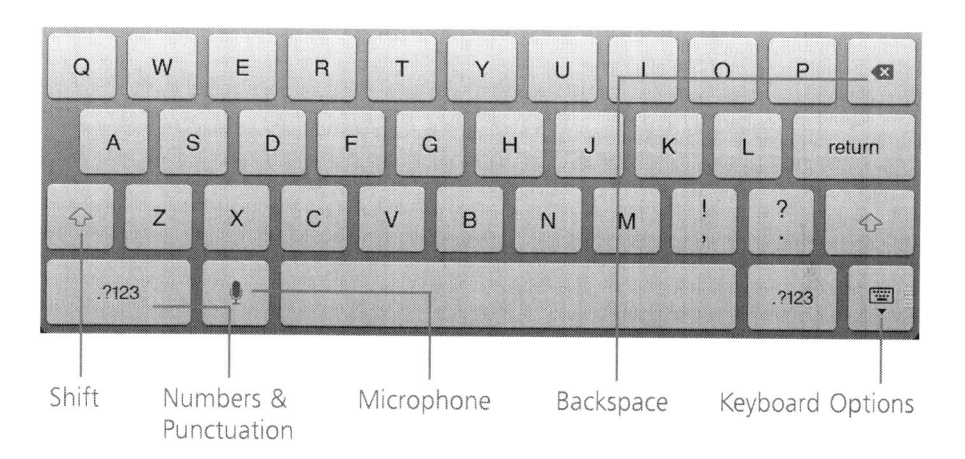

[Keyboard diagram with labels: Shift, Numbers & Punctuation, Microphone, Backspace, Keyboard Options]

Shift key – press this key to shift between upper-case and lower-case. When you have typed the upper-case character, the keyboard reverts to lower-case

Numbers & Punctuation – this key switches from letters, to numbers and punctuation marks

Microphone – if you want to use the iPad's dictation feature, then pressing this key will activate it

cont'd

Backspace key – pressing this key deletes characters to the left of the cursor. Three modes are available:

1. Press once to delete a single character
2. Press and hold down to delete continuously
3. Press and hold down for four seconds. After four seconds entire words are deleted

Return key – this key moves the cursor to the next line

Keyboard options – tap to remove the keyboard from the screen. If you press and hold, you get two options – Undock and Split. The former releases the keyboard from the bottom and moves it to the centre of the screen where, for some people, it can be easier to use.

It makes it easier to type when in Portrait mode as well.

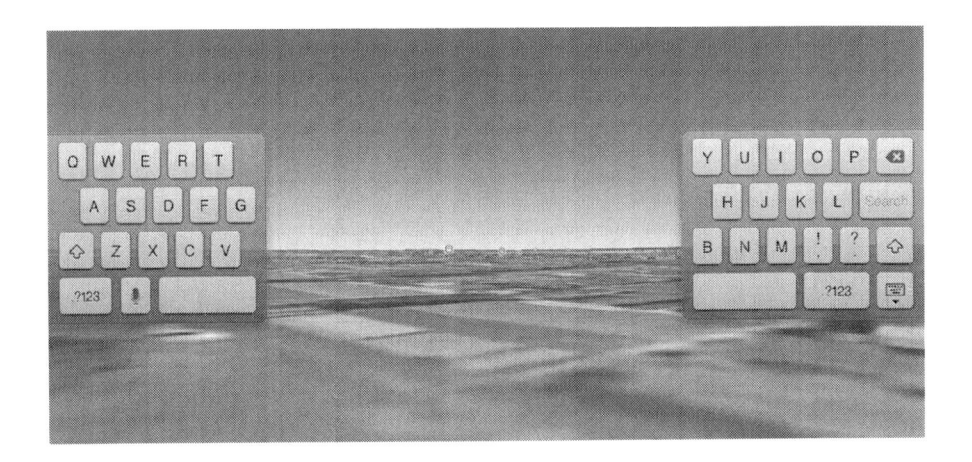

iPad keyboard undocked and split

The latter splits the keyboard into two sections – one on the left and one on the right. Again, many people find this mode easier to use, particularly those who type with their thumbs.

To revert to normal, press and hold the Keyboard options key again and select 'Dock and Merge'. If you select Merge, the keyboard becomes one again but remains in the centre of the screen

cont'd

Keyboard Tricks

There are a number of tricks and shortcuts that can be used with the iPad keyboard. For people who do serious amounts of text entry, these can be extremely useful:

- **Quickly redo incorrect keystrokes** – when you tap a key nothing is entered until your finger leaves the screen. So if you hit the wrong key, just keep your finger on the screen and slide it across to the correct one

- **New sentence quick start** – double-tapping the space bar inserts a period and begins a new sentence. If it doesn't work, check the feature is enabled in Settings > General > Keyboard

- **Quickly insert numbers & punctuation** – to insert numbers and punctuation, you press the .?123 key, press the required character and then tap the ABC key to revert to the letters keyboard

  A quicker way is to press the .?123 key but instead of releasing it and going to the required character, keep your finger on the screen and slide it to the key you want. When it has been selected, release the key and the keyboard will automatically revert to letters

- **More quick punctuation** – swiping up on the Comma key will insert an apostrophe; swiping up on the Period key inserts a quotation mark

- **Quick capital letters** – rather than engage the Shift key every time you need to type a capital letter, just press and hold the Shift key and drag your finger to the letter you want to capitalise

- **Related characters** – pressing and holding a character will, in many cases, open a list of related characters above the key. For example, accented versions of letter keys, and other currencies from the currency key

- **Phrase shortcuts** – if you type a certain phrase or sentence frequently, you can set a shortcut for it which, when typed, automatically expands to the full phrase

  To set this up, go to Settings > General > Keyboard. Under Shortcuts, tap 'Add New Shortcut' and then enter your phrase and associated shortcut. A common use for this is to quickly enter a long email address

- **Quick spacing** – tap the space bar with three fingers at the same time to get three spaces, with four fingers to get four spaces and with five fingers to get five spaces

cont'd

- **Emoticons** – if you want to insert emoticons in your emails and text messages, press the globe key at the bottom-left of the keyboard next to the left .?123 key. You will see a categorised list of hundreds of icons and emoticons as shown below:

- **Website extensions** – when you are typing a website address in a browser, instead of typing the extension, press and hold the Period key. You will see a list of common extensions such as .com, .co.uk. Just select the one you want

- **Auto features** – by default, the keyboard has a number of automatic features enabled. These include Auto-Capitalisation, Auto-Correction, Check Spelling, Enable Caps Lock, Predictive, Split Keyboard and ".". Shortcut. You can disable these individually by going to the Settings app > General > Keyboard

- **Hide the Keyboard** – when you have finished typing in your text, the keyboard becomes redundant. However, it will still be there and, in some apps, the Mail app for example, it gets in the way. Get rid of it by tapping the Keyboard options key, which you'll see at the bottom-right of the keyboard

- **Dictation** – your iPad's voice recognition feature allows you to enter text by dictation. Press the microphone icon at the bottom-left of the keyboard and speak – you will see the text appear on the screen. Press Done when you are finished

- **Third-party keyboards** – you are not restricted to using the default keyboard – alternatives are available in the App Store. When you have downloaded one, open the Settings app and go to General > Keyboard. Tap 'Keyboards', 'Add New Keyboard' and select your new keyboard from the Third-Party Keyboards section.

  Now open the default keyboard and keep tapping the globe icon at the bottom-left until you see your new keyboard

Working With Text

Editing text on a tablet is never going to be as quick as on a computer or laptop. Both the screen and keyboard are much smaller, plus touchscreen control is not as precise as it is with a mouse or touch pad. Nevertheless, it's surprising just what is possible with the iPad.

Positioning the cursor
Getting the cursor precisely where you want it is an essential part of text editing. One way of doing it is to use the Backspace key to backtrack, which of course deletes everything as it goes along. Fairly obviously, this is a far from ideal way of doing it.

A much better way is to tap and hold on the text to be edited. You will then see the text and the cursor enlarged inside a magnifying glass. By dragging your finger left and right, you will be able to position the cursor exactly where you want it.

Selecting and Copying/Moving Text
Your options here depend on whether the text is editable or non-editable. A web page is a good example of the latter and the only option you will have here is to copy.

To do this, tap and hold the required word. You will then see the word has been highlighted between two blue selection handles. Above this will be a menu offering Copy and Define options. Tap on Copy and then open the app into which you are going to paste the word. Tap once in the text field and you'll see a menu open offering a Paste option. Tap Paste and the word will be pasted into the text field.

Using this method, you can copy and paste single words, whole blocks of text or even an entire page. All you have to do is adjust the selection handles by dragging them up and down, and left and right. Once you have made your selection, click Copy and paste it where you want as described above. Below we see a selected sentence:

> Copy | Define
> Embark on a grand adventure and experience ports of call across Eastern and Western Mediterranean. Should your chosen cruise take you the length of the Adriatic Sea, you'll arrive in Dubrovnik which will delight you with its cafés and flower markets. Alternatively step onto Greek islands, like crescent-shaped Santorini, Rhodes with its stories of Crusader Knights and Mykonos.

In the case of editable text, such as text you've created in a note, email, text message, word processor, etc; the procedure is much the same.

cont'd

Tap and hold anywhere in the text. When you see the magnifying glass, remove your finger and you will see three options appear in the toolbar above the text – Select, Select All, and Paste:

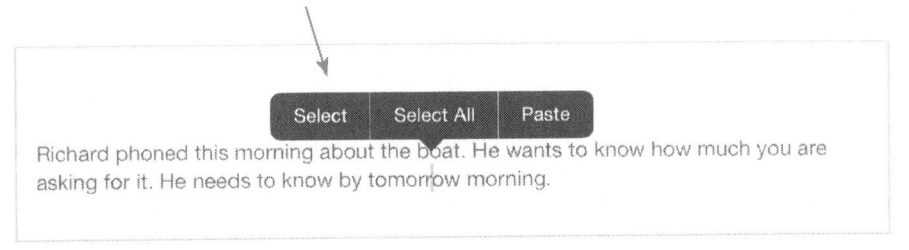

> Select | Select All | Paste
>
> Richard phoned this morning about the boat. He wants to know how much you are asking for it. He needs to know by tomorrow morning.

- **Select** – choose this option if you want to select just some of the text. You will then see the blue selection handles while the toolbar above will now offer different options – Cut, Copy Paste, Replace..., and Define, as we see below:

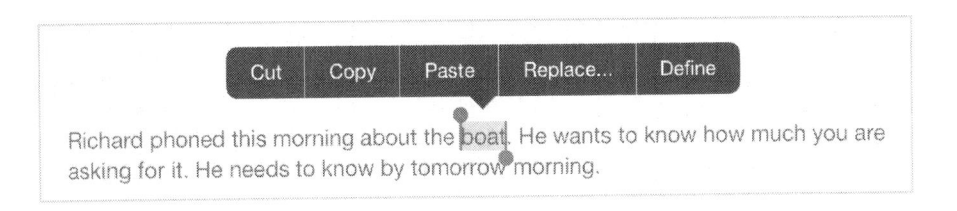

> Cut | Copy | Paste | Replace... | Define
>
> Richard phoned this morning about the boat. He wants to know how much you are asking for it. He needs to know by tomorrow morning.

Choose Cut to remove the text, Copy to copy it, Paste to replace it with text you have copied from elsewhere, Replace to replace it with a suggestion and, if it's a word, Define to see the definition of the word from the built-in dictionary

- **Select All** – tapping Select All will return the same options as above with the exception of Replace

- **Paste** – if you have previously copied some text, clicking Paste will replace the text (boat in the example above) with the copied text

Note that you get different options depending on the app in use – the Mail app is a good example of this. This app also happens to be the only default iPad app that provides text formatting options – these are limited to just Bold, Italics and Underline.

If you want to create formatted documents on the iPad, you need to download a suitable app. One that we can recommend for this purpose is the free Pages app that is available from the App Store.

CHAPTER 3

Setting Up Your iPad

When you first switch on your iPad, you will be presented with a setup wizard that walks you through a series of important configuration settings. We explain what these settings are so that you select the right options.

There are also a number of other settings that you will need to configure in order to set up the iPad to suit your own way of working, needs and personality.

Setup Wizard 36

Name Your iPad 38

Screen Brightness 38

Wallpaper 39

Date & Time 41

Sounds 42

Privacy 43

Accessibility 44

Setup Wizard

When an iPad is run for the first time, it offers a setup wizard designed to help the user get off to a flying start. Whether or not you follow the wizard is entirely up to you – if you wish, you can skip it and configure the device as you go along.

However, as the wizard does deal with some important aspects of the iPad, such as setting up an Apple ID (needed to use the Apps and iTunes Stores), setting up a Wi-Fi connection, iCloud, and Touch ID amongst other things, our recommendation is that you follow the wizard's prompts.

Most, if not all, of them will probably have to be done at some point anyway so it may as well be right at the start.

1. First, you will be prompted to select your country or region

2. Next, you will be asked to specify a Wi-Fi network in order to begin device activation. Wi-Fi is a technology that allows you to wirelessly connect to a local-area network, and will allow you to browse the Internet, connect to the App and iTunes Stores, send and receive email and use many other features of your iPad

3. Once you are connected, you will be asked whether you wish to enable Location Services. This is an iPad feature that allows location-aware apps, such as Maps and the Safari web browser, to use information from cellular, Wi-Fi, and Global Positioning Systems (GPS) networks to determine your location

    A typical example of how location services is used is Yellow Pages apps that use your location to help you find nearby coffee shops, theatres, ATM's, etc. Many of the apps available for the iPad rely on the Location Services feature, so enable it when prompted

4. At the next stage, you will be asked whether you want to set up your iPad as a new device, or restore its content and settings from a backup. You would choose the latter option if you have an older iPad and want to transfer its contents and settings to the new iPad

5. You are going to need an Apple ID, or account. If you already have one, you can associate it with the iPad now by signing in. If you don't have an ID, you are prompted to create one.

    Note that your Apple ID can be used with any other Apple devices you may have, or later acquire. It enables you to use any Apple service, such as the iTunes and App Stores, iCloud, iMessage, FaceTime, GameCenter, and iBooks

cont'd

Creating an Apple ID is very simple; all that's required is your name, date of birth, email address, a password, and a security question and answer

6. Agree to Apple's terms and conditions

7. Next, you are asked whether you wish to use iCloud. This is a service from Apple that gives you a free 5 GB of online storage space that you can use to keep your devices synchronised.

   Synchronisation is the transfer of data, such as music, pictures and documents, between your Apple devices, and iCloud does it behind the scenes for you automatically

   iCloud can also automatically backup your iPad and restore that backup should it ever be necessary to do so. Plus, of course, it can be used purely for data storage purposes

   So if you envisage ever needing to transfer data between your iPad and another Apple device, create a backup, or simply store stuff online, setting up an iCloud account is a must. We look at the subject of iCloud in more detail in Chapter 12

8. You are now offered the option to set up Apple's fingerprint recognition feature, Touch ID. This allows you to use your finger rather than having to enter passwords and passcodes

9. If you choose not to set up Touch ID, you will be asked whether you wish to set up a passcode to secure your iPad. Just enter a four digit code when prompted, and henceforth you'll have to enter the code to unlock the iPad. It's not essential that you do this but it is recommended

10. Set up iCloud Keychain. This feature keeps your website user names and passwords, credit card information, and Wi-Fi network information up-to-date across all of your Apple devices

11. Enter your phone number. This will be used to verify your identity when using your iCloud security code

12. Approve or disapprove Siri. As we have already seen, Siri is a voice recognition feature that lets you speak to your iPad to issue commands, or request information

13. Finally, you are asked whether you are willing to send information back to Apple for diagnostic purposes. Doing this will help Apple to improve the device both for you and other users, so we recommend that you do

Name Your iPad

Your iPad needs a name, which is why the setup wizard asks you to specify one. You may think it's so you can put your personal stamp on the device but actually it's more to do with backing up and recovery purposes.

Every backup you make is identifiable by the iPad's name and the date it is created. If you sync your data across several devices, by giving each device a unique name, you are able to differentiate between multiple backups.

You can change the name to something more suitable or cool sounding at any time. The way to do it is:

1. Tap the Settings app – this gives you access to your iPad's settings
2. Tap General to open the General settings screen
3. Tap About to open the About screen

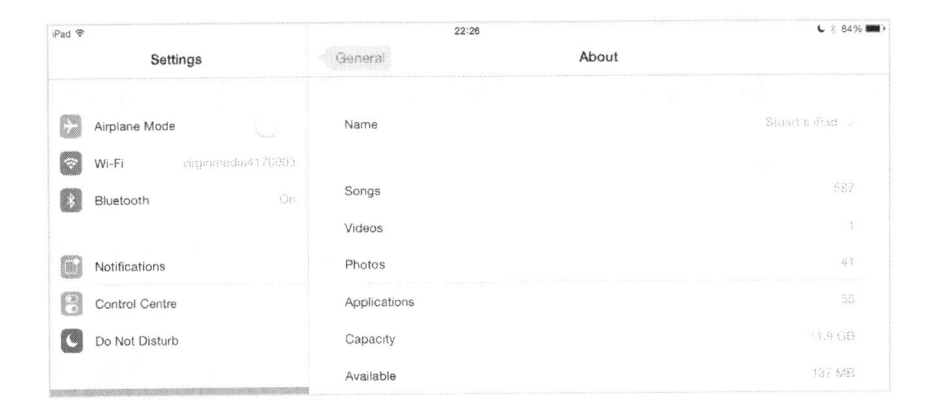

4. Tap Name at the top – you will see a Name box displaying the current name. Tap the box to open the Edit screen and then enter the desired name

Screen Brightness

The level of brightness on your iPad is an important issue in more ways than one. First, it needs to be at a level that's easy on the eye. Second, reducing the brightness reduces the device's power consumption and thus extends battery life. There are two ways to access the Brightness control:

The first, and the quickest, is to activate the Control Centre by swiping up from the bottom edge of the screen; you'll see the Brightness control at the top-right. Adjust by dragging the slider left or right.

cont'd

The second is to go to the Settings app > Display & Brightness. At the top, you'll see the Brightness control slider. Below is an Auto-Brightness option, which is enabled by default.

Auto-Brightness employs a built-in light sensor to measure the ambient light level of your surroundings. It then uses this as a reference point on which to base the automatic adjustment of the iPad's brightness.

Because the process is automatic, the brightness of the screen should always be suitable for the current reading conditions. The control dims the screen when you are in dark conditions and brightens it when you have more light around you.

Generally, the Auto-Brightness feature does a good job of handling your iPad's brightness levels and we recommend you leave it enabled.

Wallpaper

Many people are happy to use the default iPad wallpaper. Others, however, either because they simply don't like it, or because they want to personalise their device, will want to change it.

This can be done in two ways:

The first is to open the Settings app and tap Wallpaper on the left of the screen. You'll now see your current wallpaper and how it looks on both the Lock screen and the Home screen.

Tap 'Choose a New Wallpaper' to open a new screen that offers a choice of two different types of wallpaper – Dynamic (these contain moving objects within the wallpaper) and Stills. Tap the required type to bring up a list of available wallpapers.

The image on page 40 shows part of the Stills collection. Tap one and the image will open in a full-screen preview. At the bottom, you'll see options to Cancel or set it as Lock Screen, Home Screen, and Set Both.

cont'd

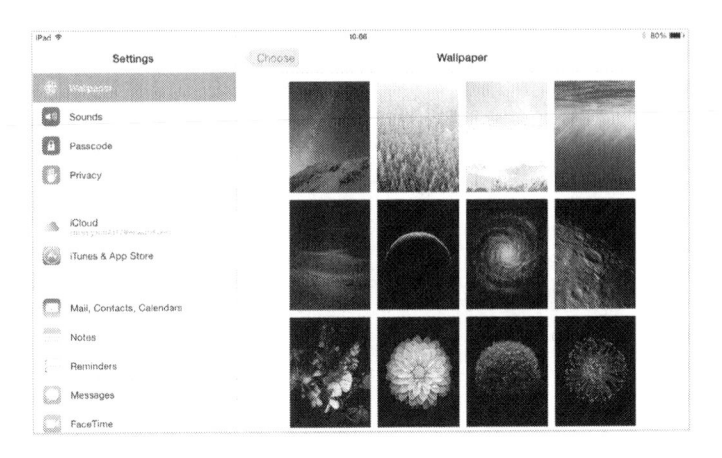

So far so good. What do you do though, if you don't like any of the supplied wallpapers? This leads us to your second option; use one of your own images:

In the 'Choose a New Wallpaper' screen, you will see a Photos section at the bottom – this lets you choose images from the Photo app. You can select from 'All Photos' or 'Recently Added'. Tap either option to see what is available. Selecting a picture is the same as for the Dynamic and Stills collections – tap the one you want and it will open in a full-screen preview.

At the bottom, you'll see the same options to set it as Lock Screen, Home Screen, and Set Both.

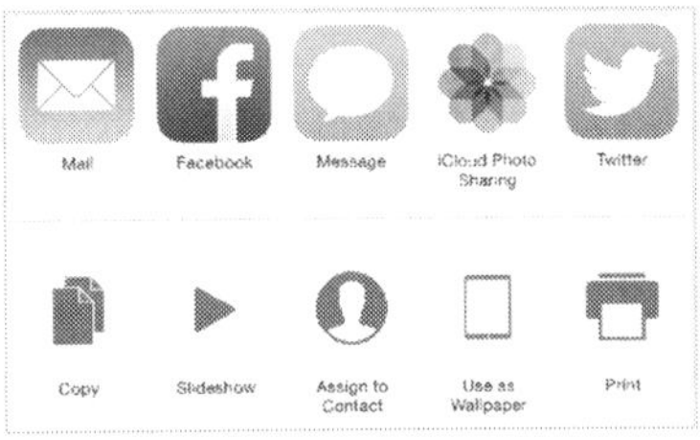

You can also set a picture as wallpaper directly from the Photos app. Open the app and select a picture by tapping it. Then tap the icon at the bottom-left of the screen. This opens a new screen that offers a 'Use as Wallpaper' option as shown on the right.

Note that pictures not supplied with the iPad will probably have the wrong dimensions for wallpaper. If this is the case, you'll see a 'Move and Scale' message at the top of the picture. Use your fingers to crop and adjust the picture by dragging it to the left or right, up or down, stretching to zoom in and pinching to zoom out. When you have it as you want it, set it as wallpaper as described.

Finally, you can also import pictures to your Photos app, either from your computer via iTunes, or from the Internet via the Safari web browser, and set them as wallpaper in the same way as described above.

Date & Time

Your iPad offers a number of date and time related functions, e.g. a clock, a calendar, reminders, as indeed do many third-party apps available from the App Store. For these to work correctly, it is essential to set the date and time, and your time zone as we explain below.

The procedure is:

1. Tap the Settings app on the Home screen

2. Tap General and then tap Date & Time

3. Choose between a 24- or 12-hour clock by tapping the 24-Hour Time button switch to On

4. Turning 'Set Automatically' on will set the date and time via any network the iPad is connected to

5. If the iPad is not connected to a network, or you would rather do it manually, disable Set Automatically and then tap Time Zone

6. Using the keyboard, enter the name of a nearby city and your iPad will calculate the correct time zone from its location

7. Underneath Time Zone, tap the date and time shown in blue

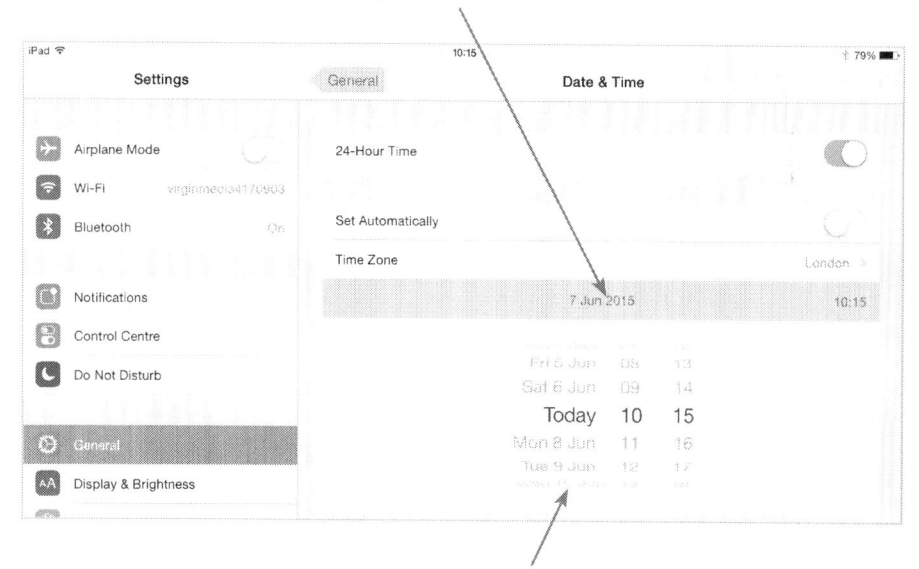

8. Spin the wheel controls to set the day, hour and minute. You can also specify that the time be displayed as AM or PM

Sounds

The purpose of some apps is keep you informed of various types of information as it comes in. News headlines, emails, text messages, and weather updates are typical examples. To bring these to your attention, the apps use alerts, both visual and audible.

Just using your iPad also generates sounds, e.g. locking/unlocking the device and tapping keys on the virtual keyboard.

Usually, you will be quite happy to hear these sounds as they do add another dimension to your use of the device. However, you may find a particular sound to be inappropriate, impractical or simply not to your liking. If so, you can change it in the iPad's settings.

Tap the Settings app on the Home screen and then tap Sounds. The Sounds options screen will open:

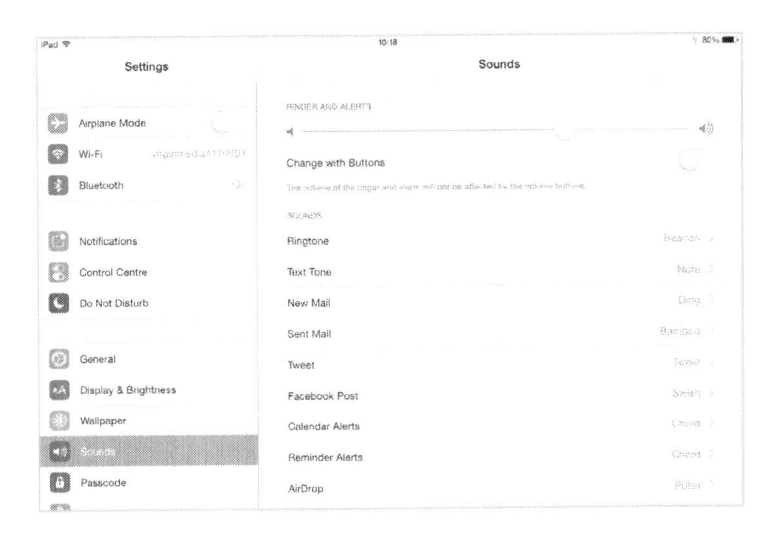

Right at the top is an option that allows you to set the volume of ringers and alerts with the volume control buttons – by default, this is turned off. If you turn the setting on, you will effectively have a universal volume control that controls all the iPad's sounds. With it off, you can have music playing at one level, for example, and alerts set at a different level.

In the Sounds section below, you can change the sound associated with the iPad's various alerts. Just tap the alert, e.g. New Mail, and you'll be presented with a list of available sounds. Tapping each sound gives you a preview and also selects it.

You'll also see options to disable the sounds made by locking/unlocking your iPad, and by tapping the keyboard's keys.

Privacy

Many of the apps you use on your iPad, both Apple and third-party, share information between themselves. For example, the Mail app can access the contents of your Contacts app in order to facilitate the quick addressing of emails.

When you first run a third-party app that wants to use data from another app, it will request your permission to do so. If you grant it, the app will continue to use that data without further requests.

Your iPad provides a feature called Privacy that not only allows you to monitor exactly what data is being accessed by third-party apps but to also revoke any permissions previously granted.

1. Tap Settings on the Home screen and then tap Privacy
2. You'll see a list of apps and services that provide data. Apps include Contacts, Calendar and Photos, and services include your Twitter and FaceBook accounts (assuming you have them set up)

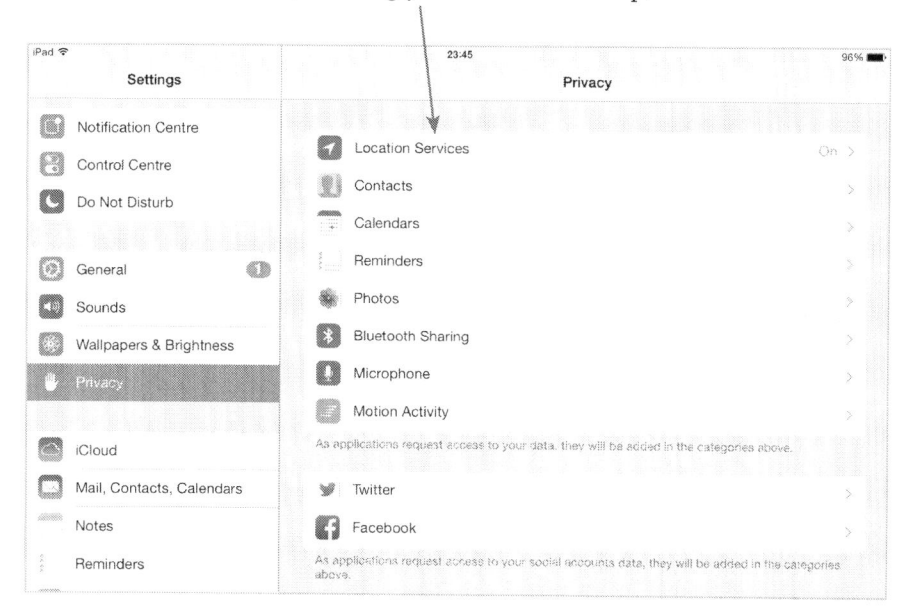

3. To see what third-party apps are accessing these apps and services, tap the relevant entry
4. If you want to deny an app in the list access to data from other apps and services, tap the switch at the right to the Off position

The privacy feature enables you to monitor who is accessing your data and, if necessary, put a stop to it.

Accessibility

For users with disabilities that make it difficult to use the iPad, the device provides a range of accessibility features that can help considerably. You can access the settings for all these features by opening the Settings app and going to General > Accessibility.

There are quite a few options here and we'll briefly run through the most important ones to see what they offer.

For the visually impaired, we have:

VoiceOver
VoiceOver is a screen reader that reads aloud, providing an audible description of everything that is happening on the iPad.

For example, it tells you the name of someone who is calling, speaks the letter being touched on the keyboard, what app your finger is on, and helps you navigate the device. The pitch, speaking rate, language and dialect of the voice can be altered if necessary.

A VoiceOver feature called the Rotor provides help specific to the navigation of web pages and documents.

Your iPad is fully compatible with many refreshable Braille displays. You can synchronise a Bluetooth wireless Braille display to read VoiceOver output. Also, Braille displays with input keys can be used to control your device when VoiceOver is turned on.

Be aware that when you activate VoiceOver, the gestures used to control your iPad will change – you'll get a warning message pop up on the screen about this. Also, some VoiceOver features are on by default and others are off. If you decide to use VoiceOver, be sure to go through the various settings to make sure you get the best out of it.

Zoom
The iPad's Zoom feature is a built-in magnifier that works wherever you are in the device. Double-tapping with three fingers instantly zooms in 200 per cent, and you can adjust the magnification between 100 and 500 per cent.

While you're zoomed in, you can still use all the usual gestures to navigate your device. Plus, Zoom works with VoiceOver to help you both see and hear what's happening on the iPad.

Invert Colors
This feature simply turns black to white and vice versa, thus increasing contrast so that content is easier to distinguish.

cont'd

Speech
If you find it difficult to read text on your iPad, Speak Selection can help by reading your email, messages, web pages and books to you.

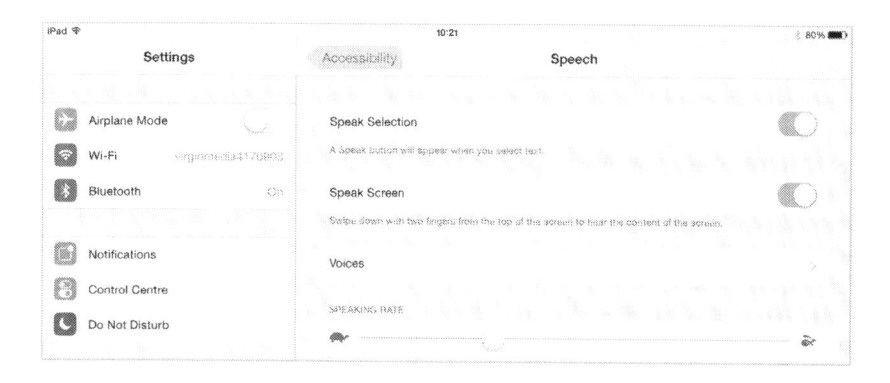

Select text in any application, tap Speak, and the selected text is read aloud. You can adjust the voice's language and speaking rate, and have words highlighted as they're being read.

Larger Text
Larger Text lets you increase font size so making it easier to read. By dragging a slider to any of 12 predetermined steps, you can alter the size of the text. Note that this only works in apps that support the feature.

For those with hearing problems, the iPad offers:

Hearing Aids
The Hearing Aids feature makes it possible to use compatible, Bluetooth equipped, hearing aids with your iPad. The hearing aid settings can be managed with your device.

Subtitles & Captioning
When enabled, this feature displays captions at the bottom of the screen, so you can read what's being said. This is useful if you are watching a video in a noisy environment, for example. However, Subtitles and Captioning only works if the video being watched supports the technology behind it.

You can choose from three built-in display styles, or create one of your own design (font, text size and colour, background, etc).

Mono Audio
People with hearing problems may miss part of a stereo recording when using headphones. This is because stereo recordings usually have distinct left- and right-channel audio tracks.

cont'd

The Mono Audio feature compensates by playing both audio channels in both ears and letting the user adjust the balance for greater volume in either ear.

For those with physical problems, the iPad offers:

Switch Control
Switch Control lets you control your iPad with a single switch, or multiple switches. These can be in the form of buttons, leaf, sip and puff, or even eye-blink switches. The switches connect wirelessly to the device and are positioned where you can easily activate them.

There are several ways in which to perform actions such as selecting, tapping, dragging, typing, and even freehand drawing. The basic technique is to use a switch to select an item or location on the screen, and then use the same (or a different) switch to choose an action to perform on that item or location.

There are three basic methods:

- **Item scanning (default)** – highlight items on the screen until one is selected
- **Point scanning** – use scanning cross-hairs to pick a screen location
- **Manual selection** – move from item to item on demand

Whichever method you use, when you select a single item (rather than a group), a menu appears so you can choose how to act on the selected item (tap, drag, or pinch, for example).

You can adjust the behaviour of Switch Control in a variety of ways to suit your needs and style.

AssistiveTouch
AssistiveTouch is a very useful application for those with impaired physical and motor skills. It enables the user to activate multi-touch gestures such as pinch-to-zoom; to trigger hardware features such as the volume and Home buttons; and even rotate the screen or take a screenshot – all with just one finger.

The user can also employ a compatible adaptive accessory (such as a joystick) together with AssistiveTouch to control their iPad.

Accessibility Shortcut
This enables a number of the accessibility features to be activated by triple-pressing the Home button. Specifically, these are: VoiceOver, Invert Colors, Greyscale, Zoom, Switch Control and AssistiveTouch.

CHAPTER 4

Apps

In Chapter Four, we take a look at the business end of your iPad – its programs, or apps as they are more commonly known. We explain what the pre-installed apps do, show how to use the App Store to get more apps, and how to keep your apps updated.

We also see how to manage your apps in terms of organisation so as to make the most efficient use of the iPad.

What is an App? 48

Pre-installed Apps 48

The App Store 51

Browsing the App Store 51

Reviewing & Installing Apps 52

Updating Your Apps 54

Managing Your Apps 55

App Folders 55

Deleting Apps 56

Reinstalling Apps 57

Reset the Home Screen 58

What is an App?

By itself the iPad is just a piece of hardware – beautifully designed and superbly constructed – but still just a piece of hardware. To do something useful, it requires instructions.

On a computer, these instructions are provided by software programs, most of which are highly complex, large in size (which means they can take a long time to install and configure), and require a considerable amount of system resources to run. Computer software can also be extremely expensive.

The app is the tablet equivalent of computer software. However, due to the power and system resource restraints placed on tablets by their reliance on battery power, and small physical size, the software used on them needs to be similarly restricted in terms of power and resource requirements.

Thus, in general, apps for tablets and smartphones are much more streamlined than their computer equivalents. They are small in size, quick to download and install, and very inexpensive. The downside is that currently, they provide limited options and are restricted to relatively simple tasks.

Having said that, as tablets become more powerful (your iPad Air 2 is twice as powerful as it's predecessor), the apps used on them will be capable of doing a great deal more.

iPads are supplied with a number of pre-installed apps that provide basic functionality, such as email, an Internet browser and the iSight camera. To increase the capability of your iPad you can, of course, download other apps from the App Store as we'll see later.

For now though, we'll take a brief look at the pre-installed apps:

Pre-installed Apps

App Store – this is basically a link that opens Apple's App Store from where you can download apps to your iPad. Many of these are free, others need to be purchased. Note that you will need an Internet connection.

Mail – this app lets you send and receive email on your iPad. It is easy to set up and, if you already have an email account, you can quickly add it to the app.

iTunes Store – this app takes you to the iTunes Store from where you can download music, films, TV programs, etc.

Safari – essentially a 'lite' version of the web browser found on Apple Macs, Safari is your portal to the Internet. Like most apps, it has a relatively sparse set of features but is still perfectly adequate for most users.

cont'd

Apps pre-installed on your iPad

Messages – for those of you who like to send text messages, the Messages app can be used to send text, photos and videos to and from other Apple devices – namely iPads, iPhones, iPod Touches and Apple Mac computers.

Music – an important app for many people, the Music app is used to play music on your iPad. You can upload music to the iPad from your computer via iTunes, or download it directly from Apple's iTunes Store.

Clock – by default, the Clock app shows you the current date and time in your location. You can also view the time in any other country. Other functions include an alarm, a stopwatch and a timer.

Calendar – typical of all digital calendars, the Calendar app lets you make and store appointments etc. By synchronising the app with iCloud, your appointments can also be viewed and edited on other Apple devices.

Photos – this app not only lets you view pictures, it provides some useful editing functions as well. Pictures can be organised in albums and shared using iCloud.

Camera – the Camera app lets you use the iPad's front- and rear-facing cameras. With them, you can take pictures and videos.

cont'd

Contacts – a critical app for many people, the Contacts app is an electronic address book in which to store the contact details of the people in your life. Entries can be accessed and used by other apps such as Mail.

Reminders – a surprisingly useful app, Reminders ensures you don't forget to do things. It can also be used to create to-do lists. Reminders can be accessed on all your Apple devices via iCloud.

FaceTime – the FaceTime app lets you make video calls to other iPad users and to people who have an iPhone, iPod Touch or an Apple Mac computer. The app utilizes the front-facing camera.

Maps – with the Maps app, you can view specific regions from around the globe, find places, and get directions from one location to another. It also has a feature called Flyover that gives a birds-eye view of many interesting places.

Tips – as the name suggests, the Tips app provides tips and tutorials on how to get the best out of the iPad. These are automatically updated on a regular basis.

Podcasts – a podcast is basically a subscription-based audio or video file that is broadcast over the Internet – the iPad's Podcasts app is used to play these files. Podcasts are an increasingly popular form of communication.

Videos – the Videos app stores TV programs, films and podcasts that you download from the iTunes Store. It also lets you play them – just tap on one to begin playback.

Notes – a very simple app you can use to jot down things that pop into your head so you don't forget them.

Settings – the Settings app is your way into the iPad. With it, you can change the default settings for most apps, set up email, configure network connections, customise your iPad, and much more.

iBooks – this app lets download books to your iPad from Apple's iBooks Store. Note that while it is very similar to Amazon's Kindle app, it cannot be used to download books from Amazon.

Newsstand – the Newsstand app lets you download magazines and newspapers. It also provides a location in which to store and view them.

Game Centre – the Game Centre is a central location for all things to do with gaming. Preview and download the latest games, play against yourself or challenge friends.

The App Store

In all likelihood, it probably won't be long before you want to increase the capabilities of your iPad by downloading a new app. Unlike Windows computers that let you download programs from virtually anywhere (together with the attendant risk of also downloading viruses and malware), you have only one place to go with regard apps for your iPad.

This is the App Store. Not only does it offer a huge range of apps that cover every conceivable purpose, you can browse and download from it safe in the knowledge that it is just about the most secure site on the Internet. All apps in the store are stringently checked before they are offered for download. Also, the very nature of apps, most of which are basically self-contained programs that do not access the outside world, makes them inherently safer than traditional computer programs.

Accessing the Store
To access the App Store, tap its icon on the Home screen. When it opens, you will see something similar to the screenshot below:

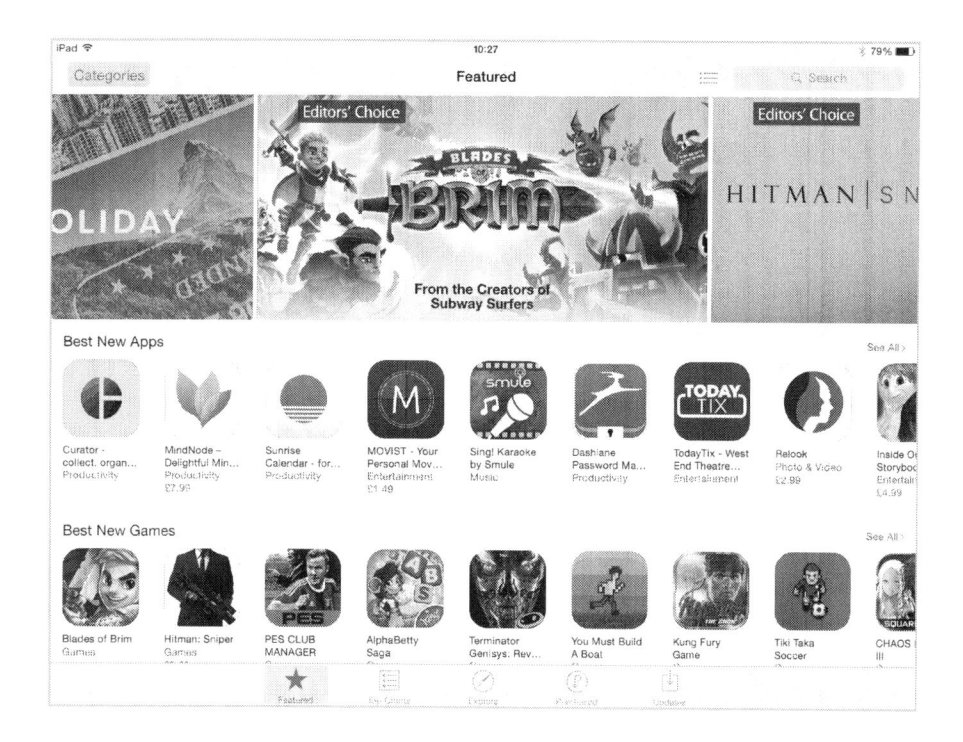

Browsing the App Store
At the top-left of the screen is a Categories link – tap this to reveal a list containing around 25 categories of apps. At the top-right is a small icon that opens your wish list. Next to that is a search box.

cont'd

Right at the bottom is a row of icons. These include:

- **Featured** – tap this to open a page showing a range of featured apps. This includes sections for Best New Apps, Best New Games, Kids Apps & Games, Best New Game Updates and more

- **Top Charts** – on this page, you'll see scrollable sections that show the highest rated Paid, Free and Grossing apps

- **Explore** – the Explore option lets you drill down by category – some of the apps shown are based on your geographical location

- **Purchased** – on this page, you will see all the apps you have bought from the App Store. If the app is on the iPad, you'll see an Open icon to the right – tapping this will open the app. If it has been downloaded at some point, either to your iPad or to a different device, but is not currently on your iPad, you'll see a download icon – tap this to re-download and install the app

- **Updates** – we look at this on page 54

So, as you can see, the App Store provides a number of ways for you to find the app you are looking for, or indeed just have a look at what's available.

If you are looking for something specific and know its name, the search box is the quickest way to locate it. Otherwise, tap Explore and drill down through the various categories.

Reviewing & Installing Apps

As you're browsing, you'll notice a box to the right of each app in which is either the word GET or a price. GET indicates the app is free – tap it and you will now see INSTALL.

The iTunes Store login window will pop up asking for your account password. Enter it and then tap OK to start the download and installation procedure.

If you see a price in the box, this is what the app costs. As there is money involved, you may wish to get some more detailed information about the app before shelling out.

cont'd

To do this, tap on the app to open the Details and Reviews screen as shown in the example below:

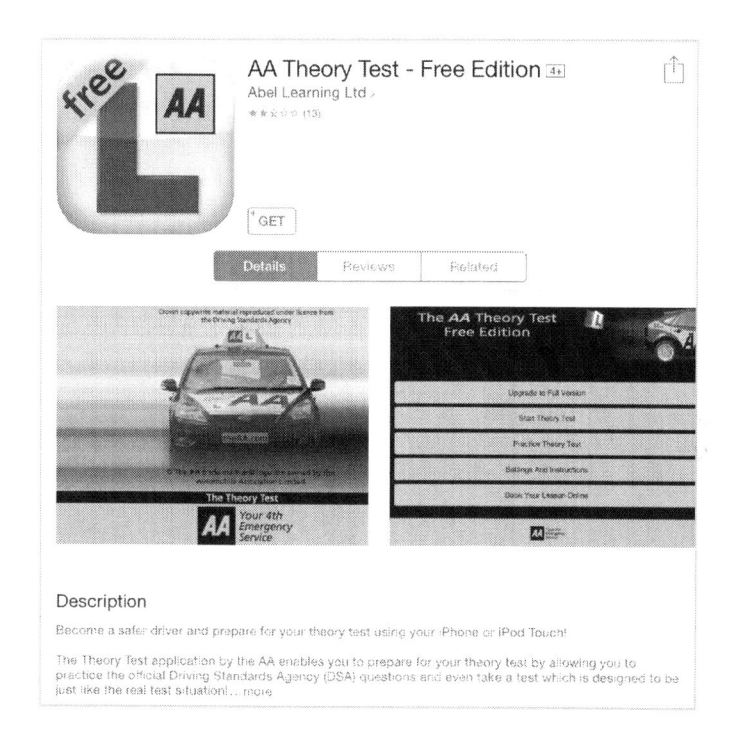

Right at the top, you'll see how the app has been rated by other users. For most apps, there will be a series of thumbnail images showing the app in action – scroll to the right to see them all. Below, will be a description of the app and other information such as its version history.

Tap the Reviews button to read the reviews left by people who have bought the app. If you decide you want it, tap the price box.

This leads to the INSTALL box, which in turn opens the 'Sign In to iTunes Store' screen. Enter your Apple password and press OK. The app will be charged to the credit card registered to your account, and then downloaded to your iPad and automatically installed.

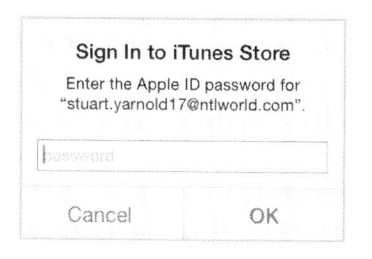

Go to the end of your Home screen (the last one if you have more than one) and you'll see the icon for your new app.

53

Updating Your Apps

All apps worth having continuously undergo development that enhance and extend their functionality and performance. This is important because the technology behind apps is fast-moving – developers who don't keep up are soon left behind.

So if you want the apps on your iPad to be current and provide top-notch features, you need to update them periodically. There are two ways you can do this: manually and automatically. We'll start with the manual method:

When updates are available for your apps, you will see a red badge at the top-right of the App Store icon that shows the number of available updates. Open the App Store and, at the bottom of the screen, you'll see the Updates button is showing the same number.

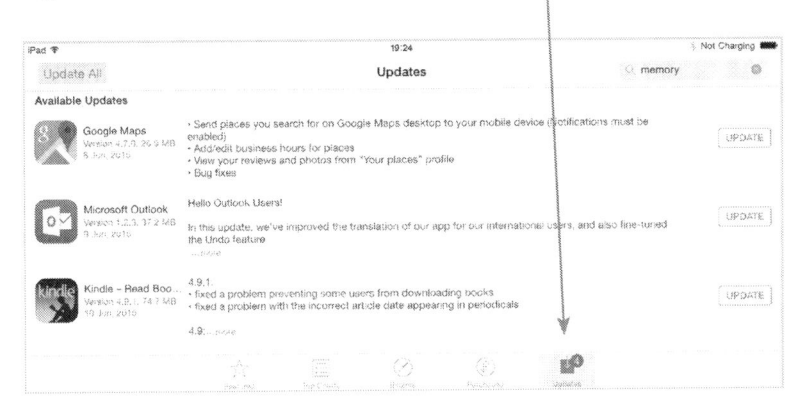

Tap the Updates button and on the screen that opens, you'll see the apps for which updates are available. Tap Update All at the top-left, or update them individually with the separate UPDATE buttons.

The automatic method is much easier. Open the Settings app and go to iTunes & App Store. In the Automatic Downloads section, simply tap the Updates button for Apps to On.

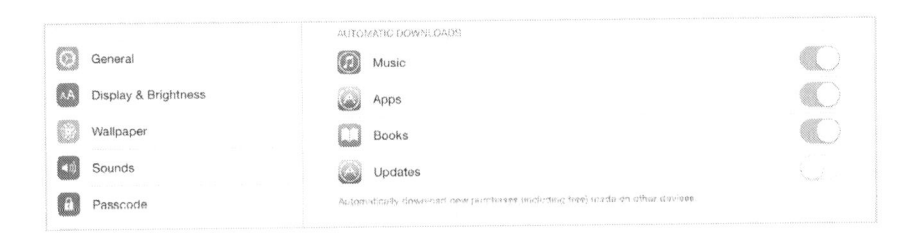

That's all there is to it. From now on, your iPad will download and install app updates as and when they are available.

Managing Your Apps

Your iPad starts you off with over 20 apps and, in time, you will no doubt download many more. To be able to use your iPad efficiently, all these apps need to be organised so you can find them quickly. This may be difficult if you have them randomly scattered across several home screens.

Moving Apps
Probably the first thing you will do is rearrange the order of your apps. To move one, press and hold it until it begins to wiggle and then simply drag it to where you want it to go. Release it and then tap the Home button.

You can rearrange the Dock apps in this way as well. Furthermore, you can change the default Dock apps by dragging the originals off the Dock and then dragging different apps to the vacated spaces, It is also possible to add another two to make a total of six.

If you don't want a particular app on your Home screen at all but don't want to go the lengths of actually deleting it, you can place it on a secondary home screen where it is out of the way. Simply drag the app to the right-hand edge of the screen and a secondary home screen is created automatically – release the app there. This is one way of dealing with the default Apple apps that you don't use.

You can create up to 11 home screens on the iPad and have 20 apps on each, plus six on the Dock. According to the maths, this makes it possible to have a maximum of 226 apps on your iPad. However, by creating app folders as we see below, it is possible to have even more.

App Folders
The ability to create folders in which to place your apps provides another method of organising your iPad. This feature can be used for various purposes – for example, grouping related apps under one icon, creating more space for apps, and making it easier to find particular apps.

Follow these steps to create a new folder:

1. Go to the home screen that contains one of the apps you want to include in the new folder

2. Press and hold the app until its icon begins to wiggle

3. Drag the app to the top of another app that you also intend to place in the folder. Then release it. Note that if the two apps are on different screens, you can drag from one screen across to the other

Your iPad will now create a new folder. Tap to open it and you'll see that it contains your two apps as shown on the next page.

cont'd

The iPad will automatically give the folder a name based on the type of apps in it. This is demonstrated in this folder where we have dropped the Photo Booth app onto the Photos app. The apps are both photography related so the iPad names it Photography.

If you want to name the folder yourself, tap the X to the right of the name and the keyboard will open. Type the name and then tap Done. If you don't see the X, press and hold one of the app icons until they begin to wiggle – the X will now be visible.

You can add more apps by dragging them onto the folder's icon. Remove them by opening the folder and dragging them out. You can also rearrange the order of the apps within the folder by pressing until the icons wiggle and then dragging them to the new positions.

Finally, if you place more than nine apps in the folder, the 10th and above apps will be put on a new screen within the folder. Swipe right to access it.

Opening & Closing Apps
To open an app, just tap the app's icon – it couldn't be simpler. What isn't so straightforward is how to close it. You can press the Home button but this doesn't actually close the app, it just returns you to the Home screen – the app is still open, albeit in a state of suspension whereby it isn't using any system resources.

The latter is an important concept to grasp as it means you don't need to close apps down at all. You can actually have any number of them running simultaneously without any noticeable performance hit on the iPad.

However, should you feel the need to do so for whatever reason, the way to close them is to double-press the Home button. This opens the multitasking interface (see page 19), which shows a mini representation of all open apps. To close one, just swipe it upwards.

Deleting Apps
When you've had a chance to play around with your iPad and see what the default apps do, it's quite likely that you'll decide some of them are superfluous to requirements, and are thus candidates for deletion.

cont'd

To do this, simply press and hold any app until the icons begin to wiggle as previously described. If the app can be deleted, an X will appear at the top-left of the icon – tap it to initiate the delete process. In the Delete window that opens, tap Delete. The app will be deleted from the iPad.

However, not all apps can be deleted. With the default Apple apps supplied with the iPad, the X will not appear – this means these apps cannot be deleted. Similarly, if you create a folder that contains an Apple app, you will not be able to delete the folder until you take the app out of the folder.

NOTE: having deleted an app/apps, if you subsequently sync your iPad with iTunes on your computer, make sure you first uncheck these deleted apps in iTunes. If you don't, they will be restored to your iPad during the synchronisation procedure.

Reinstalling Apps
You may at some point delete an app (due to lack of use, the need to reclaim storage space, etc) only to decide later that you would like it back. The App Store makes it easy to reinstall deleted apps:

Open the App Store and, at the bottom of the screen, tap Purchased. In the new screen, at the top, tap 'Not on This iPad'.

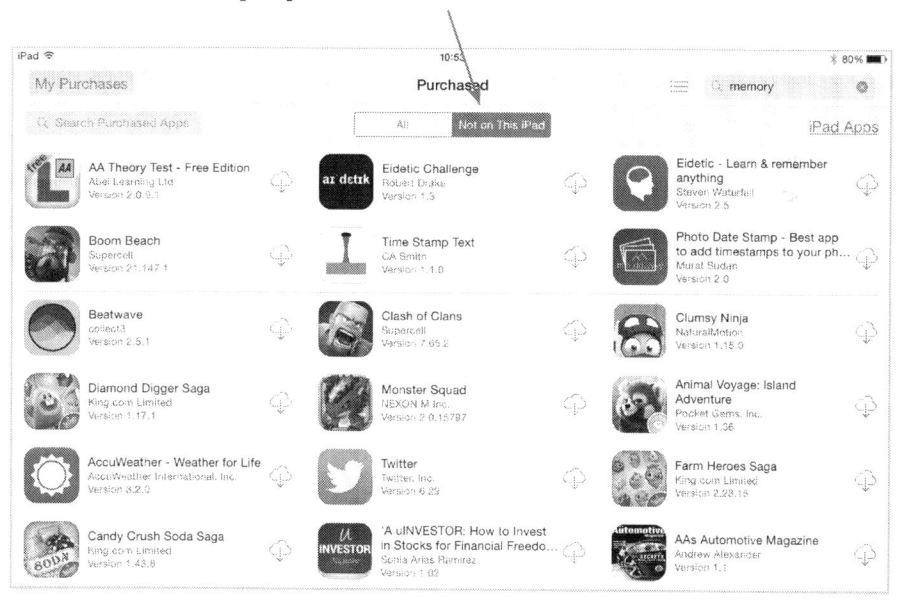

You will now see all the apps that you have installed and then deleted since your Apple account was created. Next to each app, you will see the iCloud icon with a down-arrow. Just tap the icon to reinstall the app.

cont'd

Switching Between Open Apps

You may sometimes need to use two or more apps to achieve a particular goal, and so being able to quickly switch between them will be handy. We looked at this scenario on page 19 where we saw that one way of moving between open apps is to double-press the Home button to open the multitasking screen and select them from there.

Another way is to use the four-finger gesture. Place four fingers on the screen of an open app and swipe left and right to switch between it and other apps.

Reset The Home Screen

Messing around with your apps – deleting some, moving others, and installing new ones – will alter the layout of your Home screen. If at some point, for whatever reason, you want to revert to the default layout, your iPad allows you do so easily and quickly:

1. On the Home screen, tap the Settings app

2. Tap General

3. At the bottom of the page, tap Reset

4. Tap 'Reset Home Screen Layout'

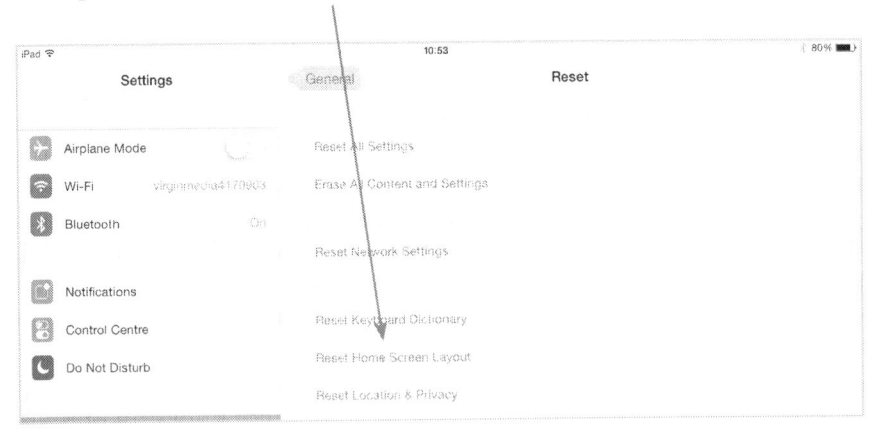

5. You will see a message warning that your Home screen layout will be reset to factory defaults. Tap Reset

Your Home screen will now be restored to how it was when you first switched on the device. Note that any apps you've subsequently installed yourself are kept on the iPad.

CHAPTER 5

Networks

Your iPad can do many things that do not require it to be connected to a network. However, the device offers so much more when it is. For example, browsing the web; downloading content such as apps, music, video, books and magazines; sending and receiving email and text messages; and navigation with apps such as Maps.

In this chapter, we explain everything you need to know with regard to networks and your iPad.

Connections Overview 60

Set Up a Wi-Fi Connection 61

Set Up a Tethered Wi-Fi Connection 63

Turn Off Wi-Fi 64

Set Up a Cellular Connection 65

Wi-Fi or Cellular? 66

Managing a Cellular Connection 67

Turn Off a Cellular Connection 68

Turn Off Data Roaming 68

Bluetooth Connections 69

Connections Overview

Your iPad will be either a Wi-Fi only model or a cellular model that can connect not just to Wi-Fi but also to cellular data networks, such as 3G and 4G. If you're not sure what model you have, open the Settings app and look at the top of the left-hand column.

If you just see Wi-Fi, that's what you have. If you see a Cellular entry as well, then you have the cellular model. A lot of people are confused by the difference between the two so we'll clarify the issue here:

Wi-Fi
A Wi-Fi only iPad can only connect to the Internet via a wireless, or Wi-Fi signal. These signals are produced by a device called a router, that typically has a range of approximately 150 feet indoors and 300 feet outdoors.

Many homes have these routers installed as part of their broadband setup, and they are also widely found in public places such as airports, libraries and Internet Cafes. The latter are known as Wi-Fi hotspots and they enable people to use their iPad's and smartphones while on the move.

The big advantage of Wi-Fi is that if you use your iPad at home, your connection is free. Some public places offer free Wi-Fi hotspots but most don't, in which case you have to pay for your connection.

However, if you are in an area where Wi-Fi is not available, you won't be able to access the Internet, send/receive email, and you'll find that any apps that rely on Internet access will not work.

Cellular
Cellular iPads, on the other hand, can connect to the Internet wherever there is cellular network coverage, in the same way that mobile phones do. This is their big advantage and one that is much valued by people who travel a lot.

Furthermore, by installing a suitable app such as Skype (available from the App Store), a cellular iPad can also be used as a phone (assuming you don't mind holding an iPad to your ear!).

Cellular iPads are designed to access a large frequency spectrum. This means they will work well in most locations globally that offer a cellular service.

Needless to say of course, there is a downside – namely cost! Cellular iPads are considerably more expensive than the Wi-Fi models. Not only that, you will also need to pay for a data service plan. This is essentially the same as the plan you buy for your mobile phone and is subject to the same data restrictions and costs.

Set Up a Wi-Fi Connection

Unlike cellular connections, Wi-Fi connections are not automatic – they have to be set up.

Immediately you initiate an action on your iPad that requires an Internet connection, e.g. opening the Safari web browser, the device will look for a Wi-Fi signal with which to make the connection.

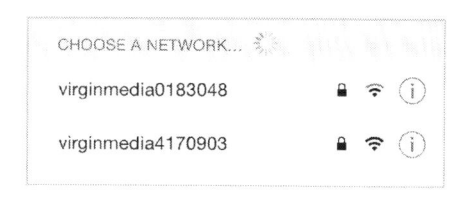

Assuming this is the first time you've initiated such an action, your iPad will then present you with a list of the Wi-Fi networks it has found, i.e. that are within range of the device.

This gives you the following information:

- On the left is the name of the network, e.g. virginmedia0183048

- On the right, you may or may not see a padlock icon. If you do, this indicates the network is password-protected

- At the far-right, is the signal strength icon. The more bars, the stronger the signal, and thus the faster and more reliable the connection

Making a Connection
Tap the Wi-Fi network you want to join. If it requires a password, enter the password at the prompt and then tap Join at the top-right.

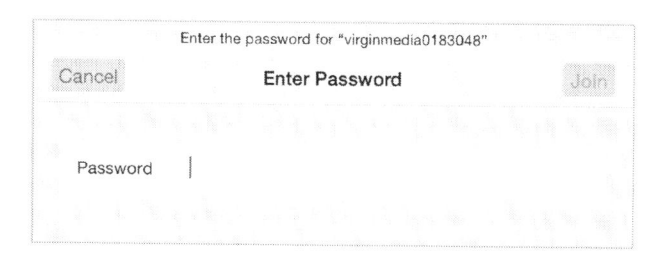

If the password is accepted, your iPad will connect to the network and, as an indication of this, you'll see the Wi-Fi network icon appear at the left of the Status bar. In the case of a commercial network that requires up-front payment, you will be asked to enter your name and credit card details before you are allowed to use the network.

Note that when you join a free network, henceforth, whenever your iPad is in range of that network, it will automatically login to it – you won't have to select it (and enter the password) every time.

cont'd

Connecting to Your Home Broadband

If you have a broadband Internet connection in your house and the setup includes a Wi-Fi router (as most do these days), you're all set for free Wi-Fi on your iPad:

1. Find your router and look at the rear of the case

2. You'll see a SSID number, e.g. virginmedia123456 and a passphrase. Make a note of them

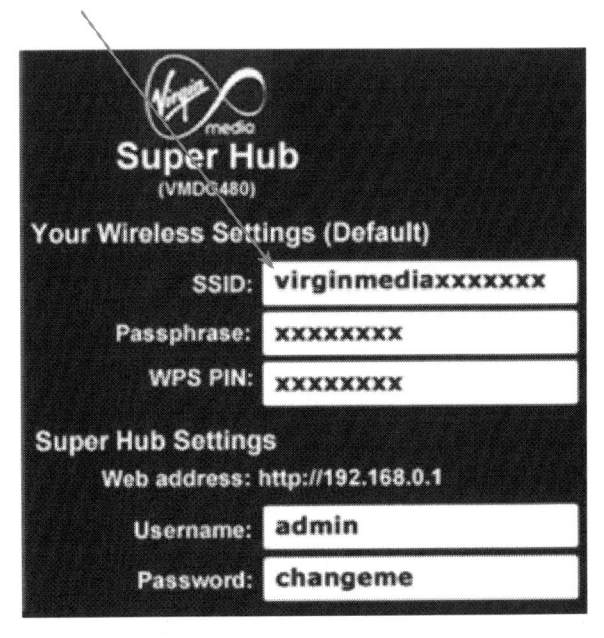

(Image: Virgin Media Super Hub (VMDG480) label showing Your Wireless Settings (Default): SSID: virginmediaxxxxxxx, Passphrase: xxxxxxxx, WPS PIN: xxxxxxxx. Super Hub Settings: Web address: http://192.168.0.1, Username: admin, Password: changeme)

3. If you haven't set up a connection on your iPad yet, follow the procedure described on page 61. When you see the dialogue box showing the list of available connections, choose the one that has the same name as the SSID number on the back of your router

4. Enter the passphrase in the password box and tap Join

Now it may be that your broadband router is the outdated type that doesn't provide Wi-Fi. If this is the case, contact your Internet service provider (ISP) and ask them to send an engineer to update your router. They should do this free of charge.

With regard to SSID numbers, note that all Wi-Fi networks are given an identifying name – this is the Service Set Identifier, or SSID for short. A typical example is shown in step 2 above – virginmediaxxxxxxx – this enables you to differentiate between networks and connect to the one you want.

Set Up a Tethered Wi-Fi Connection

From what we're written so far in this chapter, you'll be forgiven for thinking that if you have a Wi-Fi only iPad and there is no available Wi-Fi network, there is no way of establishing a connection.

However, if you have a cellular iPhone running iOS 4.3 or later, that is not actually the case. This is thanks to a feature called 'Personal Hotspot' that lets you share the iPhone's cellular connection with the iPad, thus enabling the iPad to get online by 'piggybacking'.

One proviso is that you will also need a cellular data plan that supports using your iPhone as a personal hotspot.

When you have everything you need, you can set up a tethered Wi-Fi connection as follows:

1. On your iPhone's Home screen, tap the Settings app

2. Tap Personal Hotspot (if you don't see this option, tap Cellular and then Personal Hotspot)

3. Enable Personal Hotspot by tapping the button

4. If you get a prompt for 'Wi-Fi and USB Only', select it

5. You'll see the network's name – make a note of it

6. Your iPhone now generates a password (if you prefer, you can use your own). Make a note of this as well

7. Now go to your iPad, tap Settings and then tap Wi-Fi. You will see a list of available networks, one of which is the network you've just created on the iPhone

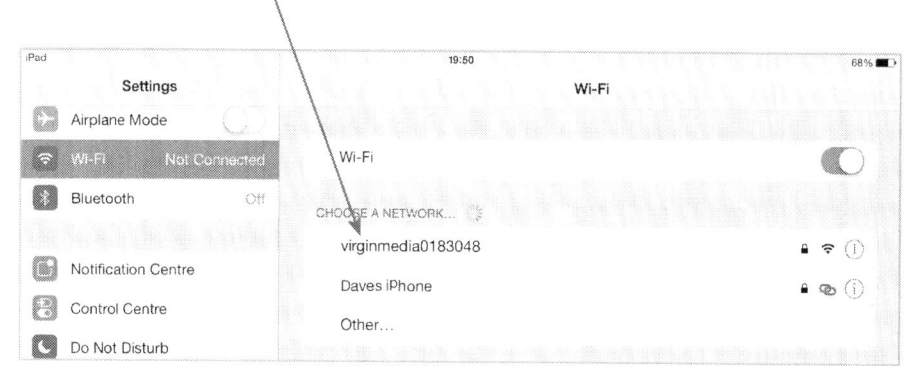

8. Tap to select it

cont'd

9. Enter the password you were given in step 6

Your iPad will now be connected to the personal hotspot via your iPhone. This will be confirmed by the presence of the Personal Hotspot icon on the iPad's Status bar – two interconnected rings.

You can use the connection to browse the Internet, send and receive email, plus all the other things you do online.

Turn Off Wi-Fi

Every single action carried out by your iPad uses up some of the charge in the battery. For this reason, it makes sense to minimise these actions as far as possible.

A common culprit in this respect is your iPad constantly seeking out nearby Wi-Fi networks. It may only be a minute hit but it's happening all the time, and does help to drain the battery.

So, whenever you are in a situation whereby you don't need Wi-Fi access, simply turn off it off. This will help to conserve the battery's charge.

You can turn off Wi-Fi in two ways. The first is in the iPad's settings:

1. Tap the Settings app
2. Tap Wi-Fi to open the Wi-Fi Networks screen
3. Switch Wi-Fi off by tapping the button to Off

The second way is to use the Control Centre:

1. Open the Control Centre by swiping up from the bottom of the screen

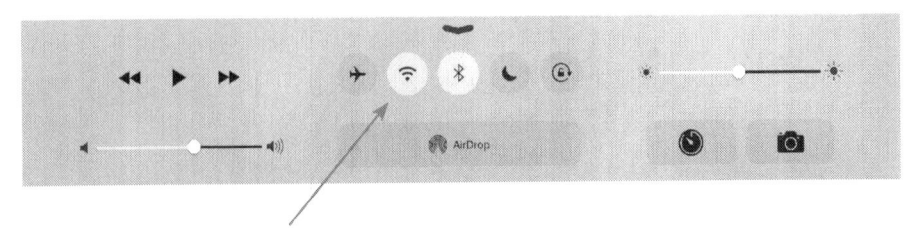

2. Tap the Wi-Fi button – this turns Wi-Fi off. Tapping it again turns it back on

Set Up a Cellular Connection

Overview

To start, a brief overview of cellular networks may be helpful as it can be a confusing topic. This is due to the fact that cellular networks use a number of different technologies, the latest being 4G (4th Generation). This is gradually replacing the older, and less capable, 3G (3rd Generation) technology, which in turn replaced EDGE (2.75G) technology.

To complicate things further, there are several different implementations of each type. For example, there are three types of 4G network – LTE, HSPA+ and WiMax. However, regardless of the minor differences between them, they all do essentially the same thing – provide data transfer rates that are some 10 times faster than 3G. Furthermore, 4G networks have the potential to provide even faster speeds in years to come.

Which type of cellular network your iPad connects to depends on your geographic location. In advanced countries, particularly in the major cities, 4G will be available. If it is not, the iPad will look for the next best type, 3G, and if it cannot find that either, it will connect to an EDGE network.

Establishing a Cellular Connection

Unlike with Wi-Fi networks, establishing a connection with cellular networks is automatic. Simply switch on your iPad and, if it is a cellular model, it will look for a compatible signal. If it finds one, it will automatically connect to it.

However, you first have to enable the feature and purchase a data plan:

1. Tap the Settings app

2. Tap Cellular Data on the left of the screen

3. Turn the 'Cellular Data' and 'Enable LTE' settings to on

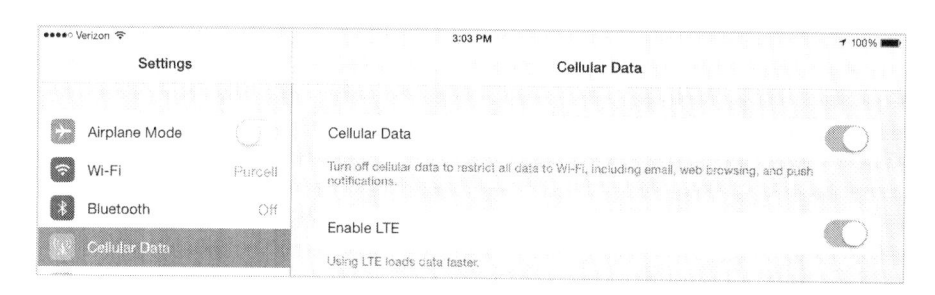

At this point, you have to set up a data plan account. If you already have one, you can transfer it to your iPad by entering the account details when prompted, e.g. name, password, post code, etc.

cont'd

If you don't yet have an account, you will have to create one:

1. Tap 'Set Up New Account'
2. Enter your details – name, telephone, email address and password
3. Choose a data plan
4. Enter your credit card information, OK the agreement and confirm

It may take a few minutes for your 4G service to be activated. When it has been, your iPad will automatically begin searching for a network. It will probably find several different types of cellular network and, if so, it will connect to the most recent type.

When connected, the iPad will indicate the type of network on the left of the Status bar. If it is 4G, you will see LTE or 4G, if it is 3G, you will see 3G and if it is EDGE, you will see E.

Note that if a Wi-Fi network is available, your iPad will connect to that rather than to your cellular network. It will only use the latter when it is not in range of a Wi-Fi network.

Mostly this is a good thing but occasionally it might not be. You may, for example, be in an area where you are getting a stronger cellular signal than Wi-Fi. In this case, just go into your iPad's settings and disable Wi-Fi.

Wi-Fi or Cellular?

This is a common question and the answer is dependant on two factors: cost and network speed.

Of the two, only Wi-Fi is free (assuming you're piggybacking on your home broadband, or using a free hotspot). Couple this with the fact that Wi-Fi networks also tend to have more bandwidth, i.e. they are faster, makes it a no-brainer in most situations.

However, if you're having to pay for the Wi-Fi, it might be a different matter. Commercial Wi-Fi can be very expensive as typically you're paying for short periods. Even so, if it is just for occasional use, e.g. when you're on holiday, it can still be cheaper than a cellular plan.

For the frequent traveller though, who is always on the move, buying a cellular data plan will be considerably cheaper. Also, if it's available, a 4G network could well be faster than a free, and thus often over-subscribed, Wi-Fi network.

Managing a Cellular Connection

As we've seen, a cellular connection requires a data plan – and these need to be paid for. To make sure you get value for your money, and also don't get burned by extortionate data roaming charges, it is important to keep on top of this type of connection.

Track Your Data Usage
The big advantage of paying for a cellular data plan is that you will almost always have access to a network regardless of where you are – your email will always work and you will always be able to connect to the Internet.

These data plans are either limited (you can only use a set amount of data, after which you are charged extra) or unlimited (there is no limit to what you can use).

If you're on the latter type of plan, you don't have an issue here. If you're using a limited plan though, you most definitely do.

Fortunately, the iPad lets you keep an eye on your data usage:

1. Tap the Settings app
2. Tap Cellular
3. Look in the Cellular Data Usage section
4. In the Current Period, you will see exactly how much of your data allowance has been used

Control Your Data Usage
Your iPad also lets you track your data usage on an app-by-app basis. Access the screen by following steps 1-2 above. Then scroll down to the 'Use Cellular Data For' section.

Here, you will see a list of all the apps that are sending or receiving data, and precisely how much. If you find that a particular app is using more than you'd like, by tapping its switch to Off you can prevent it from using any more.

Data-hungry apps tend to be media-related. Typical examples are FaceTime, the App Store, the iTunes Store, Maps, etc.

Turn Off a Cellular Connection

If you don't need a cellular connection at all, or have reached your data limit and don't want to risk triggering an over-the-odds payment for excess usage, you can turn the connection off altogether. This is the only foolproof method of ensuring no extra charges.

If the connection is left on, it's all too easy to accidentally click a link in an email, or for someone else to use the iPad without your knowledge.

1. Tap the Settings app

2. Tap Cellular

3. Tap the Cellular Data switch to the Off position

Don't forget that when you do this, your iPad will now be reliant on Wi-Fi for connectivity. If no Wi-Fi networks are available, you won't be able to send email, browse the Internet, etc.

Turn Off Data Roaming

Data roaming is a function that enables you to get a connection in areas where you are out of range of your operator (typically, this occurs when you are abroad). In this situation, your iPad will 'roam' in an attempt to find an accessible network, even it is provided by another operator.

Accessible, however, does not mean affordable! Data roaming charges can add up to astronomic amounts.

Even if you don't use your iPad, if the data roaming feature on your device is enabled, you can still get hit with an eye-watering bill. You may not be actively browsing the Internet but behind the scenes your iPad will be busily checking for email, apps will be updating, etc. A week or two of this while you're on holiday can prove to be very costly.

So, when you are outside your operator's coverage area and don't need a connection, make sure Data Roaming is turned off.

1. Tap the Settings app

2. Tap Cellular

3. Turn Data Roaming off by tapping the switch to the Off position

Note: you can always see how much of your data allowance Data Roaming has used by checking the Cellular Data Usage section in the iPad's settings as we explained on the previous page.

Bluetooth Connections

What is Bluetooth?
Bluetooth is a low-power wireless network technology designed for the exchange of data over short distances – typically, 10 metres and less. It is built into literally billions of products: from cars and mobile phones to medical devices, computers, headphones and even toothbrushes.

Bluetooth networks enable the sharing of voice, music, pictures, video and other information wirelessly between paired devices. Typical uses are connecting wireless speakers to playback devices such as smartphones, uploading pictures from cameras, and transferring files from one smartphone to another.

Do not confuse Bluetooth with Wi-Fi – although both are 'wireless', they are not the same at all. For example, Bluetooth networks use virtually no power, and because they don't travel far are theoretically more secure than Wi-Fi networks that operate over longer distances.

Setting up a Bluetooth connection is a two-stage procedure involving both the iPad and the device being connected to it, as we see below.

Make Your Devices Discoverable
The Bluetooth network is created by a tiny chip built-in to the device that you are connecting wirelessly to your iPad. For it to work, both the device and the iPad need to be made 'discoverable'.

We'll start with the iPad:

1. Tap the Settings app

2. Tap Bluetooth

3. Enable Bluetooth by tapping the switch to the On position – your iPad is now discoverable

In the Devices section, you'll see that the iPad is searching for a Bluetooth signal as shown here:

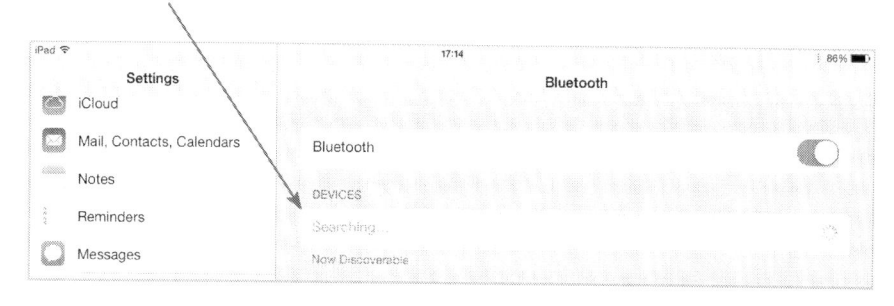

4. Now go to the Bluetooth device

cont'd

1. Switch the device on. If it has a separate switch that makes it discoverable (see the documentation if you are not sure), turn it on. The device will now be discoverable

2. Make sure it is no further than 10 metres or so from the iPad

Pairing Your Devices
Back at the iPad, look in the Devices section of the Bluetooth settings page. Instead of searching as it was before, you will now see the name of your Bluetooth device (JABRA BT2045 in this example):

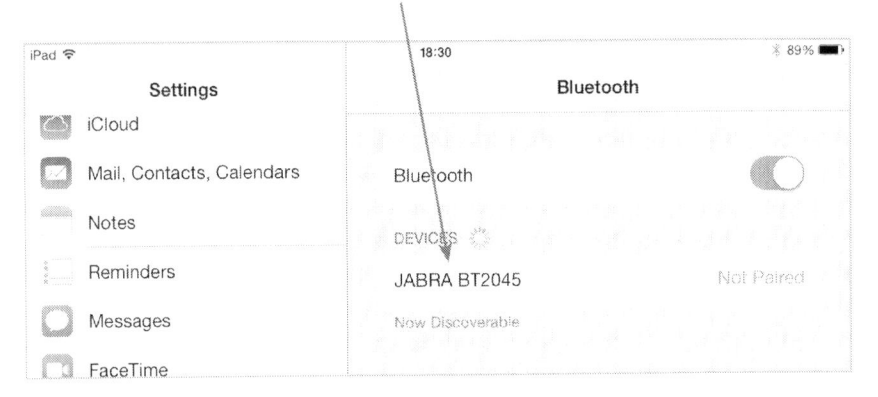

iPad 📶		18:30	📶 89%
	Settings	Bluetooth	
	iCloud		
	Mail, Contacts, Calendars	Bluetooth	⬤
	Notes	DEVICES	
	Reminders	JABRA BT2045	Not Paired
	Messages	Now Discoverable	
	FaceTime		

However, it will say 'Not Paired' – this means the two devices are not yet communicating with each other.

To fix this:

1. Tap the Bluetooth device. Depending on the device, you may be asked to enter a pin code at this point (this will be supplied with the device's documentation)

2. Pairing will now take place. Once done, instead of Not Paired, you will see Connected in the Bluetooth settings screen

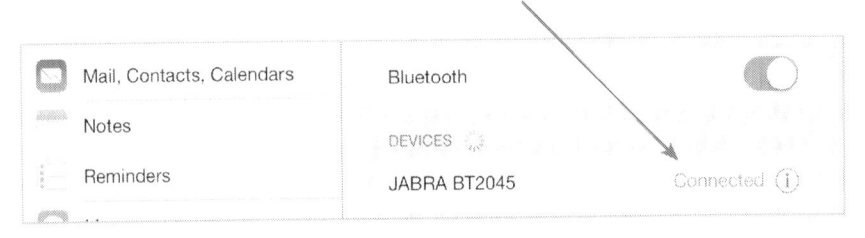

	Mail, Contacts, Calendars	Bluetooth	⬤
	Notes	DEVICES	
	Reminders	JABRA BT2045	Connected ⓘ

The Bluetooth network is now established and the two devices will be able to communicate wirelessly with each other.

CHAPTER 6

The Internet

One of the biggest boons offered by tablets in general is the ability to use the Internet while on the move. Sure, this can also be done on a smartphone but the larger screen of a tablet enhances the experience enormously.

Your iPad comes with Apple's Safari app, a web browser that provides a good range of features and functions. Quite apart from browsing, it enables you to bookmark your favourite sites, get rid of irritating in-line ads, hide your browsing tracks and much more.

We also take a look at alternatives to Safari.

Safari Web Browser 72

Opening a Web Page 73

Searching With Safari 74

Viewing & Navigating Web Pages 76

Browsing With Tabs 77

Viewing Articles With Safari Reader 79

Bookmarks & Favourites 80

Reading Lists 82

Private Browsing 83

AutoFill 84

Privacy & Security on the Internet 85

Alternative Browser Apps 86

Safari Web Browser

Before you start browsing the Internet with the iPad, it will be as well to familiarise yourself with the app you'll use to do it – the Safari web browser. Tap Safari on the Home screen to get started.

The screenshot below shows Safari's main elements, plus the controls you will use to navigate both the Internet and individual web pages:

- **Forwards/Backwards** – tap the arrows to navigate between pages

- **Address/Search Box** – this is where you enter the address of a website you want to visit. It also doubles as a search box – simply enter your search term and tap Go on the keyboard

- **New Tab** – tap to open a new tab

- **Bookmarks** – this gives you access to your Bookmarks, Favourites and Reading List. You will also find options to manage them

- **Options** – these include sharing a web page via AirDrop, text message, email, Twitter or Facebook. There are also options to bookmark a page, add it to a reading list, add it to the Home screen, copy it, and print it

- **Tab View** – tap this to open a thumbnail list of all open tabs

Opening a Web Page

To open a web page in Safari, tap in the address/search box. The keyboard will open at the bottom of the screen allowing you to type the address.

After you have been using the browser for a while, you'll notice that Safari tries to predict the address based on what you have already typed in an attempt to speed things up. If it gets it right, stop typing and tap Go on the keyboard. If it gets it wrong, just ignore it and keep typing.

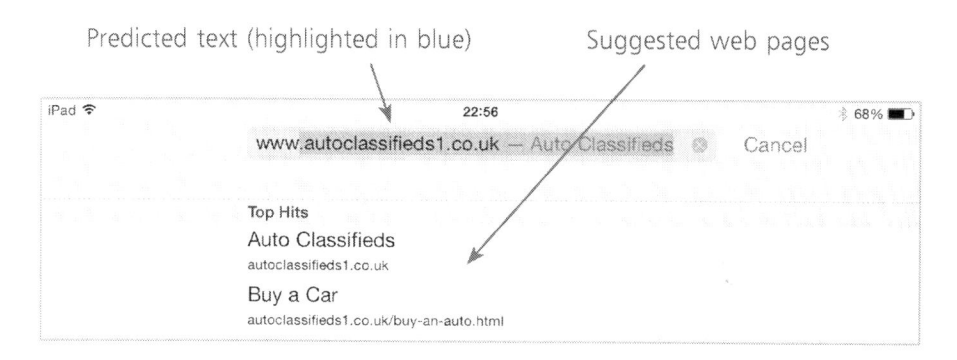

Also, as you type, Safari will suggest pages it thinks are relevant to what you are entering in the address/search box. These appear below the box and are based on pages previously visited and past searches. Just tap one of the links to go to the page.

If you find this feature annoying or simply don't need it, you can turn it off in Safari's settings. Open the Settings app and go to Safari > Search Engine Suggestions. Tap the switch to Off.

When you finish a particular browsing session and close Safari, it will remember the last page visited. The next time you open the browser, it will open that page, the address of which will be in the address/search bar.

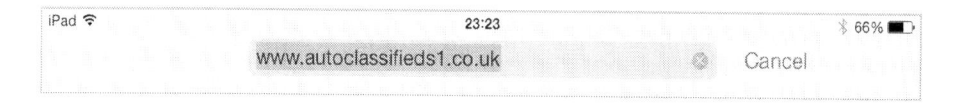

To clear the address/search box so you can enter a different address, just tap anywhere in the box. The address will be highlighted as shown above. Clear it by either tapping the X at the far-right of the box or by simply typing over it.

Searching With Safari

As we mentioned on page 72, the address box also doubles as Safari's search box. You can use this to search the entire Internet, or just a single web page.

Search the Internet
Tap in the box to bring up the keyboard and type in your search term. By default, the search is done via Google and you will see four suggestions listed below the search box. If any of these are relevant, tap to open the page.

If not, tap Go on the keyboard to open a full list of Google search results.

Search a Web Page
Open the required web page, tap in the address box to bring up the keyboard and type in your search term. At the bottom of the list of results, you will see a section entitled 'On This Page'. This will show your search term and the number of matches the search has found (you may have to hide the keyboard to see this).

On This Page

Find "australia"   7 matches

Tap the search term and you will be taken to the first occurrence of the word – this will be highlighted in yellow.

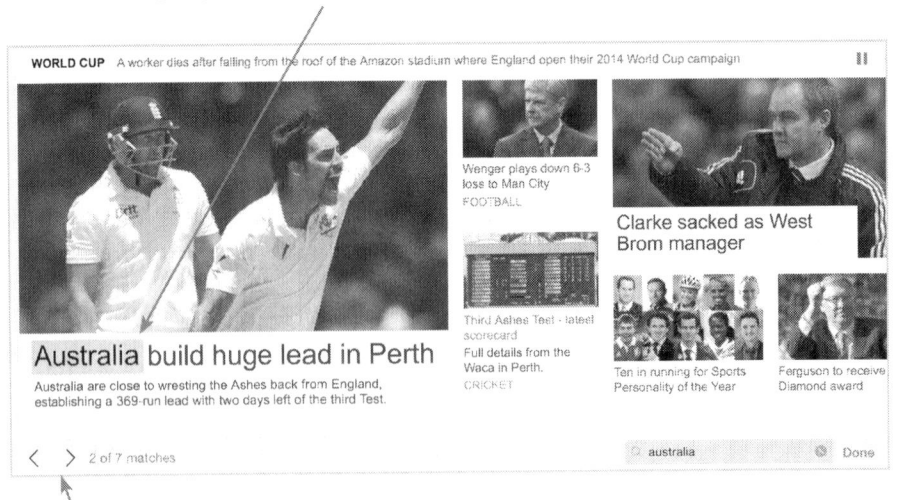

At the bottom-left of the page, you will see Next and Previous arrows that take you to other instances of the word. When you are finished, tap Done at the bottom-right.

cont'd

Change the Default Search Engine

Your iPad comes with Google as the default search provider and you will probably be quite content with this. However, should you prefer to use a different search engine, you do have a choice.

Open the Settings app and go to Safari. At the top-right, you'll see Search Engine in the Search section. Tap this to open the options window:

Google	✓
Yahoo	
Bing	
Baidu	
DuckDuckGo	

Tap the search engine of your choice. Note that Baidu is a Chinese search engine, while DuckDuckGo is a relatively new search engine that puts privacy first and, as such, does not store IP addresses, does not log user information, and uses cookies only when needed. As a result, targeted advertising and skewed search results are largely eliminated.

Search by Voice Command

On page 28, we took a look at Siri – the iPad's voice-controlled personal assistant. One of the many ways this feature can be used is to conduct Internet searches. Simply tell it what you are looking for and it will do its best to oblige. Some typical examples are:

- **Conducting a full Internet search** – e.g. 'search the web for world cup 2014', or 'search the internet for origins of apache indians'
- **A more specific Internet search** – e.g. 'bbc ashes cricket'
- **Searching with a specified search engine** – e.g. 'bing gold prices'

How you phrase the search is not critical as long as your meaning is clear.

When you are looking for a business or service, Siri uses data provided by Yelp. For example, you can locate restaurants by criteria such as cuisine, price, location, etc. It will also give you specific details of the restaurant including pictures, rating, prices, and reviews.

If you add a qualifier such as good or best, e.g. 'good thai takeaway', Siri will sort the results by their rating.

Viewing & Navigating Web Pages

Viewing and navigating a web page with a touchscreen tablet requires a different technique than the traditional computer/mouse combination. With a tablet, touch gestures are the order of the day and while they are not as precise as a mouse cursor it is, nevertheless, surprising just how effective they are.

- **Panning** – placing a finger on the screen and moving it left, right, up, and down enables you to move, or pan, the page. To move quickly, flick your finger – the faster you flick, the faster the page moves

- **Zooming** – due to the small screen size of tablets, zooming is a much more important issue than it is when browsing the Internet with a full-size computer monitor. Before you do though, try simply rotating the tablet so you are holding it in Landscape mode – this will increase the size of screen elements and may be all that's necessary

    If not, double-tap the area you want to zoom into. This may be an area of text, an image, or a form, and it will be magnified to the width of the screen. To zoom back out, double-tap again

    To zoom with more control, place two fingers on the screen and move them apart – this action zooms in. Pinching your fingers will zoom out. Note that you should place your fingers on the part of the screen you want to zoom into or out of

- **Move to the top** – if you are down at the bottom of a long page, rather than pan back up, just tap at the top of the screen – this action instantly takes you to the top of the page

- **Links** – web pages often contain links to this, that and the other. If you want to know where a link leads before actually going to it, press and hold the link. A small pop-up will appear and at the top will be the link's address

    Below this, you will see a number of options one of which is Open. Below that is 'Open in New Tab'. Tap this and the link will open in a new tab – we'll see how to configure this option on the next page

    Another option is Copy. Tap this and go to another app, such as Mail or Notes. Position the cursor, tap and then tap Paste. You can now save the link or email it, depending on the app you are using.

Browsing With Tabs

Before the concept of tabbed browsing was conceived, an Internet browsing session could be a somewhat painful experience that involved opening numerous pages, each in its own window, and constant use of the back and forward buttons. Losing your starting point, i.e. the original page, was very easy to do. Furthermore, all these open windows placed a considerable load on the PC's resources that could reduce it to a crawl.

The introduction of tabs resolved these issues and made it possible to have any number of pages open simultaneously, and to instantly switch between them without ever touching the back and forward buttons. At the same time, the original page could be kept open in case you needed to go back.

Opening Tabs
Opening a tab in Safari is very simple and can be done in two ways:

- The Tab Button – at the far top-right of any browser window, you will see an icon in the shape of a cross – tap this to open a new tab. All open tabs are shown on the Tab Bar, which is situated just below the address/search box, and can be accessed from the bar

Tab Bar showing open tabs   Open a new tab

- Links – On page 76 we saw how there are several options with regard to opening web page links, such as Copy and Open. Another of these options is 'Open in New Tab'

When you select this option, the page is loaded in the tab but the current page is kept in the foreground – just tap the new tab to switch to it. However, if you'd rather switch to the new tab automatically, you can configure this in Safari's settings:

1. On the Home screen, tap the Settings app

2. Tap Safari on the left-hand side and then on the right, tap the 'Open New Tabs in Background' option to Off

cont'd

Tab View

As we have seen, you can view your open tabs and switch from one to the other from the Tab bar. However, this is not ideal as you can't actually see what's on them.

Safari's Tab View provides the solution. Tap the Tab view ▢ icon at the top-right of the screen and you will be presented with a thumbnail view of all the tabs currently open in Safari:

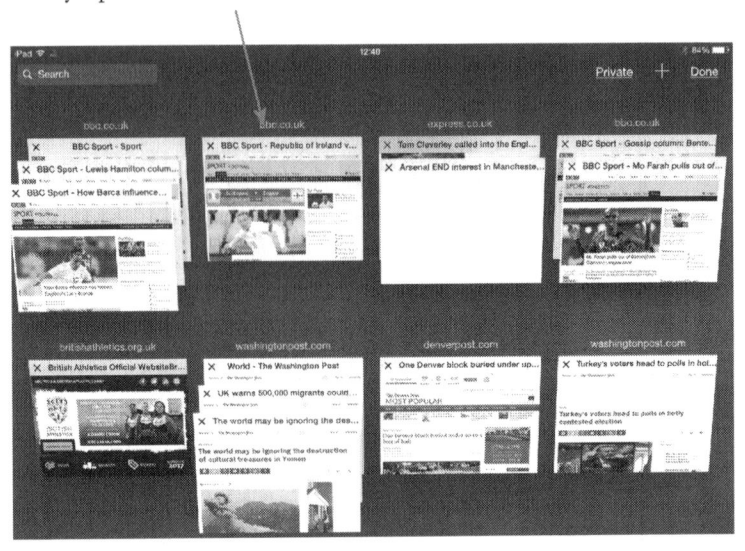

You'll now be able to see what's on the pages, making it much easier to select the one required – just tap on the thumbnail to go to it. Note that tabs from the same site are grouped together, i.e. stacked, as shown above.

iCloud Tabs

You are sitting at home reading a web page on your iPad. However, you have to leave to take someone to the hospital before you can finish the page. Wouldn't it be handy if you could just pick up where you left off with your iPhone while waiting at the hospital?

Well, with iCloud Tabs you can – any Safari tabs left open on one of your Apple devices will be accessible on all the others. However, the devices must all be signed in to the same iCloud account – we explain how to sign in to iCloud on page 185.

To test it is working, open some tabs in Safari on your iPad. Now open your other device, and tap the Tabs View icon. At the bottom, below the thumbnails, you will see a list of all the tabs open on the iPad. Just tap on one to open it.

Viewing Articles With Safari Reader

Many web pages these days contain a number of elements that can get in the way of the page's content. For example, images and adverts that contribute nothing worthwhile to a site's content. Then there is all the stuff necessary to make the site work such as sidebars, menus, links, search boxes and icons.

As a result, it is often surprisingly difficult to find and read a site's content. A solution provided with your iPad is Safari Reader. When activated, all that extraneous clutter is stripped away leaving just the article and any related images on the page. Reader is also useful for getting rid of those in-line advertising links that open in pop-up windows.

However, the feature doesn't work on all web pages. Usually, this is when a page contains two or more articles. In this case, you need to tap an article link to open it in a new window. You will then see the Reader icon appear to the left of the address bar.

Tap the icon and, as if by magic, all those banner ads, unrelated images, menus, etc, will disappear. This is demonstrated below:

Page as normal Page in Reader

Bookmarks & Favourites

The Internet is so vast that finding a useful page is a task that can take a long time and involve a lot of searching. So, having found such a page, it makes sense to ensure you can find it again, and quickly, should you ever need to.

This is where bookmarks come in. They allow you to save a link to pages you visit often, or might need to access again at some point. Favourites are simply bookmarks that are placed on the Favourites Bar at the top of the browser window. From here, they can be instantly accessed, i.e. they are your favourite bookmarks.

Creating a Bookmark
Bookmarking a page with Safari is simple:

1. Navigate to the required page in Safari

2. Tap the Options button at the left of the address/search bar

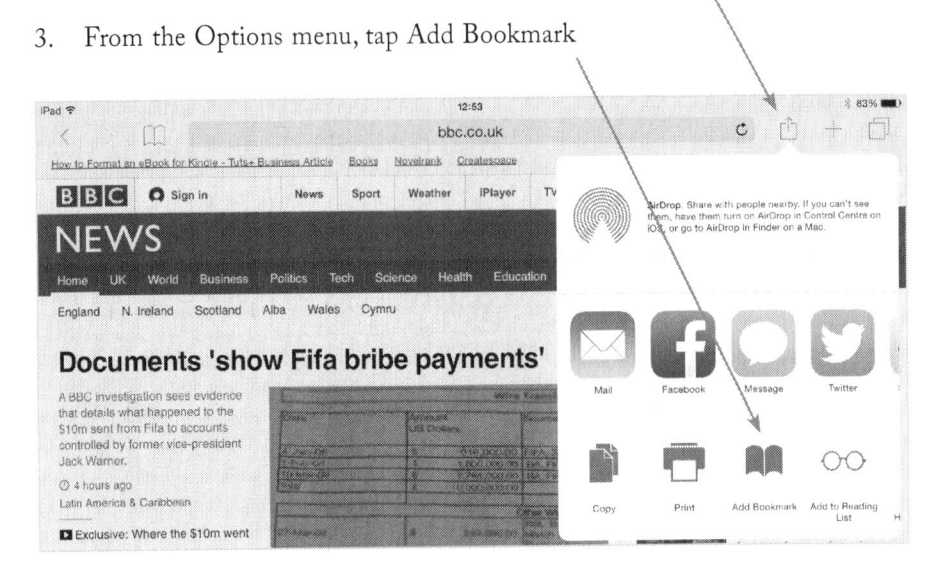

3. From the Options menu, tap Add Bookmark

4. The bookmark is automatically named with the title of the page. However, this is usually long-winded so you may prefer to name it yourself. If so, tap the X at the right of the name to delete it and then enter the name you'd prefer

5. Under the Name box, you'll see an option called Location. Tap this and you'll be able to choose between saving the bookmark as a favourite (favourite bookmark) or as an ordinary bookmark. Make your choice and then tap Save (or Done on the keyboard)

cont'd

Opening Favourite Bookmarks

Your favourite bookmarks are placed in a bar at the top-left of the browser window for immediate access. Just tap on one to open it.

Another way is to tap the + icon at the top-right to open a new tab – you will now see large icons of all your favourites in a browser window. Yet another way is to tap once in the address/search bar – this opens a pop-up window showing the same large icon view of the favourites.

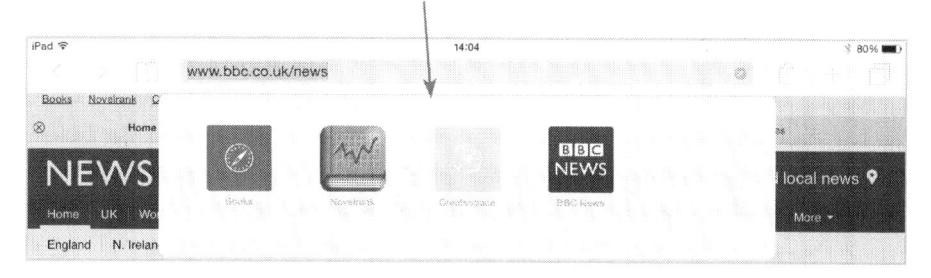

Opening Bookmarks

To open an ordinary bookmark, tap the Bookmarks icon at the left of the address/search bar.

In the window that opens, you'll see your bookmarks below the Favourites and History folders. Just tap one to open it.

The History folder contains a chronological record of every site you have visited over a period of several days.

This can be useful if you forget to bookmark a page – just scroll through the list of visited web pages until you find the one you are looking for.

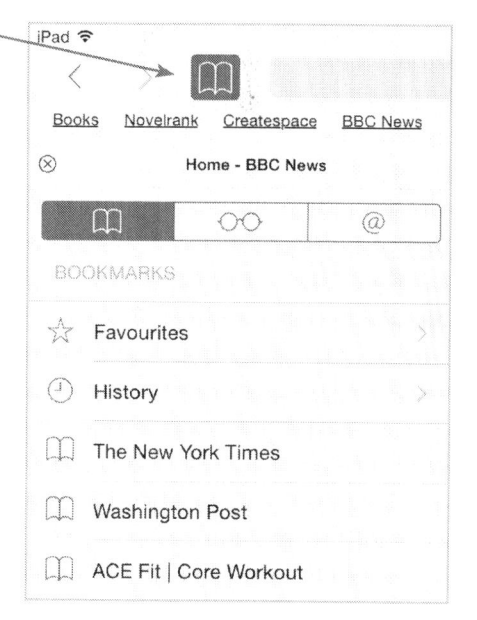

81

Reading Lists

Every now and then you'll come across an interesting web page that you don't have time to finish reading. Or you may be looking for information on a certain topic for later perusal.

Whichever, Safari has it covered in the form of its Reading List feature. This works by downloading the page to the iPad so you can read it at your leisure. Furthermore, because it is stored on the iPad, you do not need to be connected to the Internet to do so.

Add a Page to Your Reading List
Having found a page you want to save for reading at a later time, the way to add it to your reading list is:

1. Tap the Options button at the right of the address/search bar
2. In the pop-up window that opens, tap 'Add to Reading List'

Copy   Print   Add Bookmark   Add to Reading List

Accessing Your Reading List
When you are ready to read some of the pages in your reading list, access the list by:

1. Tapping the Bookmarks icon at the left of the address bar
2. Tapping the Reading List icon (shaped like spectacles). You will now see a list of all the pages saved. Tap any item to open the page
3. At the bottom of the list, you will see either 'Show Unread' or 'Show All'. The latter shows all the pages in your list; the former just the ones that haven't been opened yet

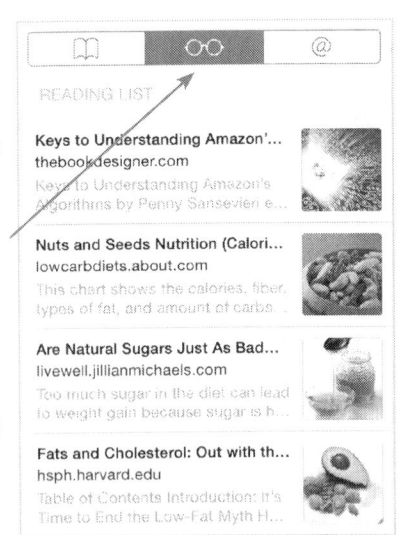

Private Browsing

If you are security conscious, you may want to take a look at your iPad's Private Browsing feature. This allows you to browse the Internet without leaving any traces of what you have been doing.

When in Private Browsing mode, Safari doesn't save any website data so there is no way for anyone else to see what you've been up to.

For example:

- Web pages are not stored in Safari's History list
- Text and images are not stored
- Search box entries are not saved
- Autofill is disabled
- Web pages cannot be seen on your other iOS devices via iCloud tabs

To activate Private Browsing:

1. Open Safari and tap the Tab View icon at the far top-right
2. In the window that opens, tap Private
3. You will now see the screen below saying you are in Private Browsing Mode. Tap the + button at the top-right to open a new tab

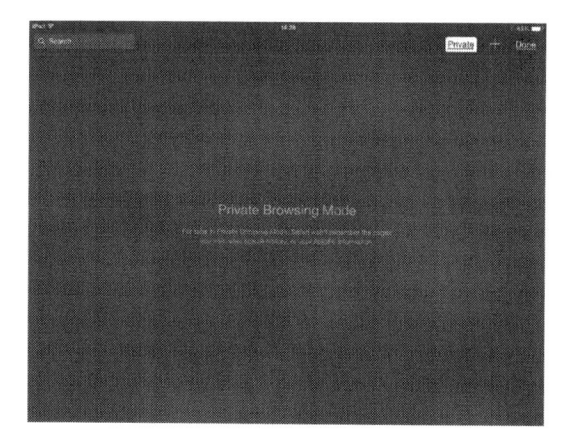

4. The top of the browser now turns dark indicating you are in Private Mode. From this point, you are browsing in complete privacy
5. When you want to return to normal browsing, tap the Tab View icon again, tap Private and then tap Done

AutoFill

Many sites these days require you to create an account – this will include personal details, such as your home and email addresses, phone number, etc. To log in to these accounts, you'll need to enter a password. Then there is online shopping, which requires you to enter your credit card details.

To save having to constantly enter this type of information, Safari provides a feature that can speed things up considerably – it is called AutoFill.

When enabled, AutoFill does the work for you by automatically entering the requested information in the various fields (it takes the info from your contacts profile) – all you have to do is tap a button.

To set up AutoFill:

1. If you haven't already done so, create a contact for yourself in the Contacts app. Include all the information you are likely to need online

2. Tap the Settings app to open it

3. Go to Safari > Passwords & AutoFill

4. Tap 'Use Contact Info' to On

5. Tap 'My Info' and then select your contact profile

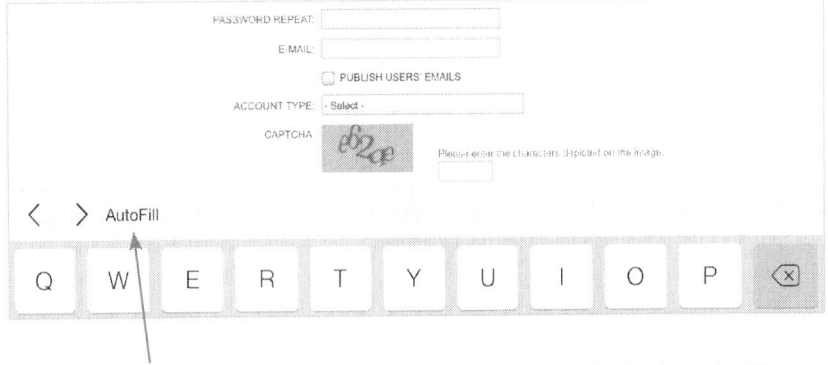

From now on, when you tap a text field in a web page, the keyboard will open as normal but with the addition of an AutoFill option at the top as shown above. Tap an email field for example, then tap AutoFill, and your email address will be entered automatically.

As we mentioned at the top of the page, you can also enable the automatic entry of usernames, passwords, and credit card info. Fairly obviously, however, there are security issues with these options, so you may wish to consider carefully before enabling them.

Privacy & Security on the Internet

The Internet is a dangerous place, particularly for the uninitiated or unwary. Not only is your privacy at risk but your wallet as well!

Things you need to be aware of include:

- **Phishing** – phishing is when a fake website purports to be something respectable, a well known corporation perhaps, in order to gain your trust. Having done so, it will ask you to enter personal details such as passwords and account numbers, and then relieve you of your money

- **JavaScript** – JavaScript is a programming language used in web sites to add useful applications. Generally, it's a good thing but in the wrong hands it can be used to compromise a user's computer

- **Pop-ups** – a pop-up is a little window that quite literally pops-up unexpectedly when you are browsing a site. They may contain an annoying ad or something useful such as a login page

- **Cookies** – a cookie is a text file that websites download to your iPad. They store information about your current browsing session; a typical example being a shopping cart. However, they can also be used to track what you are doing and serve up related ads

- **History List** – Safari keeps a chronological list of all the sites you visit, which can be useful should you need to find a certain site again. However, anyone snooping through the list will be able to see exactly what you've been up on the Internet

If any of these concern you, open the Settings app and tap Safari. Go to the 'Privacy and Security' section where you will see various options:

The 'Fraudulent Website Warning' setting lets you turn phishing protection on or off. By default, it is on and we suggest you leave it on.

'Block Cookies' is also enabled by default. However, if you visit certain types of site you may want to change this. Tap the setting and you will be able to choose from a number of options.

In the General section, you'll see that pop-ups are blocked by default. This can result in a considerable loss of functionality in many websites, so you may want to have this off for some sites and on for others.

Tap Advanced and you'll be able to toggle JavaScript support on or off.

With regards the History List, tap 'Clear History and Website Data'. Then tap Clear – this removes your history, cookies and other stuff.

Alternative Browser Apps

Safari is a good app and offers most of what is required from a web browser. There are, however, a lot of other browsers available from the App Store. While you may find Safari adequate, it could be that one of the others provides a feature that you need and that Safari doesn't provide. Or, you may just want to try something different.

Whatever, some browser apps you can try include:

- **Google Chrome** – Chrome is a popular alternative for people who use Google services. For example, if you use Chrome on your Mac or PC and save bookmarks, the app can sync them across your devices. You can also sign into your Google account with the app and all your settings and preferences will be right there

- **Opera Mini** – Opera Mini is reckoned to be the fastest browser available. This does come at a price though, as many of the features found in other browsers have been sacrificed accordingly. However, if speed is what you need, the Opera Mini is the one to go for

- **Dolphin** – due to its support for gestures and the use of sidebars, Dolphin provides a more intuitive way of browsing the web. It offers many useful options that include a downloads manager, a choice of search engines, tab browsing and much more

- **Mercury Browser Pro** – Mercury takes the best bits of Safari and Chrome and rolls them up into one of the best browsers available. Features include ad blocking, social network integration, and excellent support for gestures. It will even sync bookmarks and data across all your devices with both Firefox and Chrome

- **Puffin** – the feature that really defines Puffin is its speed. From loading web pages to tabbing through menus, it's smooth and quick. There are also numerous add-ons to choose from, the ability to download files, and much more besides

- **Atomic** – Atomic is a highly flexible browser that allows the user to set up advanced privacy controls, choose from several colour themes, activate an ad-blocker, customise the search engine bar, view the source of a web page, and more

CHAPTER 7

Email

Your iPad comes equipped with a decent email app called Mail – this does everything you'd expect of an email client. We take a close look at Mail in this chapter and see just what it has to offer.

For the uninitiated, we explain how to set up an email account, how to sync accounts, and how to manage accounts.

You will also learn how to use Siri to send and receive email, and see some interesting alternatives to the Mail app.

Email Accounts 88

Email Services & Protocols 88

Setting Up an Email Account 89

Syncing Email Accounts 90

Managing Email Accounts 91

Receiving Email 94

Sending Email 97

Sending Images 98

Sending Links & Attachments 99

Managing Email 101

VIPs 101

Thread Organisation 102

Emailing With Siri 103

Email Apps 104

Email Accounts

As with any type of computer, before you can use your iPad for email, you must first set up an email account. This is very easy to do – if you currently use one of the popular email services such as iCloud, Gmail, Yahoo, etc, it's even easier as much of the work is already done for you – just a few taps is all it takes.

If you decide to use a different service, such as the one from your ISP, you will need to provide more information though.

Email Services and Protocols

The easy way to set up an account is to use one of the six preconfigured email services provided with your iPad. These are all web-based and use the IMAP protocol (except for Microsoft Exchange, which uses the MAPI protocol).

Your iPad knows how to connect to all these services – all you need to supply is the email address and account password. If, however, you don't use any of these services, you will have to supply more information.

Apart from the email address and account password, you will also need to provide the names of the incoming and outgoing mail servers, plus any security info required to send email. You will also need to specify if the account is POP or IMAP.

All this information will be available from your email service provider – just ask them for it and you'll be ready to go. However, before we go into the mechanics of setting up an email account, we'll explain the difference between the email protocols, POP and IMAP.

- **POP (Post Office Protocol)** – with POP, emails are stored temporarily on your Internet Service Provider's (ISP's) server. When you connect to the server, the messages are downloaded to your iPad and then deleted from the server

  The advantage of POP is that because all your emails are stored on the iPad, they can be re-read at any time without the need to reconnect to the server. The disadvantage is that they can only be viewed on the iPad to which they were downloaded

- **IMAP (Internet Message Access Protocol)** – IMAP essentially works the other way. Messages are not downloaded to your iPad (although it may seem as though they are). They are actually stored permanently on the ISP's server and you simply read them from there.

  The advantage with this method is that your email can be accessed via any device regardless of its location. The disadvantage is that in order to do so, an Internet connection is necessary

cont'd

Setting up an Email Account

Get started by tapping the Settings app on the Home screen. Then:

1. Go to Mail, Contacts, Calendars on the left of the screen. Then tap Add Account. You will see the list of email services shown below. These are the iPad's six preconfigured email services that we mentioned on the previous page

2. Lets say you want to use Yahoo. Tap the Yahoo link and a configuration screen will open. Here, you will enter a name for the account, the email address, an account password and a description for the account

3. Tap Next. Your iPad will look up the details you have just provided. Assuming they check out, the account is set up without further ado

4. Tap Save

However, if you want to use an email service not preconfigured with the iPad, such as the one provided by your ISP, you will need to select the Other option at the bottom of the list.

While the procedure is much the same, you will need to also specify whether the account is POP or IMAP, and provide incoming and outgoing mail server addresses. Contact your ISP if you don't have this information.

When you do:

1. Tap Other and then tap 'Add Mail Account'

2. Enter the account name, email address, password and description in the relevant boxes. Then tap Next

3. Specify the type of account by tapping POP or IMAP

4. Under 'Incoming Mail Server', enter the host name, the username and the password in the respective fields

5. Under 'Outgoing Mail Server', enter the host name in the Host Name box

6. Tap Save

Your iPad will now verify the settings and, when done, add the account to your Accounts list.

cont'd

Syncing Email Accounts

Another way to get emailing with your iPad is to sync, or transfer, an existing email account from your computer to the iPad. This can be done with Apple's iTunes software.

If you don't already have iTunes have on your computer, download it from Apple's website and install it (the program is free by the way). Once you have it up and running, do the following:

1. Connect the iPad to your computer. By default, iTunes should open automatically – if it doesn't, open it manually

2. At the top-left of the screen, under the menu bar, click the iPad button

3. On the sidebar under Settings, click Info

4. Check the 'Sync Mail Accounts from' box and select your email program from the drop-down list (Outlook in the example below). Then check the account (or accounts) that you want to sync to your iPad

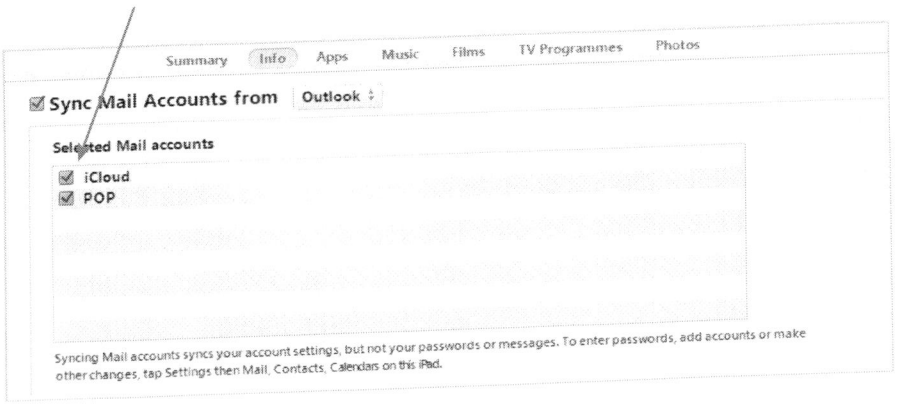

```
              Summary   Info   Apps   Music   Films   TV Programmes   Photos

☑ Sync Mail Accounts from   Outlook ▾

   Selected Mail accounts
   ☑ iCloud
   ☑ POP


   Syncing Mail accounts syncs your account settings, but not your passwords or messages. To enter passwords, add accounts or make
   other changes, tap Settings then Mail, Contacts, Calendars on this iPad.
```

5. Click Apply at the bottom-right of the window

iTunes will now sync the email account you have selected across to your iPad.

Note that this procedure only transfers the account settings, i.e. your username, password, mail servers, etc – it does not transfer your messages so you will not be able to read them on the iPad.

If the transferred account is an IMAP account, however, you will be able to read your messages on the iPad from the ISP's server.

Managing Email Accounts

Your iPad provides a number of settings with which to manage your email. Knowing what these are can make a considerable difference to how effectively you use the Mail app. We'll take a look at these next:

Setting the Default Account
You will only need do this if you have more than one email account on your iPad. If so, one of them has to be set as the default account, otherwise Mail won't know which one to use.

To this end, Mail automatically configures the first account to be set up as the default. If you are happy with this fine, but if you are not you can change it to a different one:

1. Tap Settings on the Home screen
2. Tap Mail, Contacts, Calendars
3. At the bottom of the Mail section, tap Default Account. In the list that opens, you will see all the email accounts that have been set up on the iPad

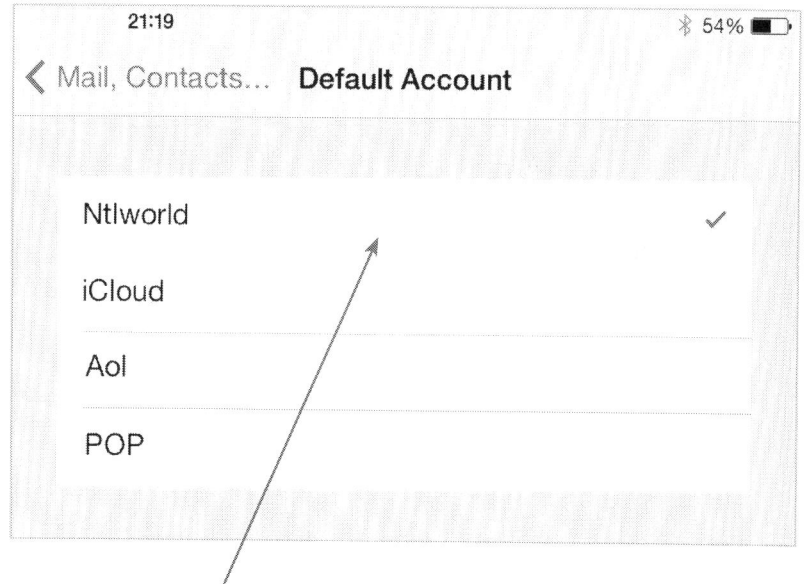

4. Tap the account that you want to set as the default. You will now see a checkmark to the side of it

Close the Settings app and then tap the Mail app. It will open showing the inbox of the account you have just selected.

cont'd

Deleting Accounts

You may, at some stage, decide that you no longer want or need a particular email account. If that's the case, you may as well get rid if it. The procedure for doing so is:

1. Open the Settings app

2. Tap Mail, Contacts, Calendars

3. In the Accounts section, tap the account to be deleted

4. At the bottom of the screen, in red, you will see 'Delete Account'. Tap this and you will then be asked to confirm the command

5. Tap Delete and the account will be removed from your iPad

Disabling Accounts

Rather than delete an account, you may prefer to disable it. Possible reasons for this include:

- It may be temporarily redundant

- Reducing the load on the battery. The Mail app checks for new messages at regular intervals – this makes a hit on the battery and the more active accounts you have, the greater the hit

1. Open the Settings app

2. Tap Mail, Contacts, Calendars

3. Tap the account you want to disable

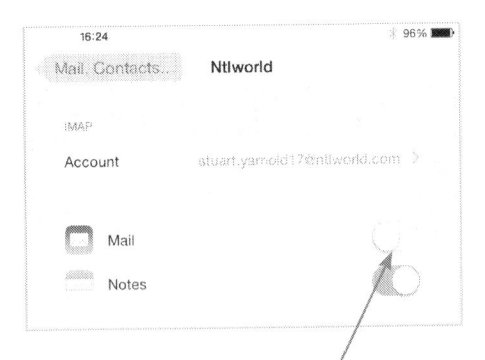

4. Tap the switch next to Mail to Off to disable the account

When you want to re-enable the account, simply toggle the switch back to the On position.

cont'd

Switching Accounts

Many users will have two or more email accounts and may at times want to switch between them – there are a number of reasons this might be necessary.

Tapping the Mail app on the Home screen will open the first account that was set up, i.e. the default account. But how do you go about accessing the other accounts?

Do it as follows:

1. Tap the Mail app on the Home screen

2. Hold your iPad in Portrait mode and then tap Inbox at the top-left of the screen

3. Tap the account name at the top-left of the screen

4. You'll now see the Mailboxes screen. At the top is 'All Inboxes' – tap this to show messages from all your email accounts in one unified list

   Below All Inboxes are links to the individual inboxes for each account

5. In the Accounts section, you will see a list of all your accounts (Ntlworld, iCloud, Aol, POP in our example on the right)

6. To see the folders associated with a particular account, tap on the account

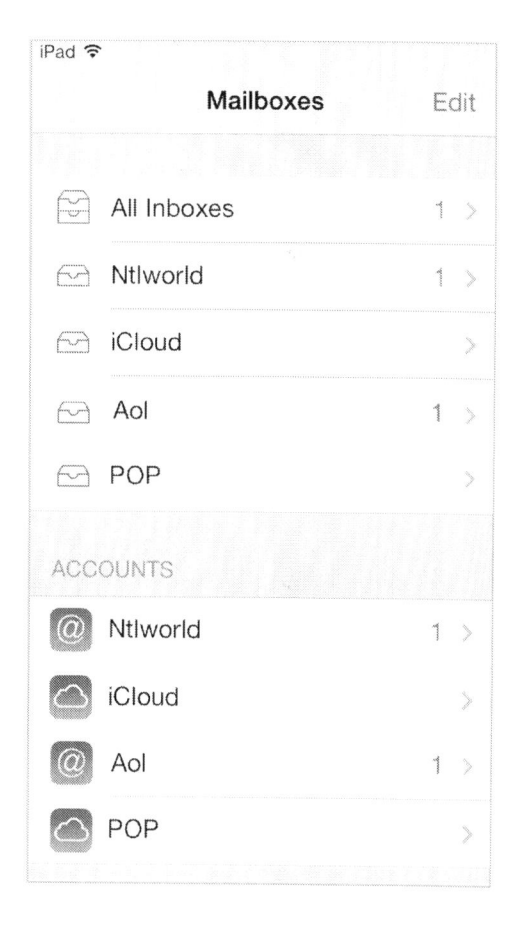

7. Tapping an account also makes it the default account

When you've finished, before closing the screen, remember to tap the account that you want the Mail app to use as the default account.

Receiving Email

Once an account is set up, incoming emails will be received by the Mail app. New mail will be indicated by a red badge at the top-right corner of the app – this shows the number of new messages.

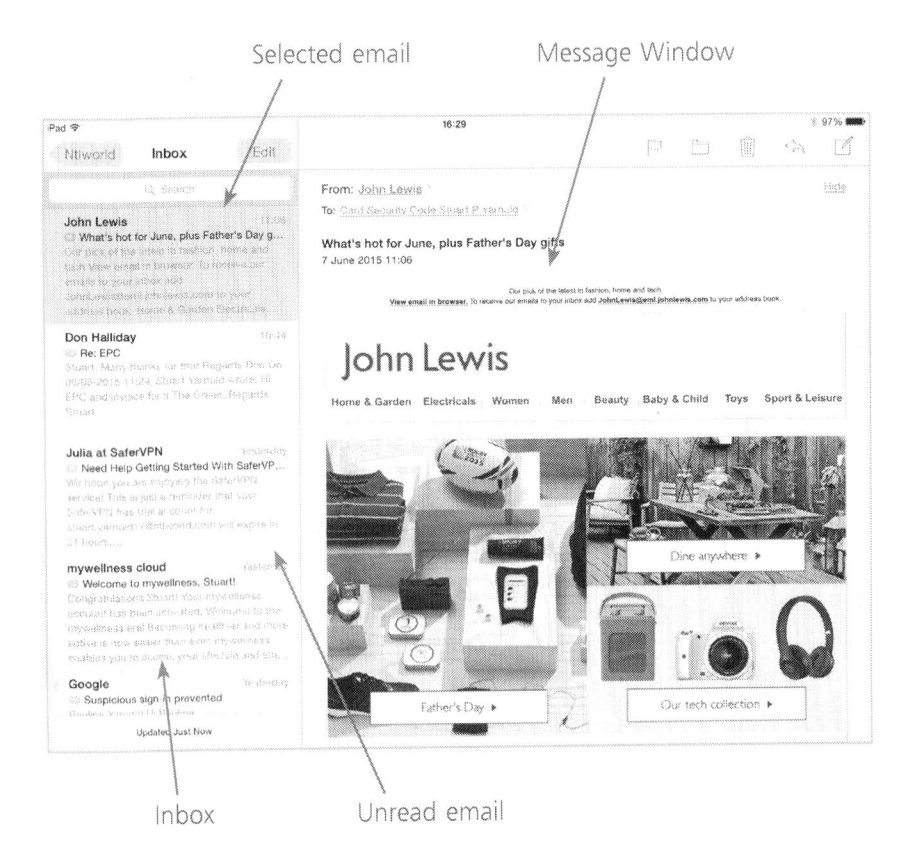

Tap the Mail app and it will open as shown above. The inbox will appear on the left of the screen showing a list of all your emails. Messages that you haven't read yet are marked with a blue dot.

To read a message, just tap on it – this will highlight it in grey, and on the right of the screen (assuming you are holding the iPad in Landscape mode), it will open in the message window.

As soon as you open the Mail app, it automatically checks for new mail – this is indicated by a 'Checking for Mail ...' message at the bottom of the inbox. You can also initiate a manual check at any time by dragging downwards on the inbox and then releasing – it will move down and then spring back up – this action queries the server for any new messages.

cont'd

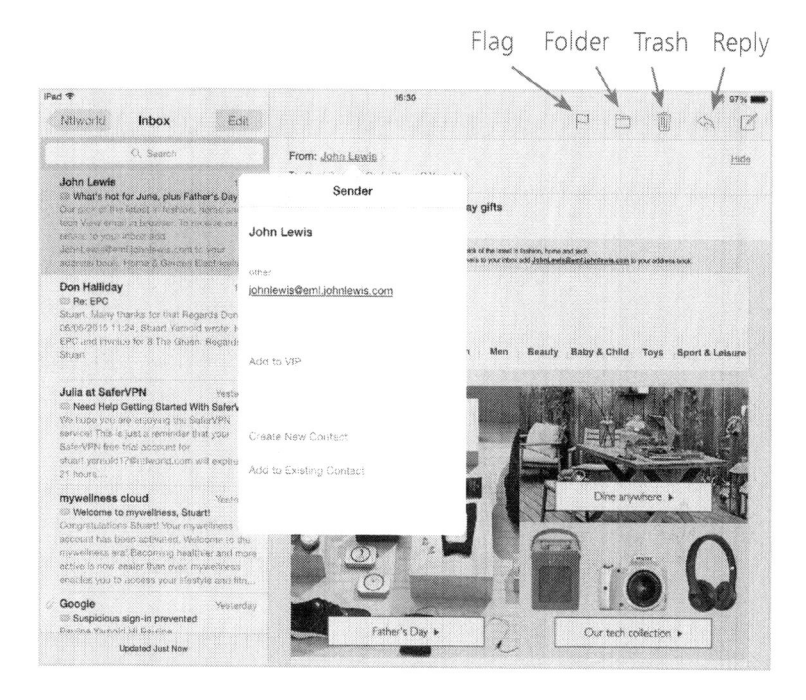

At the top of the message, tap the name or email address of the person sending the email. This opens a pop-up screen offering several options:

- Tap 'Add to VIP' to add the sender to your VIP inbox (see page 101)
- Tap 'Create New Contact' to add the sender to your contacts list
- Tap 'Add to Existing Contact' to add the sender's email address to an existing contact

The icons at the top-right provide more options:

Flag – this offers various options. These include flagging messages with a red dot to highlight them, marking messages you have read as unread, moving messages to the junk folder, and requesting notification of replies

Folder – this opens a list of all the mailboxes associated with the email account. Tap one of the mailboxes to move the message to that mailbox.

Trash – tap the Trash icon to send the message to the Trash folder from where it can be subsequently restored or deleted permanently.

Reply – this provides three options: The first enables you to reply to the message, the second enables you to forward the message, and the third, Print, enables you to print the message.

cont'd

Options for Receiving Email

Your iPad provides three options for the delivery of email to the device – Push, Fetch and Manual. This is an issue that affects battery life so you need to be aware of the differences between the three:

- **Push** – Push is the most active option as it automatically retrieves new messages as they arrive at your server. Choose Push if you want to receive your mail as soon as possible. Be aware though, that it makes a greater hit on the battery than either of the other options

- **Fetch** – with Fetch, your iPad will check for messages at set intervals of 15, 30, or 60 minutes. This means the app doesn't have to maintain a constant Internet connection, which in turn means battery power consumption is less than with Push

- **Manual** – with the Manual option, no email is received by the iPad until initiated by the user. Messages are received only when the Mail app is opened or when the screen is refreshed by dragging down on the inbox list. With regard to conserving battery charge, this is the best of the three options

To select the required option:

1. Open the Settings app and tap Mail, Contacts, Calendars. Tap 'Fetch New Data'

2. If you want to use Push, tap to enable it

3. If you don't select Push, the iPad will use Fetch by default. In the Fetch section, select how often you want to check for mail

4. If you prefer to use the Manual option, this is also available from the Fetch settings

If you have more than one account, you can customise the settings for each one by tapping the relevant account – this brings up the Push, Fetch and Manual options.

As already mentioned, if you are concerned about data usage the recommended option is Manual.

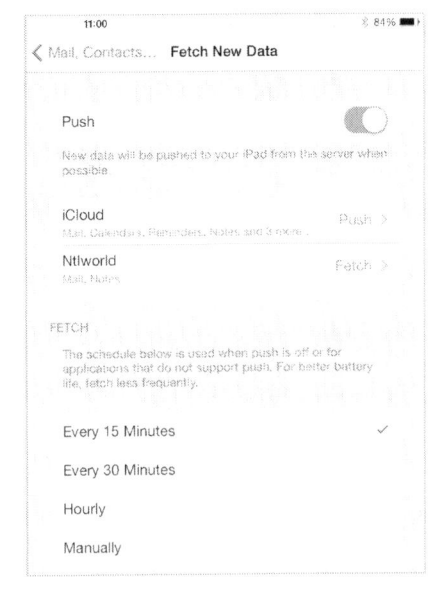

Sending Email

Sending email messages with the Mail app is very straightforward. It may not provide some of the features and options found in more complex email clients such as Microsoft Outlook and Mozilla Thunderbird, but the ones it does provide are perfectly adequate as we will see.

Composing an Email Message
To write an email message on your iPad, tap the Mail icon on the Home page; it will open at the last received message. At the top-right of the screen tap the New Message icon. A new message window will open as shown below:

1. In the To: field, type the email address. Alternatively, tap the blue + icon at the top-right to open your Contacts list from which you can select the recipient

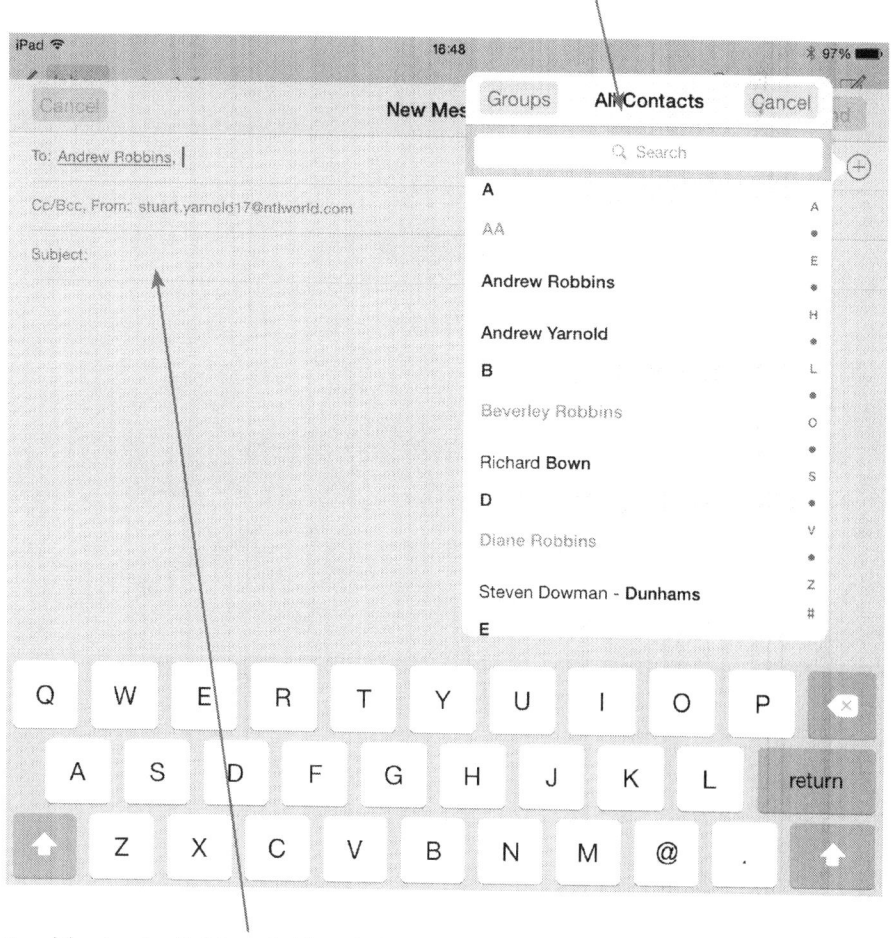

2. Tap in the Subject field and then type the subject

cont'd

3. Tap in the Message field and then type your message
4. Tap Send at the top-right of the message window

Formatting an Email Message
We mentioned at the beginning of the previous page that, in general, the Mail app provides limited options compared to many email programs. This certainly applies to the formatting options on offer, which amount to Bold, Italics and Underline – nothing else.

If you want to use any of these options:

1. Tap and hold on the text to be formatted
2. In the menu bar that appears above, tap Select
3. Drag the blue selection handles to select all the text to be formatted
4. Tap B*I*U to reveal the Bold, Italics and Underline options

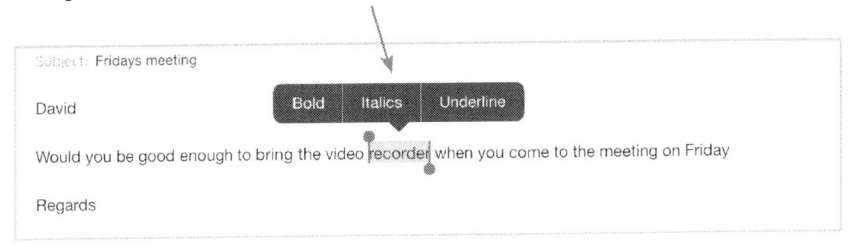

> Subject: Fridays meeting
>
> David
>
> Would you be good enough to bring the video recorder when you come to the meeting on Friday
>
> Regards

5. Tap the required option to format the selected text
6. Tap an empty part of the screen to close the formatting options

Note that if you have to stop writing a message for some reason, you can always finish it later. To do this, tap Cancel at the top-right of the message, which brings up Delete Draft and Save Draft options.

Tap Save Draft to save your incomplete message. When you are ready to finish it, navigate to the Mailboxes screen. Tap the relevant account and then tap the Draft folder. Then tap the message to open it.

Sending Images
Sometimes you may wish to send an image with your email. With traditional computer email programs there are two ways to do this:

1. Embed the image in the body of the email
2. Send it as an attachment to the email

cont'd

The Mail app though, only lets you send embedded images; you cannot send them as an attachment. To do this:

1. Tap and hold in the email until a magnifying glass appears – in the magnifying glass, you'll see the cursor. Use your finger to drag the cursor to where the image is to be inserted

2. When you release the cursor, you will see the following set of options:

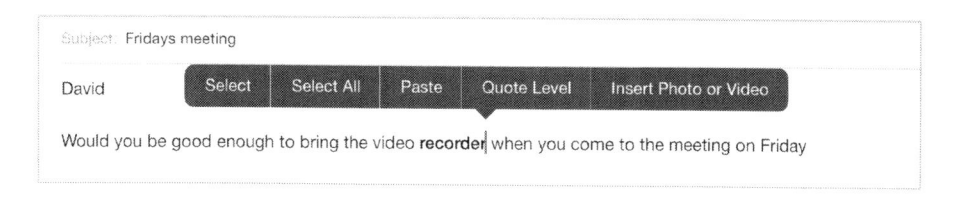

3. Tap 'Insert Photo or Video' – this will open a list of all folders on your iPad that contain images. Select a folder to reveal all the images within it

4. Tap the image to be embedded and then tap Use at the top-left of the screen

5. The image will be inserted into the email at the place you specified with the cursor

Sending Links and Attachments
Almost all of us will, at one time or another, discover something on the Internet that we want to share with someone else by sending them a link. It could be an entire page, an article, a video or picture.

One obvious way of doing this on your iPad is to copy the link's address in Safari, open the Mail app and then paste the link into the message. However, this is a long-winded method of carrying out such a simple task.

Try doing it this way:

1. In Safari, browse to the link to be sent and tap it

2. Tap the Options button at the right of the address bar

3. In the list of options that appears, tap Mail

4. A new email message window will open. As can be seen in the screenshot on the next page, the link's title is placed in the Subject field and its address in the body of the email

cont'd

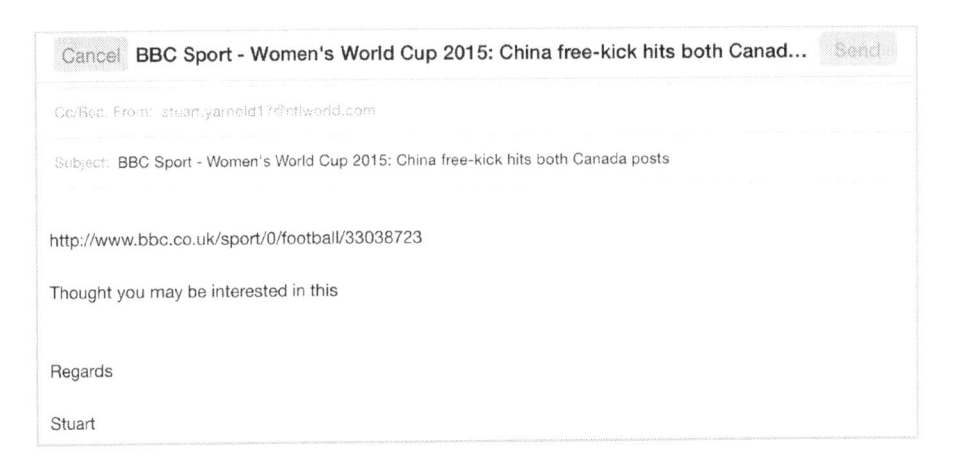

> Cancel BBC Sport - Women's World Cup 2015: China free-kick hits both Canad... Send
>
> Cc/Bcc, From: stuart.yarnold17@ntlworld.com
>
> Subject: BBC Sport - Women's World Cup 2015: China free-kick hits both Canada posts
>
> http://www.bbc.co.uk/sport/0/football/33038723
>
> Thought you may be interested in this
>
> Regards
>
> Stuart

All you have to do now is address the email, add some text if you want to and tap Send.

Don't forget, with regard to adding attachments to an email, it is not possible to do this with the Mail app.

Create a Signature

Regardless of whether or not you sign your emails, by default, the Mail app will add 'Sent from my iPad' at the bottom of all the messages you send.

If you are happy with this, fine. If you're not though, you can choose to get rid of it completely or amend it to something more to your liking:

1. On the Home screen, tap the Settings app

2. Tap Mail, Contacts, Calendars

3. In the Mail section, tap Signature

4. Tap the box that contains the current signature. You can then delete it and have no signature, or you can delete it and then add one of your own

5. Tap All Accounts if you want the signature to be used on all your email accounts. If you just want it to be used on a specific account, tap Per Account and delete it from accounts you don't want it used with. Or, you can add different signatures for different accounts

Managing Email

Create New Mailboxes
If you do a lot of emailing, it can be very helpful from an organisational point of view to place your messages in related folders, or mailboxes. You can create any number of mailboxes for this purpose:

1. With the iPad held in Landscape mode, open the Mail app and tap the back arrow at the top-left of the screen

2. In the Accounts section, tap the required account

3. At the top of the inbox, tap Edit

4. At the bottom of the inbox, tap New Mailbox

5. Give the new mailbox a name and then tap Save

6. You will be returned to the folder list for that account where you will see the mailbox

Moving Messages
To move messages to your new mailbox, tap the required message in the inbox to select it. Then tap the Folder button at the top-right of the screen – this opens the folder list for the account. Tap the new mailbox, or indeed any mailbox, and the message will be moved to it.

VIPs
iOS 8 provides an email feature called VIPs. This enables you to separate important email from the tidal wave of rubbish that no doubt washes inexorably into your inbox.

It works by creating a separate inbox called VIP to which all email that you classify as VIP mail is automatically copied. Note that these messages will still be in the main inbox. Furthermore, you will get a Notification Centre alert whenever a message arrives from one of your VIPs (you can, of course, choose to stop this in the settings).

To set up your VIP list:

1. Open the Mail app and go to the Mailboxes screen (tap the back arrow at the top-left of your inbox)

2. On the VIP line, tap the blue circle icon at the right-hand side

3. Tap 'Add VIP...' at the bottom – this opens your All Contacts list

4. Tap the contact you want to designate as a VIP. Repeat steps 3 and 4 to add further contacts

cont'd

Another way to add to your VIP list is to open an email from someone you want as a VIP and then tap their name at the top of the message.

This opens a pop-up screen, where you will see a 'Add to VIP' option. Note that you can remove a VIP from the list in the same way.

At the bottom of the VIP list, you will see a VIP Alerts link. Tapping this takes you to the Notification Centre settings where you can customise how you want the alert to appear and sound.

Any messages in your inbox that have been copied to the VIP list will have a star icon at the left of the sender's name.

Thread Organisation

By default, the Mail app groups messages by thread. This can be very useful as the original message and all the replies to it are grouped together, making it easy to follow the 'thread' of the conversation.

In your inbox, messages that are part of a thread have a double arrow at the right of the date, as shown here.

However, while it can be convenient, not everyone likes the Thread Organisation feature.

If this applies to you, it can be turned off, thus reverting to the standard chronological way of displaying messages.

To do it:

1. Open the Settings app
2. Tap Mail, Contacts, Calendars
3. Tap the 'Organize By Thread' switch to Off

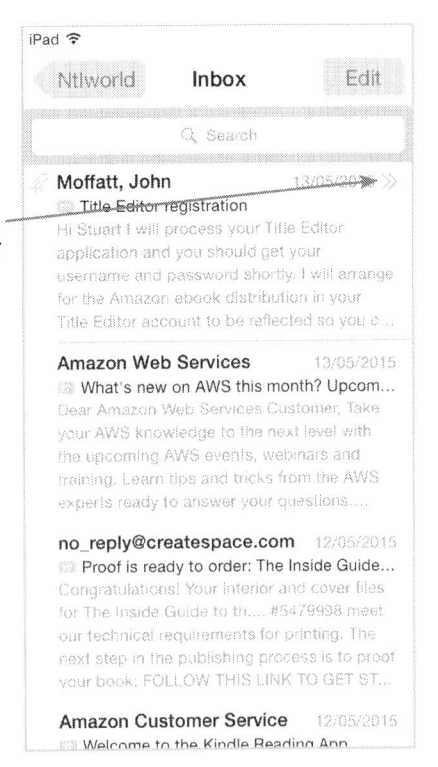

Emailing With Siri

If you don't want to get your hands dirty with the Mail app, give Siri a try – you will be surprised at just how much you can do with it.

Probably the best approach is to start off by experimenting with various voice commands to see what works and what doesn't. The following do work, however:

Reading Email

- To display all unread emails, say 'open new mail'
- To display all emails from a specific account, say 'open new email from xxx account'
- To display emails from a specific person, say 'show all email from xxx'
- To display all emails in your inbox, say 'show inbox'

Sending Email

- To send a message, say 'email xxx' where xxx is the name of someone in your contacts list. If Siri recognizes the name, it will open a new email addressed to that person and then ask you what to put in the subject line. Then it will ask what message you want to send. Dictate your text and Siri will ask if you are ready to send it – just say yes or no. If you are not ready, you can make corrections at this point

There is a quicker way to do all this though. Instead of going through the question and answer routine above, just give Siri all the information it needs to send the email in one go. Do it by using these keywords – 'email xxx', 'about', 'and say'.

In practice, this will look like:

> **email mike** (recipient) **about** (subject) **and say** (message text)

Siri will fill in everything automatically and then just ask you if you want to send or cancel the email.

Replying to Email

- To reply to an email, open the email, activate Siri and say 'reply'. Siri will ask what you want to say – dictate your text and say yes when asked if you are ready to send it

These are just some of the commands you can use to control the Mail app with Siri – there are many more.

Email Apps

The Mail app supplied with your iPad is a fairly typical example of its type. A quick search of the App Store will throw up some interesting alternatives. These include:

- **CloudMagic** – the Cloud Magic app is a simple yet powerful app for managing multiple email accounts. Its fast account switching and All Inboxes features let you easily send and receive emails from different accounts. CloudMagic supports all major email services and has an excellent search function. Other features include notifications, reminders, passcode lock, and swipe gestures

- **Boxer** – Boxer relies heavily on gestures and supports all major email services and IMAP accounts. Features include push notifications, calendar and Evernote integration, support for Gmail labels, To-Do lists, 'Likes' for messages, profile pictures and much more. It also has a passcode feature that secures emails with a password

- **my Mail** – the myMail app features a fresh look and animations that really help it to stand out. It supports all major mail services, multiple accounts, avatars, push notifications, and more. The app also has a powerful search feature that allows users to search multiple inboxes. The pane-based navigation system is another nice touch

- **Seed Mail** – Seed Mail is an email client that has been designed for performance. The app features integration for standard calendar and contact apps that allow users to easily manage their schedules and meetings. Seed Mail supports multiple accounts, plus features that include push notifications, voice mail, scheduling, Dropbox and Evernote integration, passcode lock support and more

- **Mail+ for Outlook** – Mail+ for Outlook puts all of your core needs right into one application: email, contacts, calendar, and – unique among email apps – Outlook's tasks. It connects to any Microsoft Exchange and Outlook account. If your productivity is based on the Microsoft platform, this is the email app for you

- **Dispatch** – Dispatch is not only one of the most versatile and powerful email apps, it also supports a number of other third-party apps, including TextExpander, Pocket, Evernote, Things, and Omnifocus. Dispatch also supports email aliases, image attachments, Touch ID, fetch and badges

CHAPTER 8

Organisation

In Chapter 8, we see how your iPad can be gainfully employed in helping to organise your life. This is done with the aid of four apps supplied with the device – Contacts, Calendar, Reminders and Notes. Of these, Contacts and the Calendar are most useful and will make it easy to stay in touch with the people in your life.

The Reminders and Notes apps help you to remember all the little things that need attention during your day. We also take a brief look at the Maps app and see what can done with it.

Creating & Editing Contacts 106

Finding & Using Contacts 108

Contacts App Settings 109

Syncing Contacts 110

Using Contacts With Siri 111

The Calendar App 112

Adding Events to a Calendar 114

Working With Multiple Calendars 115

Adding An Alert to An Event 117

The Reminders App 118

Hiding & Deleting Reminders 119

Working With Lists 120

The Notes App 121

Using Maps 123

Creating & Editing Contacts

Addresses and landline telephone numbers are no longer enough – these days there's also mobile numbers, email addresses and website addresses to be remembered. Step forward the electronic version of the traditional address book – the Contacts app.

Adding Contacts
When you first open it, the Contacts app will be empty. If you're like most people though, it won't be that way for too long.

1. Having opened the app from the Home screen, tap the + sign at the top of the screen – this opens the New Contact window

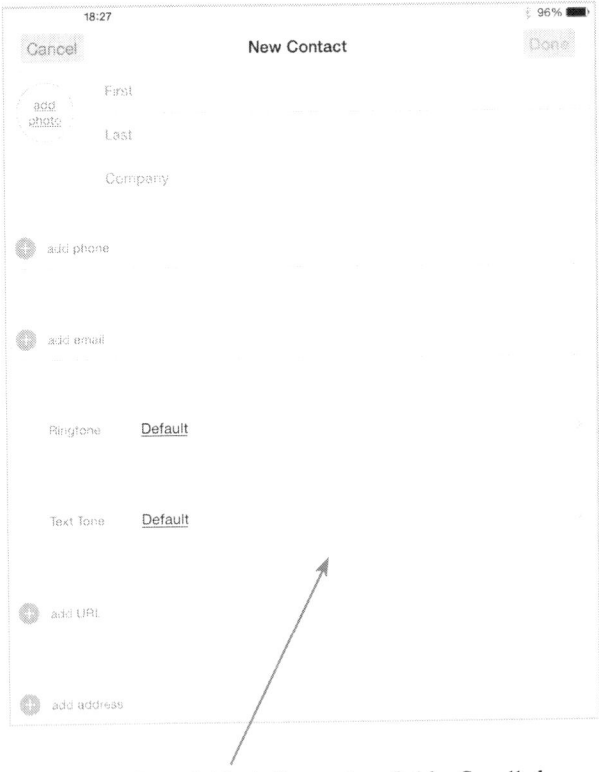

2. You will see a list of available information fields. Scroll down to see them all

3. The three fields at the top are for the contact's first and last names, plus Company. Tap in each field and then enter the names. If you wish to assign a picture to the contact, tap 'add photo'. You will see two options: 'Take Photo' and 'Choose Photo'. The former opens the Camera app allowing you to take a picture and the latter opens the Photos app from where you can select a picture

cont'd

4. Next, you'll see 'add phone'. Tapping this will enable you to enter the contact's home phone number. If you tap it again, you'll be able to enter a work phone number. Keep tapping and you will see even more phone number fields

   If you tap a field name, e.g. home, a list of available fields will open as shown on the right. This includes an 'Add Custom Label' option that lets you create your own field

5. Below 'add phone' is 'add email'. Available fields here include home, work, iCloud and other. You can also create your own field as described above

6. Moving down the screen, you'll see options for 'add URL', 'add address', 'add birthday', 'add date', 'add related name', 'add social profile', 'add instant message' and 'add field'

   With all these fields, tapping the field name opens a list of available fields. The last field, 'add field' enables you to create your own fields and, with it, you can add information of any conceivable type to a contact

Editing Contacts

Having created a list of contacts, you will no doubt want at some point to edit one or more of them. This is very easy to do:

1. Open the Contacts app

2. Tap the contact to be edited

3. Tap Edit at the top-right of the window

4. The original information is now available and can be changed where necessary. When you are finished, tap Done at the top-right – your changes will be saved

Deleting Contacts

Should you wish to delete a contact, open the contact's Edit screen as described above and scroll down to the bottom. Here, you'll see a Delete Contact option in red.

Finding & Using Contacts

Tap the Contacts app – it will open in the following view:

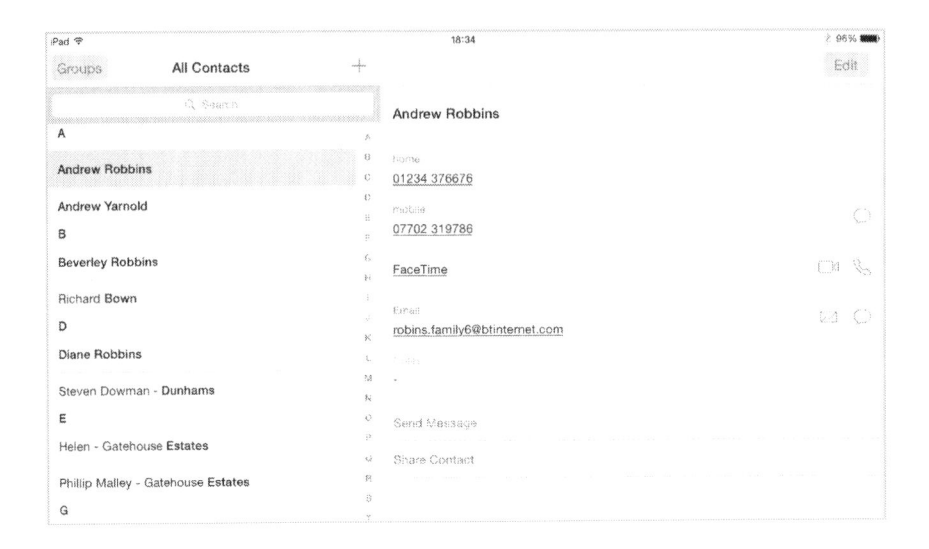

[Screenshot of Contacts app showing All Contacts list on the left with names including Andrew Robbins, Andrew Yarnold, Beverley Robbins, Richard Bown, Diane Robbins, Steven Dowman - Dunhams, Helen - Gatehouse Estates, Phillip Malley - Gatehouse Estates; on the right showing Andrew Robbins's details with home number 01234 376676, mobile 07702 319786, FaceTime, and email robins.family6@btinternet.com]

On the left of the screen, you will see an alphabetical list of all the names for which the app holds information. On the right, the details of the selected contact are displayed.

Finding Contacts
If you have a long list of contacts, you may have to scroll down the screen to find the one you want. You can avoid the need to do this by tapping the relevant blue capital letter at the right of the contacts list – all contacts filed under this letter will now be moved to the top of the list.

Alternatively, you can use the search box, which you will find at the top. As you type in letters, the search box will quickly whittle the list down to the required contact.

Using Contacts
Tap the desired contact and, on the right of the screen, you will see all the information held for that contact. If you have a cellular iPad, just tap a phone number to initiate a call to it; for email, tap any email address to open a pre-addressed message window in the Mail app; and tap any website address to open the site in Safari.

At the far-right, you'll see various icons: The bubble icon next to mobile phone numbers opens the Messages app; the camera and phone icons next to FaceTime open FaceTime video and phone links respectively; while the envelope and bubble icons next to email addresses open the Mail and Message apps respectively.

Contacts App Settings

As with many apps on your iPad, the Contacts app has a number of settings that can be changed to suit your method of working or requirements. These can be accessed by tapping the Settings app on the Home screen and then tapping Mail, Contacts, Calendars. Scroll down to the Contacts Section.

Sort Order	Last, First >
Display Order	First, Last >
Show In App Switcher	On >
Short Name	>
My Info	Card Security Code Stuart P Yarnold >

The options are:

Sort Order – this lets you sort your contacts from A to Z by 'First Name, Last Name' or 'Last Name, First Name'.

Display Order – this lets you specify how your contacts names are displayed – 'First Name, Last Name' or 'Last Name, First Name'. Together, these two settings provide four possible combinations for sorting and displaying your contacts.

Show in App Switcher – the App Switcher (or multitasking screen as it is also known), is accessed by double-pressing the Home button. When the screen is open, recently used contacts are displayed at the top. If you don't want to see these, this setting lets you get rid of them by toggling the switch to the Off position.

Short Name – by default, both the Messages and Mail apps only show the first name of a contact in a conversation thread. For those of us that have more than one 'John' in our contacts, for example, this can be the cause of unnecessary confusion. The setting lets you turn Short Names off completely or choose from various options such as 'First Name & Last Initial', 'First Name Only', etc.

My Info – My Info is your personal details and it is used by the iPad's AutoFill feature – see page 84. It tells Siri your name and any relationships you have, and also works with Find my iPhone. To use it, you have to first create a contact for yourself and then select that contact by tapping My Info.

Syncing Contacts

If you have a long list of contacts, entering them all manually into the Contacts app will be a tedious and time consuming task. However, if you already have the contacts on a Windows or Mac computer, you can quickly and easily sync them across to your iPad:

1. Connect your iPad to the computer

2. Start iTunes

3. In the iTunes Devices list, select your iPad

4. Click the Info tab

5. Check the 'Sync Contacts with' checkbox

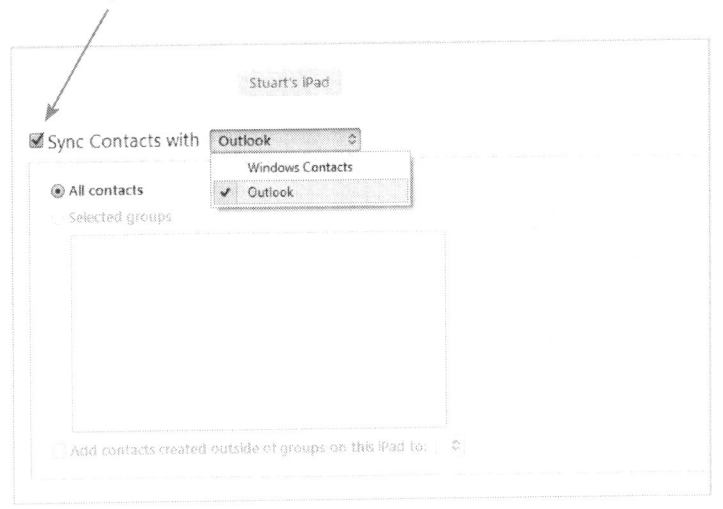

6. In the dropdown box, select the contacts list you want to sync – Outlook in the example above

7. Click Apply at the bottom-right of the screen

The contacts on the computer will now be transferred across to the Contacts app on your iPad.

You can be selective in the contacts you sync – you don't have to sync them all. To do this, you must first create contact groups on the computer that contains the contacts you want to move to the iPad.

Then, in iTunes, select the 'Selected groups' option to display the groups you have created, and then select the groups to be synced. Finally, click Apply.

Using Contacts With Siri

You can ask Siri to access and query your contacts rather than do it manually – very handy in some situations. Activate Siri by pressing and holding the Home button down until it springs to life.

With Siri, you can:

- **Display information for a specific contact** – simply say the contact's name, i.e. 'fred bolton'. All the information held for that contact will be displayed

- **Display information from a relation** – if you have defined a contact as being a relation, say 'show xxx' where xxx is sister or brother, etc

- **Display information from multiple contacts** – if your contacts list has more than one person that share common criteria, say 'show people xxx' where xxx is the criteria. For example: 'show people named Clark', 'show people living in London', etc

- **Display all email from a contact** – if you want to read recent emails from a contact, say 'show email from xxx'. Siri will display a list of emails from the contact

- **Send a text message** – you can send a text message to a contact. For example, say 'text fred I'll be home at 10 tonight'. The message will appear on the screen and Siri will ask 'ready to send it?' Reply 'send' or 'yes' and the message will be sent

- **Send an email** – to send an email to a contact, say 'email fred' (you can also use a relationship such as husband or sister if they are set up). If the contact has multiple email addresses, you will be prompted to choose which one you want to use. Siri will then ask you to dictate the subject line and the message body. When prompted, say 'send'

You can also use Siri and the Contacts app to get a specific piece of information about a contact. For example:

- 'What is fred bolton's work number?'

- 'When is my brother's wedding anniversary?'

- 'Where does paul live?'

- 'What is the name of david's oldest son?'

- 'What is davis & co's website address?'

The Calendar App

People live busy lives these days – they have places to go, people to see. The busier they are, the more things they have to remember and this is where the electronic calendar comes into play.

Provided with your iPad is an amazingly useful calendar app that will ensure you never again forget a birthday, business appointment, lunch date, or anniversary. The app remembers all these dates and times and can also prompt you with reminders just to make sure you don't forget.

On the Home page, tap Calendar:

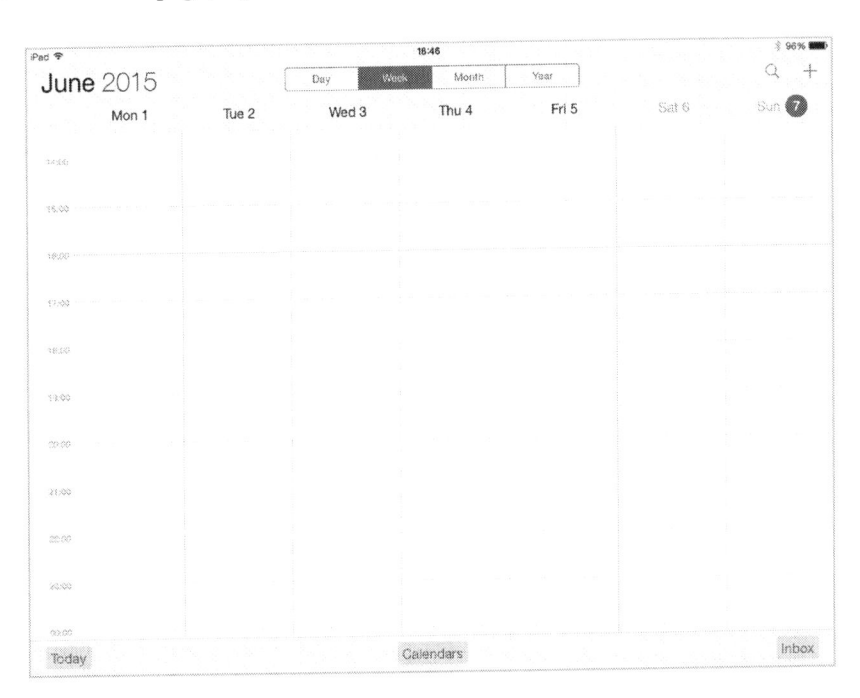

The app has four views and opens at the view in use when it was last closed down. These are Day, Week, Month and Year, and can be selected at the top of the screen.

- **Day** – in this view, you see the events for the selected day. A timeline and list of events is displayed on the left, and details of the events on the right. A red horizontal line indicates the current time

- **Week** – this view shows all the events in any given week and the time they are scheduled for – you may have to scroll down to see them all

- **Month** – in the Month view, you see all the events in any given month, and the days and times they are scheduled for

cont'd

- **Year** – this view shows the full calendar year with the current day highlighted in red. No other information is shown. Tap any month to go to the Month view for that month

At the top-right of the screen is a 🔍 icon. Tap this to open a search box that is very useful with busy calendars. As you type, relevant entries appear in a list – when you see the one you want, tap to go to it.

At the bottom is a navigation bar that provides three options – Today, Calendars and Inbox. Tapping Today will immediately take you to the current day wherever you are in the calendar; Calendars opens a list of all your calendars (we'll see more on this later); and Inbox shows any calendar invitations you may have received, plus any replies you have made.

With the iPad in Landscape mode and Day view selected, tapping the days of the week at the top of the screen takes you to those days. You can also move between days by flicking left and right at the left of the screen.

In Week view, you can move between weeks by flicking left and right anywhere on the screen.

In the Month and Year views, scroll up and down to move between months and years respectively. Also while in these two views, tapping an event opens a window that displays the details of that event.

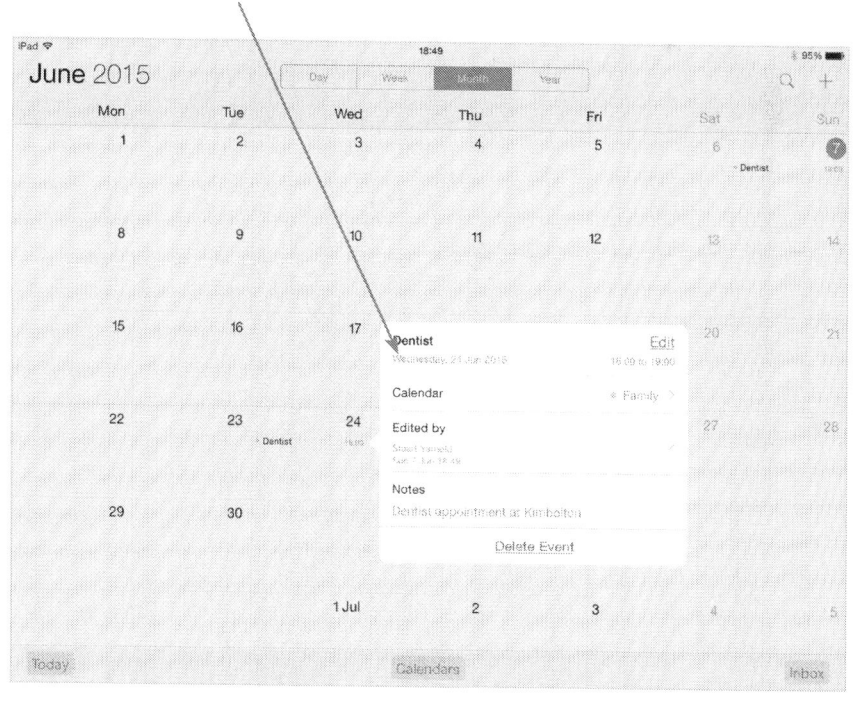

Adding Events to a Calendar

An 'event' is calendar-speak for an entry. To add an event to a calendar, follow these steps:

1. The first thing to do is select the day on which the event is to occur

2. Next, tap the + icon at the top-right of the screen. This opens the New Event window shown right

3. Tap in the Title box and type in a suitable name for the event

4. Do the same in the Location box

5. Tap in the Starts box and select a time for your event to begin. Note that you can also set the date here

6. Do the same in the Ends box

7. If the event is a recurring one, tap in the Repeat box and select one of the provided options

8. Again, if the event is recurring, set an end date in the End Repeat box

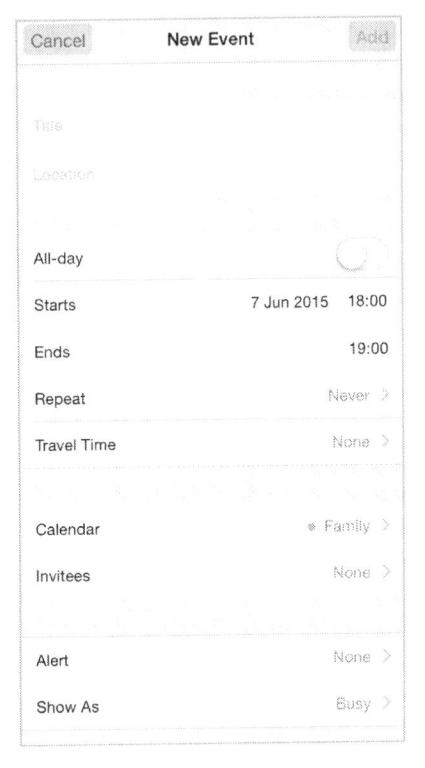

9. The Travel Time section lets you specify the travelling time allocated to the event

10. The Invitees section lets you invite people to the event. Tap in the box and then tap the + icon – this opens your contacts list from where you can add the invited person's email address

11. To ensure you don't forget the event, tap in the Alerts section. This opens a window providing a number of alert options, ranging from 5 minutes to 1 week before

12. The Show As section lets you specify your availability status during an event – options are Busy and Free

13. You can also make notes regarding your calendar by tapping in the Notes section and typing them in the box

Should you ever wish to change the details for an event, go to the event, tap Edit at the top-right, make the changes and then tap Done.

Working With Multiple Calendars

A great feature of calendar apps in general is that they let you create any number of calendars – you are not restricted to just one. This also applies to the iPad's Calendar app – it provides four default calendars – iCloud, Home, Calendar and Work. You also have the option to create more.

Accessing Calendars

To access your calendars, open the Calendar app and tap Calendars on the navigation bar at the bottom of the screen. This opens a window that shows the four calendars provided with the app.

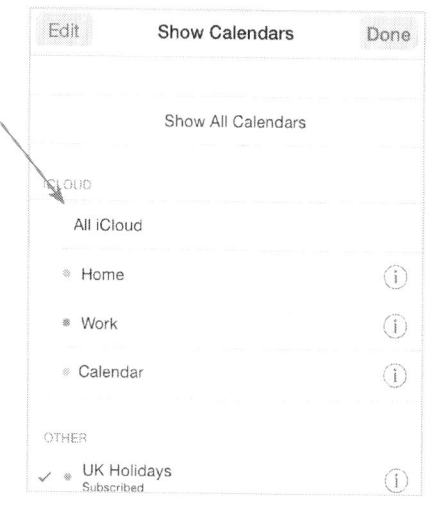

You will notice that each has a different colour dot to the left – these are for identification purposes. Any calendars that you create will also be shown here.

Should you wish to, you can edit the calendars (apart from the iCloud calendar) by tapping Edit at the top-left and then tapping the calendar to be edited. You will be able to rename the calendar and change the colour of the dot associated with it.

If you scroll down the window, you will also see a Delete option that lets you delete the calendar.

Creating Calendars

If you need more calendars than supplied with the app, you can create them easily:

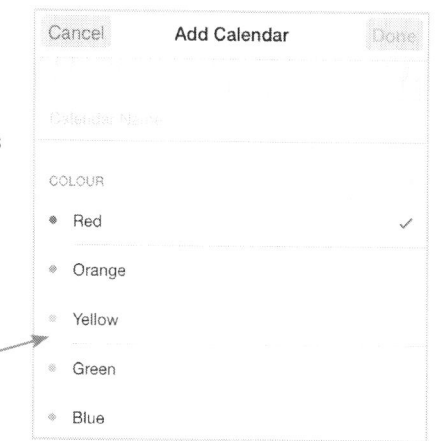

1. Open the Show Calendars screen as described above and tap Edit

2. In the Edit Calendars screen, tap 'Add Calendar...'

3. In the Add Calendar screen, give your calendar a name and select a colour for it

4. Tap Done and then Done again

In the Show Calendars window, your new calendar will now be listed.

cont'd

Viewing Calendars

By default, all calendars are lumped together, i.e. events from all of them appear on the same calendar. For example, if you have a dentists appointment on April 27th on your Home calendar and a business meeting also on April 27th on your Work calendar, when you open the Calendar app and go to April 27th, you will see both events even though they are on different calendars.

This also applies to events on any calendars you create yourself. You can always tell which event belongs to which calendar by the coloured dot to the left of the event's name. However, you may only want to see events from a specific calendar, in which case:

1. Open the Calendar app
2. Tap Calendars on the navigation bar at the bottom of the screen
3. The Show Calendars window will open displaying a list of all your calendars
4. You will see each calendar has a checkmark to its left, indicating it has been selected. Deselect the ones whose events you don't want to see by tapping them to remove the checkmark

As you deselect a calendar, its events are removed from the calendar.

Default Calendar

When you have a number of calendars, you will need to know which one is in use when you create a new event, i.e. which is the default calendar.

You can set this by opening the Settings app and going to Mail, Contacts, Calendar. On the right, scroll down to the Calendars section. At the bottom of this you will see 'Default Calendar' and, to the right, the current default calendar.

If you want to make a different calendar the default, tap on 'Default Calendar' to open a list of all your calendars – just select the one you want as the default by tapping it.

• Home	✓
• Work	
• Stuart's Calendar	
• Family	

Adding an Alert to an Event

If you're the type of person who tends to forget things, one of the most useful features of electronic calendars may provide the answer. We're talking here about the Calendar app's Alert feature, which will let you know about an upcoming event a set period beforehand.

Setting an Alert
To ensure you don't forget a birthday or whatever:

1. Open the calendar and go to the date that contains the event

2. Tap the event and the event information window opens

3. Tap Edit

4. The Edit Event window opens – tap Alert

5. You will see a number of options – At time of event, 15 minutes before, 1 hour before, 1 day before, etc – select the one you want

   Note that if you are setting an alert for an all-day event, the options are slightly different

6. Tap Done

Should you feel the need, you can also set a backup alert in case the first one doesn't get your attention.

1. Follow steps 1 to 3 above

2. Tap Second Alert

3. Select the required alert period and tap Done

When the alert activates, the Calendar app will automatically display a reminder of the event on the screen. Just to make sure you get the message, your iPad will also emit a beep.

> **Mum's Birthday**
> Today at 22:00
>
> Close   Options

Finally, the Calendar app provides a useful time-saving feature that lets you set default alert times for different types of event. Open the Settings app on the Home screen and go to Mail, Contacts, Calendars.

Tap 'Default Alert Times' and you'll be presented with options for setting alert periods for Birthdays, Events and All-Day Events.

The Reminders App

The Calendar app is excellent for tracking appointments, meetings, etc. You can also make sure you don't forget the appointment or meeting by adding an alert to it as we saw on page 117.

But what about the multitude of daily tasks that need to be done at specific times but do not really warrant a calendar entry and alert? Examples include taking the cake out of the oven, watching a program on the TV, calling someone, etc.

The solution is another of your iPad's apps – the Reminders app:

Setting a Reminder
Reminders can be set up in the following way:

1. Open the Reminders app

2. On the left-hand side, you'll see two lists – Reminders and Scheduled – tap the Reminders list

3. In the Reminders screen on the right, tap anywhere and type the name of the new reminder

4. Tap the ⓘ button at the far-right of the reminder

5. The Details window opens. Tap the 'Remind me on a day' switch to the On position

6. Tap Alarm – set the required date and time for the reminder

7. If you want the reminder to be a recurring one, tap Repeat and select the required option – Every Day, Every Week, Every Month, etc

8. You can specify a priority level for the reminder by tapping the required level – !, !!, or !!! – the latter is the highest priority level

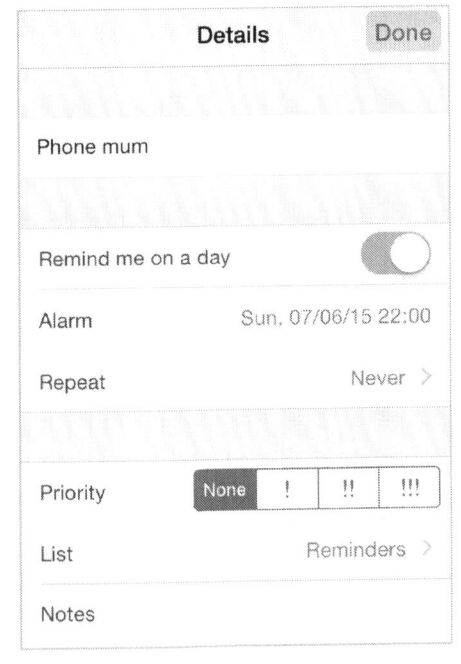

9. If you want to include a note re the reminder, tap Notes and type in your text

10. Finally, tap Done at the top-right of the window

Hiding & Deleting Reminders

When you have finished with a reminder, there are two ways to get rid of it – complete it or delete it.

Completing Reminders
Open the list containing the reminder to be completed. To the left of the reminder, you will see a round radio button.

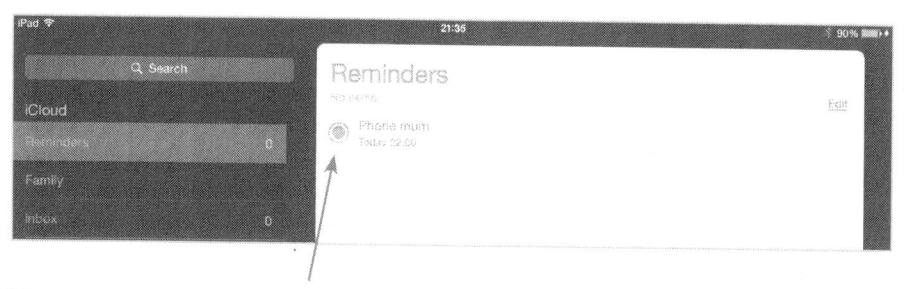

Tap the button and a coloured dot will appear inside it, which indicates the reminder is now complete, i.e. there is no further use for it. Now close the list. The next time you open it, the reminder will be gone.

However, this doesn't mean the reminder has been deleted. If you wish to see it again for some reason or to reactivate it, tap 'Show Completed' at the bottom of the list it was in. This displays a list of all the reminders you have created in that list. To reactivate one, tap the radio button to remove the coloured dot.

Deleting Reminders
Open the list containing the reminder to be deleted. Place your finger to the right of the reminder and drag it to the left. This will reveal a More button and a Delete button, as shown below:

Tap the Delete button to remove the reminder permanently. The More button opens the reminder's Details window from where you can edit it if you so wish.

Working With Lists

As we have seen, the Reminders app provides you with two reminder lists – Reminders and Scheduled. You will see them on the left of the screen.

Creating Lists

You may find, though, that these are not enough. You might, for example, need some extra lists to keep your home and work reminders separate. Whatever the reason, you can create your own lists as we see below:

1. Open the Reminders app
2. At the bottom-left of the screen, tap Add List
3. Type the name for your list

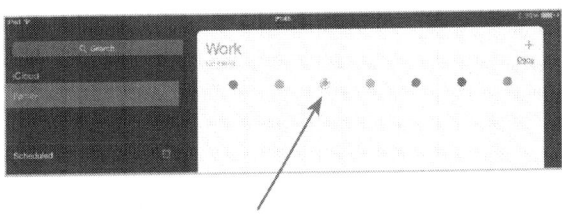

4. Tap to select an identifying colour
5. Tap Done

Your new list will now be available on the left of the screen.

Moving and Deleting Lists

You can easily rearrange the order of your lists:

1. At the bottom-right of the Lists section, tap Edit
2. You'll see a ☰ icon appear to the right of each list. Place your finger on it and move it up or down to move the list. Then tap Done

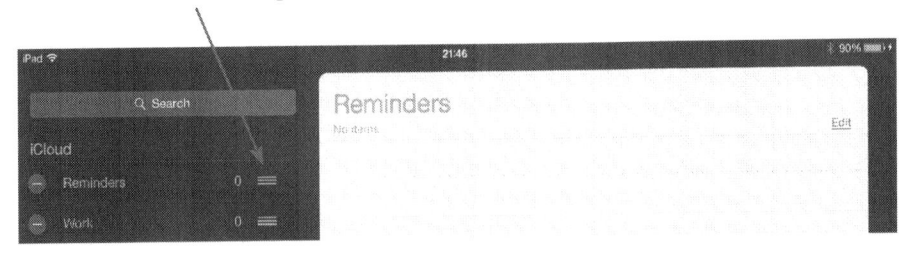

To delete a list, tap the red icon at the left of the list. The red Delete button slides into view at the right. Tap it and then tap Delete in the confirmation window that appears.

The Notes App

The Notes app is a standard iPad application that allows you to quickly jot down notes as they come to mind. While there are many apps of this type available in the App Store, some offering more features, the Notes app is straightforward and easy to use.

Creating Notes

Creating a note with the Notes app is extremely simple. To do it:

1. Open the app by tapping Notes on the Home screen

2. At the top-right of the screen, tap the New Note icon

3. A new note automatically opens and the keyboard slides into view - just type your note

4. When you are finished, the app automatically saves the note – you don't have to tap a Save button

5. At the left is a list of all your notes together with the time they were created (assuming it was done within the last 24 hours). The time-stamp will change to a date-stamp if the note goes back further than a day

Editing Notes

To edit a note, tap its name on the left to open it in the editing window on the right. Tap anywhere in the window and the keyboard will open allowing you to make your changes to the note.

cont'd

Formatting Notes

Quite apart from changing the note's text, you can also change the way it is formatted. It is also possible to insert a picture in your notes.

Lets take a look at the latter first:

1. Open the note into which you want to insert a picture. This could be an existing note or a new one

2. In the open note, tap and hold at the point where you want to insert the picture until you see the round magnifying glass

3. Remove your finger from the screen and a menu bar offering four options will appear

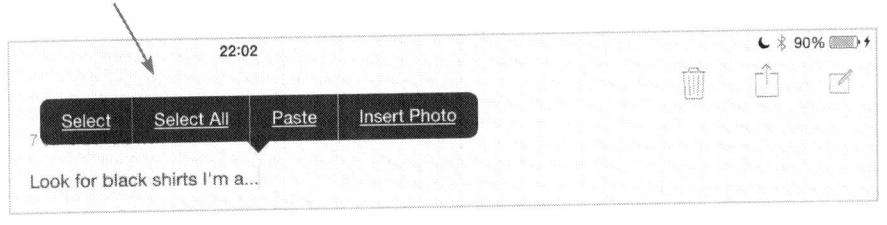

4. Tap Insert Photo and then browse to where the picture is located

5. When you have found it, tap Use at the top-right – the picture will be automatically down-sized and inserted into the note

With regard to formatting, activate the menu bar as described above. Having done so:

1. On the menu bar, tap Select or Select All. You will now see different options on the bar

2. Tap B*I*U – this reveals three options – Bold, Italics and Underline. Tap the option required and then tap anywhere in the screen to remove the editing bar

Deleting Notes

Notes that you no longer want can be deleted in two ways. The simplest is to open the note and then tap the Trash icon at the top-right. Then tap Delete Note in the confirmation window.

Alternatively, open the account that contains the list the note is located in. All the notes in that account will now be listed on the left of the screen. Slide your finger from right to left on the note to open the Delete button.

Using Maps

The Maps feature provided with your iPad is an extremely handy application that can be used for a number of purposes. These include getting directions to a particular place, getting information about a place, finding out your current location, getting live traffic information, and more.

Getting Directions

Your iPad always knows where it is – cellular models have a built-in GPS receiver and Wi-Fi models use nearby Wi-Fi hotspots to get an approximate fix. As a result, it can give you precise directions to and from any location. You can use these to guide you when walking or driving.

1. Tap the Maps app – it opens showing the iPad's current location

2. Tap Directions at the top-left

3. In the pop-up window, enter the start location in the Start: box and the destination in the End: box

4. The map view will now zoom out and show you two or three of the best routes – tapping on each shows the distance and travelling time involved. Tap anywhere on the route you want to use

5. At the top, tap Drive or Walk. Then tap Start at the bottom

As you travel, you will be given turn-by-turn directions, such as 'In 50 yards, turn into Kings Road'. You can see your position on the route, distance and time remaining, a text list of all turns, and much more.

cont'd

Live Traffic Information
The Maps app may say a certain route will take, say, 30 minutes but out in the real world traffic conditions will probably be dictating something completely different.

To find out, tap the Information button at the bottom-right of the screen. In the information window, tap Show Traffic.

If there are any known hold-ups in the selected route, a dashed red line will be displayed on the affected section of the route. Also, labelled icons on the map will show the location of construction sites, roadworks, etc.

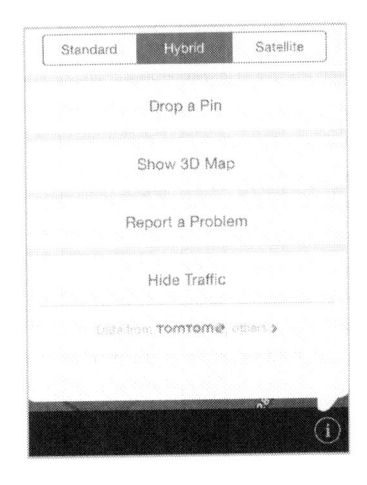

Get Information About a Place
To bone-up on a particular place, open the Maps app and type the place's name or address in the search box at the top. Assuming the app recognizes the place, it will drop a red pin on its location on the map.

Tap the blue car icon at the left to open the directions screen as shown on the previous page. Otherwise, tap on the right to open the Information window. Here, you will see phone numbers, address, website address, pictures, and reviews (taken from Yelp).

Find Out Your Current Location
When you're out-and-about in an unfamiliar town, perhaps on holiday, it's always good to know exactly where you are. If your iPad is to hand, the Maps app will ensure that you always do.

Open the app and then tap the Tracking button at the bottom-left of the screen. The map will zoom in and indicate your precise location with a blue dot. Tap the dot for more information.

Refreshments
Once you've established where you are, it may be nice to relax with a beer or get something to eat. Once again, your iPad can help. If it's food you want, type restaurant in the search box – the Maps app will immediately drop red pins on all the restaurants it knows about.

Tap on each pin to get directions, the distance, the telephone number, the address, the opening hours, and reviews (taken from Tripadvisor).

CHAPTER 9

Pictures

Your iPad comes with two built-in cameras – one front-facing and one rear-facing. While no match for a dedicated camera, these produce pictures that are of perfectly acceptable quality.

In this chapter, we'll see how to use these cameras, in conjunction with the Photos app, to create, view, edit, organise and share your digital creations. This app provides so many related options that it is an integral part of photography with the iPad, and so features highly in this chapter.

We also look at other ways of getting pictures on to your iPad, such as from a computer, and a digital camera.

The iPad's Cameras 126

Taking Pictures 127

Viewing Your Pictures 129

Creating Photo Albums 131

Uploading Pictures to the iPad 132

My Photo Stream 134

Moving Pictures 135

Deleting Pictures 136

Sharing Pictures 137

Editing Pictures 139

Printing Pictures & Documents 141

Adding Pictures to Your Contacts 142

The iPad's Cameras

As mentioned in the introduction to this chapter, your iPad comes with two cameras. The rear-facing iSight camera takes 8 mega-pixel pictures and 1080 pixel high-definition (HD) video, while the front-facing FaceTime HD camera takes lower quality pictures and video.

The latter is intended for use on social media websites, such as Twitter, Facebook and the like.

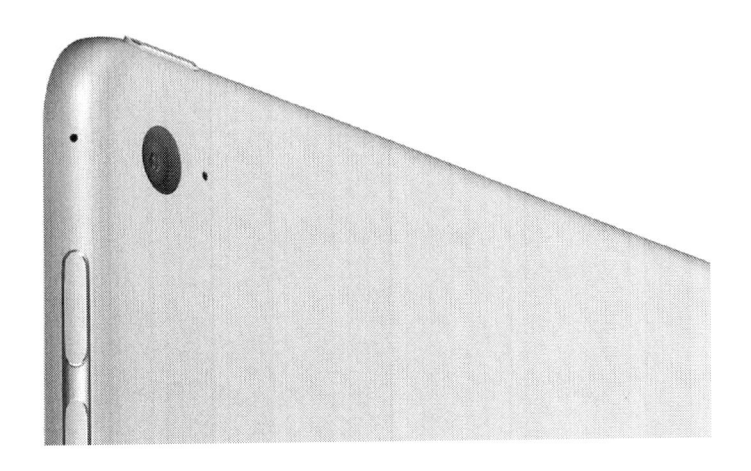

With regard to pictures, features offered by the iSight camera include:

- 8 mega-pixel sensor
- Autofocus
- 2.4 aperture
- Face detection
- Rear illumination
- Hybrid IR filter
- Tap to focus
- Exposure control
- Photo geotagging
- Panorama mode
- Burst mode
- Timer mode
- Five-element lens
- 3264 x 2448 native resolution

Camera features new to the iPad Air 2 include Burst mode, which takes 10 pictures per second, and Time-lapse mode, which compresses into a few seconds video events that last anywhere from 30 minutes to 30 hours.

Taking Pictures

To take a picture with the iPad, tap the Camera app on the Home screen. Alternatively, open the Control Centre by swiping upwards from the bottom edge of the screen and then tap the camera icon to open the app.

When the app is open, you'll see the camera controls at the right of the screen.

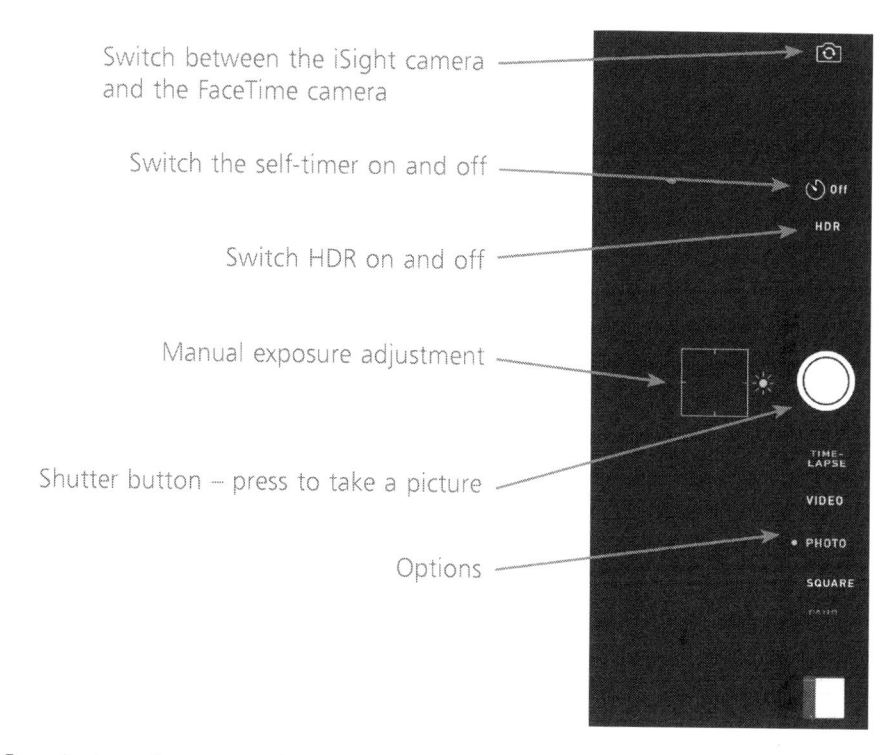

Switch between the iSight camera and the FaceTime camera

Switch the self-timer on and off

Switch HDR on and off

Manual exposure adjustment

Shutter button — press to take a picture

Options

Lets look at these controls in more detail to see what they do:

- The camera button at the top lets you choose either the iSight camera or the FaceTime camera

- The self-timer enables you to set a 3 or 10 second delay when taking pictures — this is great for when you want to be in the picture yourself. Compose your shot, then tap the shutter button — a numbered countdown will begin on the screen to indicate that the timer is counting down

- HDR stands for High Dynamic Range image and the feature combines two pictures, each shot at a different exposure. The best parts of these images are put together into one image that brings out details in both the shadows and the highlights — information that would normally be lost in a single exposure

cont'd

- The manual exposure adjustment enables you to set the exposure yourself. To do it, tap on the screen – this will open a yellow square with a sun icon to the right of it

  If you think the exposure could do with adjusting, i.e. the image is either too bright or to dark, swipe your finger up to brighten it or down to darken it. Then take the picture

- Tap the shutter button to take a picture

- The Options section lets you do the following:

  1. The time-lapse feature enables you to film a video and then speed up the replay so that everything appears to move much more quickly. For example, a 40 minute clip will take about 20 seconds to play back

  2. Select Video to switch the camera to Video mode

  3. Select Photo to switch the camera to Photo mode

  4. Select Square if you want to take a picture that is square – these are currently in vogue on social media websites

  5. Select a slow-motion video feature that can shoot 720p video at a frame rate of 120 frames per second (normal frame rate is 30 frames per second). As a result, the video can be played back at a quarter of the speed

  6. Short for Panorama, PANO mode lets you capture panoramas – much larger pictures that would otherwise be possible with the iSight camera. It does this by taking a video-like stream of successive frames and then stitching them together to create a single panoramic picture

The Camera app also provides Burst mode. To use this, you must select either Photo or Square. Then, instead of tapping to take individual pictures, hold the shutter button down to take a rapid series of pictures (10 every second).

Burst mode is ideal for situations where you don't want to risk not getting a good picture. Having taken a series of pictures in this way, you can then examine them individually in the Camera Roll, select the ones you want, and delete those that are not up to scratch.

Viewing Your Pictures

Having taken some pictures, you will now want to view the results of your photographic endeavours. To do so, tap the Photos app on the Home screen.

The Photos app
The Photos app keeps all the pictures and videos you shoot together in one place. This makes it easier to find them later when you want to view, edit, or share them with someone else.

The app automatically sorts your pictures and videos into three 'smart groups', based on time and location. The smallest group is Moments, the next is Collections, and the largest is Years. These enable you to instantly see the date each picture was taken, group them by month, and see the exact location where they were taken on a map.

Navigating Between Smart Groups
Moving between groups can be confusing initially. To do it, tap the back button at the top-left of the screen to move to a larger group. The button will be labelled with the name of the group you'll be moving to – Collections in the example below:

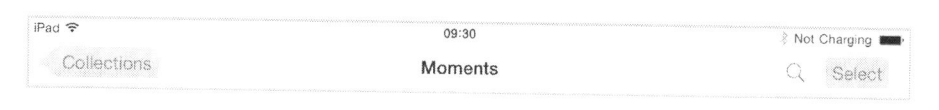

When you want to move the other way, i.e. to a smaller group, simply tap any picture or video thumbnail.

Viewing Picture and Video Locations on a Map
Not only do the Moments, Collections, and Years smart groups tell you where your pictures and videos were taken, they can also pinpoint those locations on a map.

To do it, simply tap on the name of the location. A map will open showing a thumbnail of the picture and its precise location on the map.

cont'd

Viewing Pictures
To view a picture, you need to be in the Moments view. If you happen to be in the Years view, tap anywhere on the screen to go to Collections. Find the thumbnail of your picture and tap it – you will now see a larger view of it in Moments. Tap this and it will open in a full-screen view.

While in the Moments and Collections views, you will notice that picture thumbnails are arranged by date taken and, if taken away from your home, by the location they were taken at.

In the Years view, they are grouped by year and location (this includes all the various locations).

Manipulating Pictures
Unlike some picture-viewing devices, the iPad provides you with a number of ways to view your images. These include:

- **Scrolling or flicking** – if the iPad is in Landscape mode, you can move from one picture to the next, or to the previous one, by flicking left and right (or up and down if in Portrait mode).

  You can also tap the screen to bring up a row of thumbnails at the bottom of the screen – run your finger along them to quickly view the entire collection

- **Rotating** – when you view a portrait shot in Landscape mode, there will be a blank area on either side of the picture. Rotating the iPad into Portrait mode will display the picture in full-screen view

- **Flipping** – if you wish to show a picture to someone, rather than laboriously turning the iPad round, simply flip it so that what was the top is now the bottom. The picture will also be flipped so it is the right way up

- **Zooming** – if you want a close-up of a picture, you can zoom into it. This can be done in two ways:

  1. Double-tap on the part of the picture you want a close-up of – the picture will double in size. Double-tap again to return it to its normal size

  2. Place two fingers on the picture and spread them to zoom in. Close them to zoom back out

- **Panning** – when you are zoomed in on a picture, you won't be able to see all of it on the screen. Place your finger on the screen and drag it about, or pan, to move the picture about

Creating Photo Albums

It is very common for people to organise their pictures into photo albums so it is easy to find them later on. On the iPad, this is another of the functions provided by the Photos app:

1. Open the Photos app

2. At the bottom of the screen, tap Albums

3. At the top-left of the screen, tap the + icon

4. In the New Album window that opens, type a name for the album and then tap Save. In the example below, we have created an album in which to place holiday snaps taken in Las Vegas

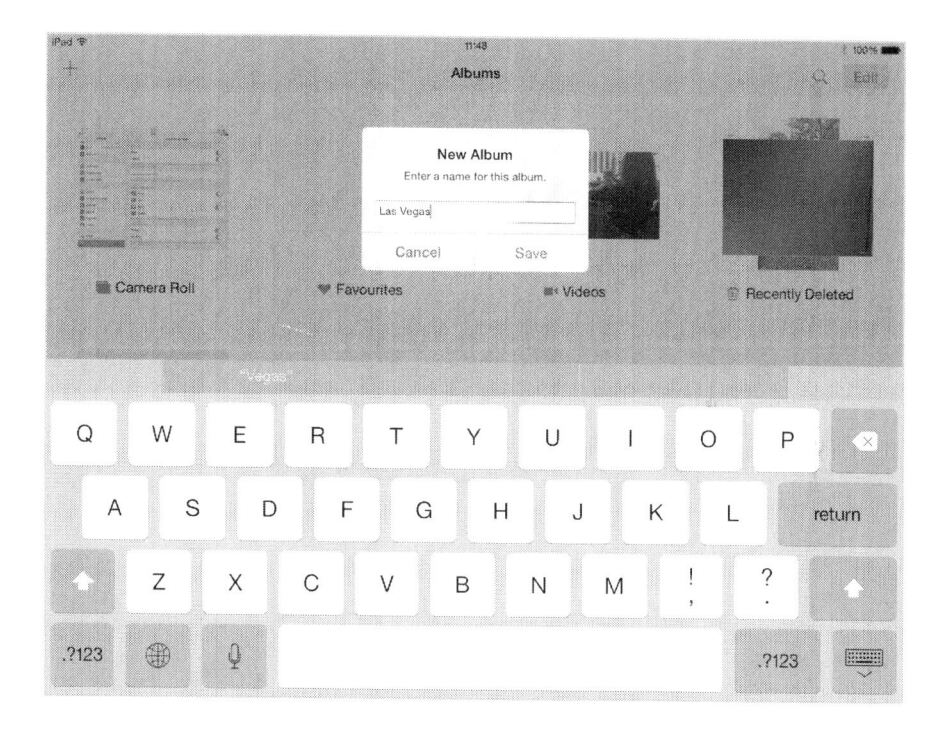

5. The Photos app will now switch to the Moments view

6. Using the Select buttons on the right of the screen, select the pictures to be placed in the new album

7. Tap Done

8. The Photos app now switches to the Album view where you will see your new album. Open the album and the pictures you selected in Step 6 will be there

Uploading Pictures to the iPad

While the iPad's iSight camera takes pictures of decent enough quality, those taken by a digital camera are definitely of a higher standard. However, where the iPad does shine is its large screen, which is much better at displaying pictures than the small screen offered by the typical digital camera.

For this reason, many people use a digital camera to take their pictures and then upload them to the iPad for showing to friends and family. There are two ways this can be done:

Uploading from a Computer to the iPad

The first is to upload the pictures from a computer (perhaps after editing) to the iPad. To do this, you will need to use iTunes:

1. Connect the iPad to the computer

2. Start iTunes

3. In iTunes, look at the top-left of the screen for the iPad icon. Click it

4. In the new window, click Photos on the sidebar at the left. You will now see the screen shown below

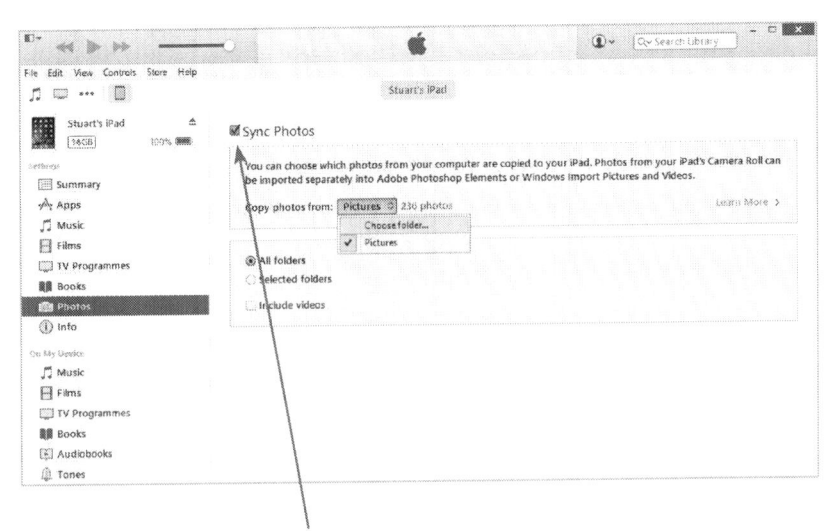

5. At the top, check the 'Sync Photos' checkbox

cont'd

6. Click 'Copy photos from', select 'Choose folder', and then browse to the folder that contains the required pictures

7. When you have chosen your folder, click 'Select Folder' at the bottom and then click Apply at the bottom-right of the iTune's screen – the pictures will be now be uploaded to the iPad

8. When the upload is complete, go to the iPad and tap the Photos app

9. Tap Albums at the bottom of the screen to show the Album view. You will see a new folder containing the uploaded pictures

At this point, you may think the job is done – the pictures are on the iPad, what else is there to do? However, if you leave the newly uploaded pictures where they are, the next time you use this method to upload pictures, they will be overwritten by the new ones. So your final task is to move them to a different folder as described on page 135.

Uploading from a Camera to the iPad
The second way to upload pictures to your iPad is to transfer them directly from a digital camera. This requires the use of a specially designed adaptor. Apple provides two types:

- **Lightening to USB Camera Adaptor** – the camera adaptor has a USB interface that plugs into the dock connector port on your iPad. Then you attach your digital camera with a USB cable

- **Lightening to SD Card Camera Reader** – connect the SD card reader to your iPad, then insert your camera's SD card into the slot

Whichever adaptor you use, after the connection is made, your iPad automatically opens the Photos app. This lets you choose which pictures to import, prior to organising into albums.

Note that both adaptors are supplied with Apple's Camera Connection Kit.

My Photo Stream

We've just looked at two ways to get pictures on to your iPad. In both cases, having done so, you can then view them wherever you happen to be as they are physically stored on the device. However, there is another way to do this. This is courtesy of a feature called My Photo Stream. With this method, though, although you can view the pictures on the iPad, they are not actually stored on the device – they are on the Cloud.

With My Photo Stream, pictures taken with any iOS device are automatically uploaded to a My Photo Stream album located on iCloud – Apple's cloud-based storage service. From iCloud, the My Photo Stream album is streamed to all devices that have the feature activated.

Activate My Photo Stream on the iPad
To set up My Photo Stream on your iPad (or indeed any iOS device):

1. Tap the Settings app

2. Tap iCloud on the left-hand side

3. Tap Photos, and then tap the My Photo Stream switch to On

Set Up My Photo Stream on a Windows PC
It is also possible to use My Photo Stream to stream pictures from your computer (we are assuming here it's running Windows 8 or higher).

1. You must first install 'iCloud for Windows' on your computer – this program can be downloaded from Apple's website

2. Open any folder on your computer. On the sidebar, you will see an 'iCloud Photos' link in the Favourites section. Click this to open it

3. In the new window, double-click My Photo Stream

4. At the top-left of the window, click Add photos

5. Browse to the pictures you want to upload. Then click Open

6. The selected pictures will now be uploaded to the My Photo Stream album on iCloud. From there, the album is streamed to all iOS devices that have the feature activated

Assuming My Photo Stream is activated on your iPad, if you now open the Photos app, you will see a My Photo Stream album in the Albums view. Tap the album to see the pictures it contains.

Don't forget though – an Internet connection is required for My Photo Stream to work – this is its inherent weakness.

Moving Pictures

Should you ever wish to move a picture from an existing location to a new one, follow this procedure:

1. Open the Photos app in either the Moments or Albums view. If you are in the former, tap Select at the top-right of the screen. If you are in the latter, open the album containing the pictures to be moved and then tap Select at the top-right of the screen

2. In the Select Items screen, locate the desired pictures and tap them once. They will fade slightly and a blue checkmark will appear at the bottom-right of each one indicating they have been selected

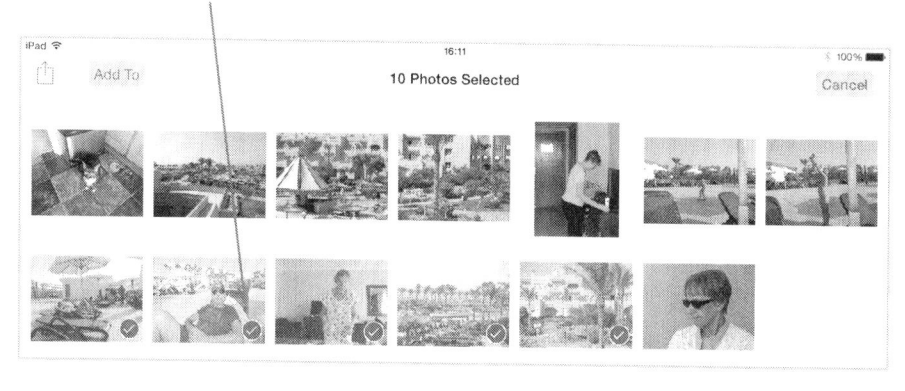

3. Tap Add To at the top-left and the 'Add to Album' screen will open as shown below. This contains a newly created album for you to use. Alternatively, you can select an existing album

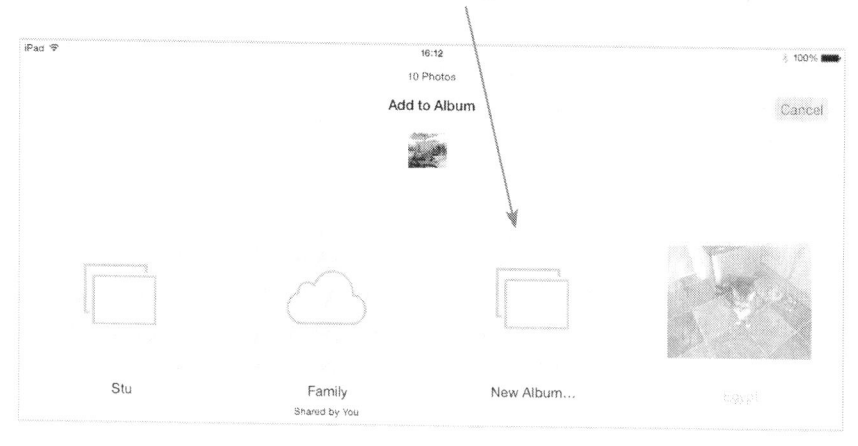

4. Tap 'New Album...', type a name in the Name box and then tap Save. Or, tap an existing album. In either case, the pictures will be moved to the specified album

Deleting Pictures

On the face of it a simple task, deleting a picture is somewhat complicated by the fact that your iPad differentiates between two types of picture:

- Pictures created directly on the iPad. These include those taken with the cameras, copied from an email, the Internet, or some other source

- Pictures copied from a computer and uploaded to the iPad via iTunes

To delete pictures created directly on the iPad:

1. Open the Photos app

2. Locate the picture to be deleted

3. Open the picture by tapping on it. At the bottom-right of the screen you will see a Trash icon. Tap it then tap Delete Photo

However, if you don't see the Trash icon, it means the picture is a copy uploaded via iTunes and so cannot be deleted with the Photos app. In this case, you need to use a different method:

1. Go to the folder on the computer that contains the original picture and remove it from the folder

2. Connect your iPad to the computer and start iTunes

3. Click the iPad button at the top-left of the screen and then click Photos on the left-hand side

4. In the new window, check the 'Sync Photos' checkbox

5. In the 'Copy photos from' dropdown menu, browse to and select the folder from which you have removed the unwanted picture

6. At the bottom-right of the screen, click the Sync button

iTunes will now synchronise the picture folder on the computer with the Photo app on the iPad. Any pictures on the iPad that are not in the folder will be removed from the iPad.

Sharing Pictures

The iPad is the ideal device for sharing your snaps with people around you. How about those who are farther afield though? Actually, there are several ways you can do it. These include:

- Email

- Messages

- Photo sharing sites such as Flickr and iCloud Photo Sharing

- Social media sites such as Twitter and Facebook

All the above methods can be used by carrying out the procedure explained below:

1. Open the Photos app and locate the picture you want to send

2. Tap the Actions button at the bottom-left of the screen

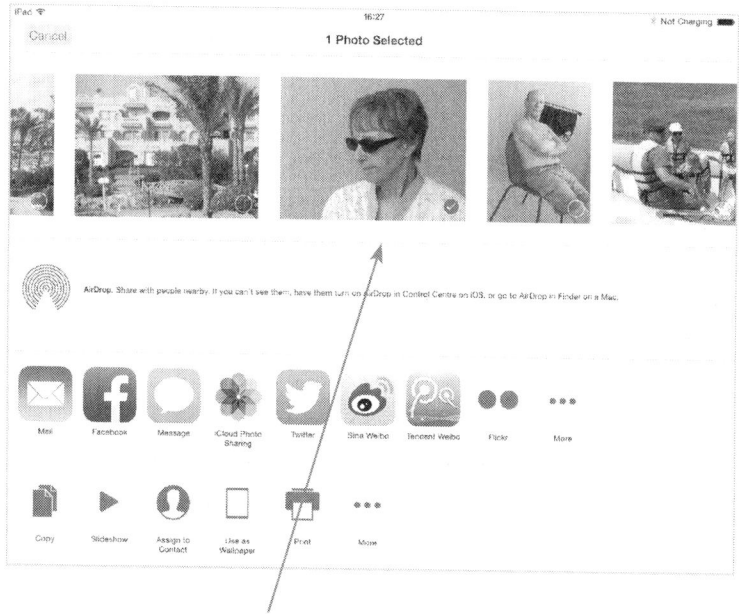

3. At the top, you will see the selected picture – by scrolling to the right you can select other pictures in the album. Below the pictures are the various sharing options open to you. These are:

Message & Mail
Having selected your pictures, to text them with the Messaging app, tap Message – a new message window for the Messages app will open. Select the person you want to share the picture with by tapping the ⊕ icon.

cont'd

This opens your contacts list from where you can select the recipient. Then tap Send at the bottom-right.

To share a picture by email, tap Mail and follow the same procedure as for Message. Note that you have to tap in the To: field to reveal the ⊕ icon.

Twitter & Facebook
To share pictures via Twitter and Facebook, you first need to set up Twitter and Facebook accounts on your iPad and then sign in to them.

Then (using Facebook as an example), tap Facebook in the Photos app's Actions screen. You will see your picture.

Type in your message (if there is one). Then tap in the Album field to choose which album to post it in, tap Location to specify where you are posting the picture from and, finally, tap Audience to select who can see the picture. Tap Post at the top-right and the picture will be posted to your Facebook timeline.

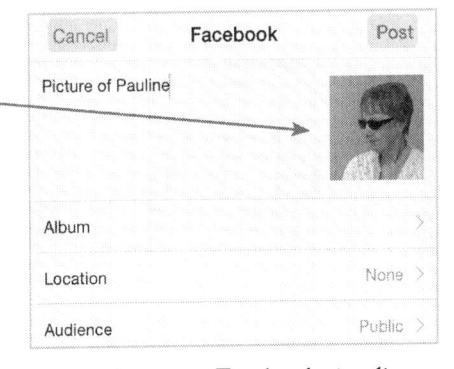

Flickr & iCloud Photo Sharing
Photo sharing websites allow you to post pictures to a website. You then send the web address of the pictures to whoever you want to share them with. We'll take a look at how to do it with iCloud Photo Sharing:

1. Turn on iCloud Photo Sharing. Do this by opening the Settings app on the Home screen and going to iCloud > Photos. Tap iCloud Photo Sharing to turn it on

2. Next, you need to access the iCloud Photo Sharing options. You can do this via the Photos app's Actions screen as already explained. However, a more intuitive method is to tap the Shared icon at the bottom of the screen in the Photos app

3. In the new window, tap the + button at the top-left, enter a name for the shared album and tap Next. In the To: field, enter the email address of the person you want to share with. Alternatively, tap the ⊕ button to open the All Contacts list and select it from there

4. Finally, tap the Create button. The person you want to share with will be now sent an email that contains a link to the web page on which the picture is displayed

Editing Pictures

Your iPad not only lets you take pictures, it also lets you edit them. The editing tools it provides are:

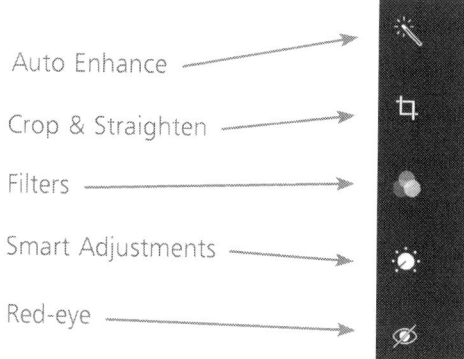

- Auto Enhance
- Crop & Straighten
- Filters
- Smart Adjustments
- Red-eye

To access the editing tools:

1. Open the Photos app and then open the picture to be edited
2. At the top-right of the picture, tap Edit
3. You will now see the five editing tools shown above appear on the screen

Lets see what you can do with them:

Auto Enhance
Auto Enhance is basically an all-in-one control. It automatically improves a picture's overall darkness or lightness, colour saturation, and other elements such as red-eye.

Crop & Straighten
This tools allows you to do several things:

First, it allows you to straighten a picture that has been taken at an angle. At the left of the picture, you will see a small section of compass. Place your finger on this and move it up and down to adjust the angle.

Second, you can remove parts of a picture that you don't want – this is known as cropping. It works by specifying a rectangular part of a picture that you want to keep – the rest is discarded.

Cropping can be done manually by dragging the sides of the picture in and out. Alternatively, you can choose from a range of pre-determined crop sizes (shown on the right) by tapping the icon at the bottom-left of the screen.

Original
Square
3:2
5:3
4:3
5:4
7:5
16:9

cont'd

Filters
The Filter tool provides a range of eight built-in filters. These let you make various changes to the look of your pictures.

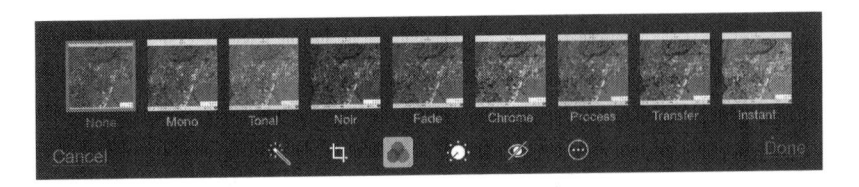

Smart Adjustments
The Smart Adjustments tool is basically three tools in one – Light, Colour and B&W.

Selecting each tool opens a 'smart slider', which previews the picture with a range of values. Just drag the slider up and down to alter the picture.

The tools intelligently adjust values like saturation, exposure, brightness, and contrast as you move the slider. For more precision, you can also adjust each value individually.

To access these controls, tap the icon on the right side of the list (or bottom depending on the iPad's orientation), then select the value you want to change. For example, for the Light control, you will see the controls shown on the right.

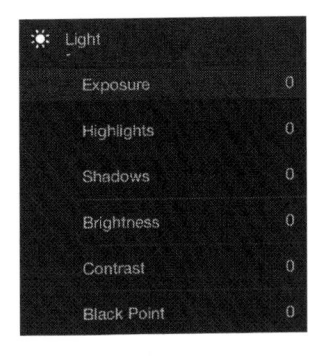

Red-eye
No matter how careful you are, red-eye will occasionally be present in one of your pictures. The last of the Photo app's editing tools is designed to deal with this issue.

Simply tap each eye afflicted with red-eye and then tap Done.

Tip: if the affected area is very small, zoom into the picture by double-tapping. Doing this will make it easier to select the desired area.

Printing Pictures & Documents

Whatever type of document you want to print from your iPad, be it an email, picture, or web page, the procedure is the same.

However, you will need a printer with Apple's wireless AirPrint technology built-in. If your existing printer isn't AirPrint-enabled, then you will not be able to print anything from your iPad.

To print from your iPad:

1. Open the app containing the document or picture to be printed

2. Look for the Actions menu in the app. For example, in the Mail app tap the button. In the Photos app and Safari tap the button

3. When you have the Actions menu open, tap Print

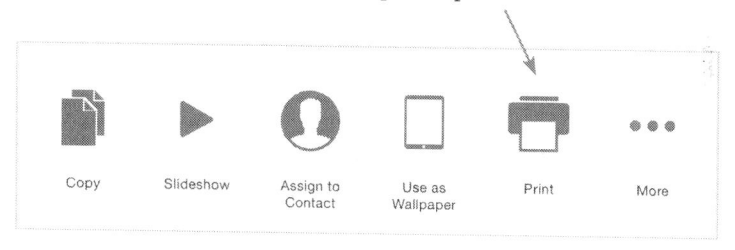

   | Copy | Slideshow | Assign to Contact | Use as Wallpaper | Print | More |

4. If this is the first time you have used the iPad to print something, you will have to associate a printer with it. In the Printer Options screen, tap 'Select Printer >'. The iPad will then look for any wireless printers in the vicinity and display a list of those it has found

5. Tap your AirPrint printer. The iPad will add it to the Printer Options dialogue, and activate the Print button at the bottom

6. In the Copy field, tap the + sign to specify the number of copies to be printed

7. Depending on the printer being used, you may see other options. Configure these as necessary

8. Tap Print. The iPad sends the document across your wireless network to the printer where it is printed

If you have any problems, check that your iPad and printer are both connected to the same Wi-Fi network and are within range.

Adding Pictures to Your Contacts

These days, contacts lists are very important to many people and are used frequently. Associating pictures with the names in your list not only helps to identify them, it also brightens up the list, i.e. it's a cool thing to do!

This can be done in two ways: direct from the Photos app or through the Contacts app. We'll take a look at the latter method:

1. Tap the Contacts app on the Home screen to open it
2. On the left of the screen, select the desired contact
3. At the top-right of the screen, tap Edit

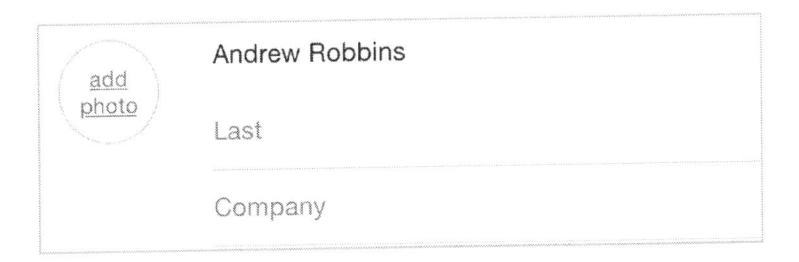

4. Tap 'add photo' at the top-left
5. You will be given two options: the first, Take Photo, opens the Camera app and the second, Choose Photo, lets you choose a picture from the various albums in the Photos app
6. Having taken a picture with the camera or selected one from the Photos app, you can then centre it by dragging, and scale it to the required size by placing two fingers on it and spreading them
7. When you are happy with the picture, tap Use Photo at the bottom-right of the screen (for pictures taken with the camera) or Use at the top-right (for pictures taken from the Photos app)

The picture will now be added to the contact's details page in the Contacts app.

CHAPTER 10

Video

Excellent multimedia device that it is, the iPad is a very handy tool for recording video. It is capable of producing high-resolution recordings and can be used wherever you happen to be – ideal for capturing those impromptu moments.

It really comes into its own, however, when you want to watch video. An endless supply of films and TV programs are available from the iTunes Store, plus, of course, your own recordings.

Another interesting feature is FaceTime, which allows you to make free video calls with your iPad.

The iPad's Video Cameras 144

Recording Video 145

Locating Your Videos 145

Playing Back Your Videos 146

Editing Video 147

Uploading Home Videos 148

Uploading Films & TV Programs 150

Video Storage Space 152

Uploading Video to Facebook 153

FaceTime Video Calls 154

Play iPad Video on a TV 155

Mirror the iPad's Screen on a TV 156

The iPad's Video Cameras

As we saw on page 126, the iPad's main camera is the rear-facing iSight camera. Not only can it take pictures, it can also record high-definition (HD) quality video. You choose the required mode with a switch.

When the iSight camera's video mode is selected, the following features and functions are activated:

- f/2.4 aperture
- 1080p HD video recording
- Video image stabilisation
- Slow motion (120 fps)
- Rear illumination
- 3 x video zoom
- Time-lapse video
- Video geotagging
- Face detection

The iSight camera is driven and controlled by a powerful image signal processor, which is built-in to the iPad's A8X microprocessor. This is a key factor in the quality of video produced by the camera.

The iPad's second camera – the front-facing FaceTime HD camera – takes lower quality video that is intended for use with social media sites such as Facebook, Twitter, and Flickr.

The video features and functions offered by this camera include:

- f/2.2 aperture
- 720p HD video recording
- Rear illumination
- Video geotagging
- Auto HDR videos
- FaceTime video calling

Recording Video

Although it's not the ideal device with which to record video due to its somewhat awkward dimensions, the iPad will do when nothing better is to hand. To record a video:

1. Tap the Camera app on the Home screen

2. Slide the mode switch on the right from Photo to Video. The Shutter/Record button turns from white to red

3. Tap the camera icon at the top to select the camera you want to use – iSight or FaceTime

4. Tap the screen to automatically adjust the focus. If you need to adjust the brilliance as well, drag the yellow slider up or down to do so

5. Tap the Record button to start the recording. A timer on the right of the screen will show the length of the recording

6. To stop recording, tap the Record button again

Locating Your Videos

As with pictures, all videos recorded with the iPad are stored in the Photos app. So when you want to find those videos, this is where you need to go:

1. Open the Photos app and tap Albums at the bottom of the screen

2. You will see an album named Videos

3. Open the Videos album and you'll see all videos recorded on the iPad

You can also view your videos in the Camera Roll. However, in this view, they will be mixed up with your pictures.

To differentiate between the two, videos have a camera icon at the bottom-left and the recording time at the bottom-right of the thumbnail, as shown on the right.

Note that videos created with the iPad are stored in the Photos app. Videos uploaded from a computer or the iTunes Store are stored in the Videos app.

Playing Back Your Videos

Playing back your videos is just as simple as viewing your pictures. Do it as follows:

1. Locate the video as described on page 145

2. Tap on the video to open it

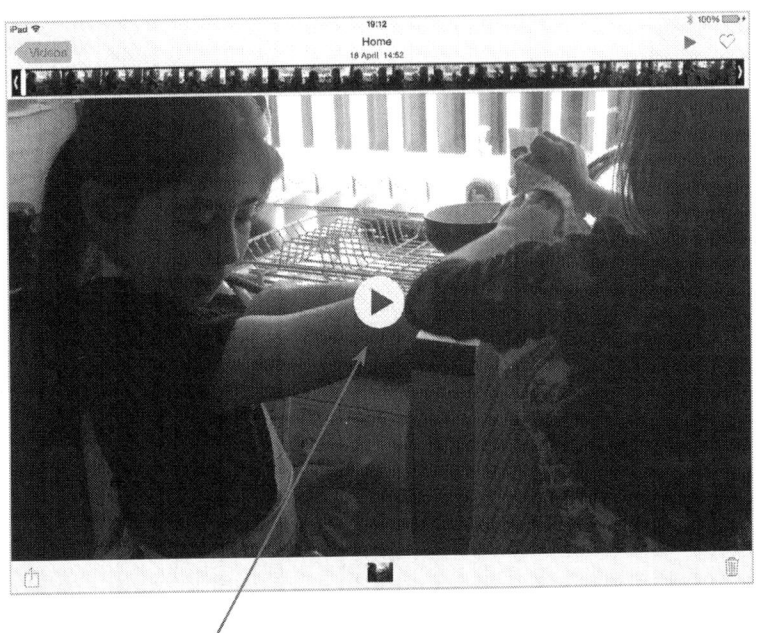

3. Tap the Play icon in the middle of the screen to commence playback

At the top of the screen, you'll see a timeline – this shows all the individual frames in the video. If you don't see it, just tap once on the screen. By grabbing the white marker on the timeline and dragging it backwards and forwards, you can quickly move about in the video.

To pause or stop playback, tap on the screen to open the Status bar at the top. At the right of this, you'll see a blue Pause button – tap it to stop the video. The icon now changes to a Play button. Tap this to recommence playback.

Next to the Play/Pause button, is a heart-shaped Favourites button. Tap this and your video will be saved in a Favourites album in the Photos app. To 'unfavourite' a video, tap the Favourites button again.

At the bottom of the screen are the Actions button, thumbnails of other videos in the current folder or album, and a Trash button.

Editing Video

A common problem with recording video is that you end up with stuff you don't really want or need. With this in mind, the Photos app provides you with a way of ditching unwanted footage.

On the previous page, we showed how to use the timeline to quickly and easily move about in videos. Well, the timeline has another function – it can also be used as a Trim tool:

1. Open the Photos app and locate the video to be edited

2. Tap on the video to open it. You will now see the timeline above it

3. At the beginning and end of the timeline, you'll notice small black handles

4. Tap and hold either of the handles and then drag it slightly to the left or right. The entire timeline will now be highlighted in yellow

5. Next, drag the handle at the left across to the right thus setting the start point of the video. Then drag the handle at the right across to the left to set the end point of the video

6. The selected frames in the timeline will now be highlighted in yellow

7. Tap Trim at the top-right of the screen. Then select 'Trim Original' or 'Save as New Clip'

8. The frames not selected are removed from the video, which is then saved in the Photos app

Uploading Home Videos

Many people starting out with the iPad will already have home videos on their computer and may want to transfer them to the iPad. After all, it does provide an excellent way of watching videos while on the move.

However, the process of uploading video from a computer to the iPad is complicated by the issue of video formats. Basically, the video to be uploaded has to be in a format the iPad will recognise – otherwise it won't be able to play it. Video formats that the iPad can play are:

- H.264 video

- MPEG-4 video

- Motion JPEG (M-JPEG)

If your home video is not in one of these formats, you must convert it to one before uploading it. You can do this with iTunes on your PC:

1. Open iTunes and go to File > Add File to Library

2. Browse to and select the video – then click Open

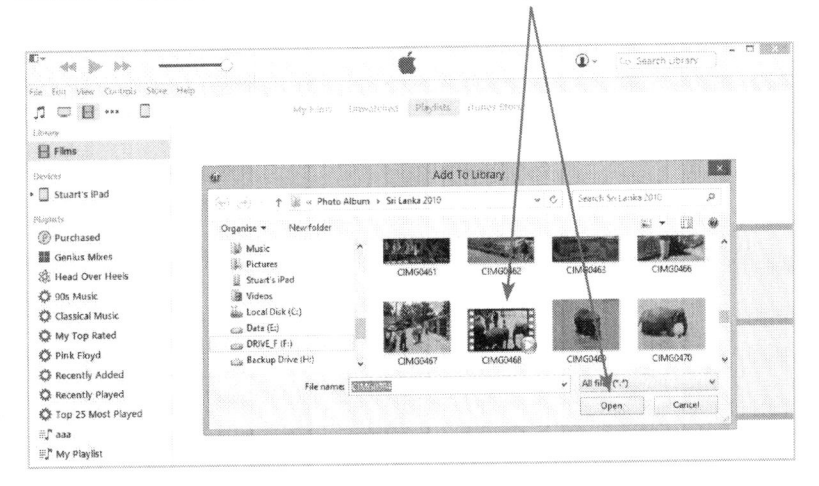

3. iTunes copies the video into the Films library – note that this can take some time depending on the length of the video

4. Open the Films library by clicking View on the menu bar and then going to More > Films

5. Select the video

6. Go back to the menu bar and click File > Create New Version > Create iPad or Apple TV Version

cont'd

iTunes will now convert the video to the MPEG-4 format. This done, you can then upload it to the iPad. The procedure for this is:

1. Connect the iPad to your computer

2. Open iTunes and, at the top-left, click the Films button

3. On the File menu, click 'Add File to Library'. Select the converted video and then click Open

4. After a few moments, you will see a new category called Home Videos appear at the top of the screen between the Unwatched and Playlists categories

5. Click the Home Videos category – you will see your video listed at the top of the screen. Hover the mouse over the line the video is on and you'll see this ••• icon. Click it

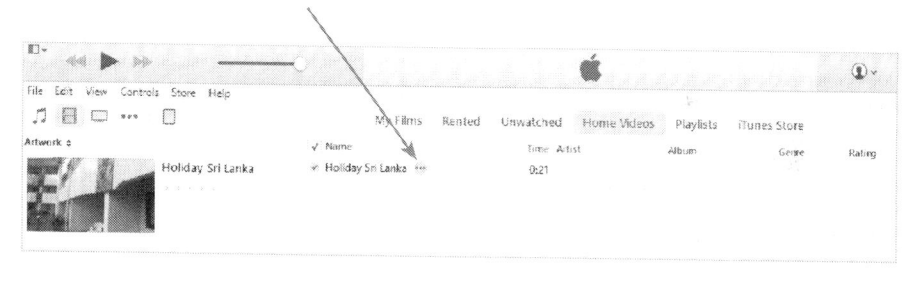

6. Click Add To and then select your iPad

7. Now click the iPad button below the menu bar to open the sidebar at the left-hand side of the screen. Select Films under Settings

8. In the new window, check the Sync Films box. Your video will be listed below in the Films section. Check this as well

9. Click the Sync button at the bottom-right

The video will now be uploaded to your iPad. When the transfer is complete, open the Videos app and then tap Home Videos at the top of the screen. This is where you will find your uploaded video.

Uploading Films and TV Programs

Apart from home videos, you may also have films and/or television programs on your computer that you want to move to your iPad. If so, the same rules as for home videos apply – you must first import them to iTunes and then convert them into the correct video format, as we describe on pages 148-149.

If, however, you have bought your films via Apple's iTunes Store, they will already be in iTunes and also correctly formatted.

Uploading Via iTunes
When everything is ready as per the above, you can use the following procedure to upload your films and TV programs from computer to iPad:

1. Connect the iPad to your computer

2. Open iTunes

3. In iTunes, click the iPad button below the menu bar to open the sidebar at the left of the screen. Under Settings, select the appropriate option – Films or TV Programmes. Then check the 'Sync' box at the top

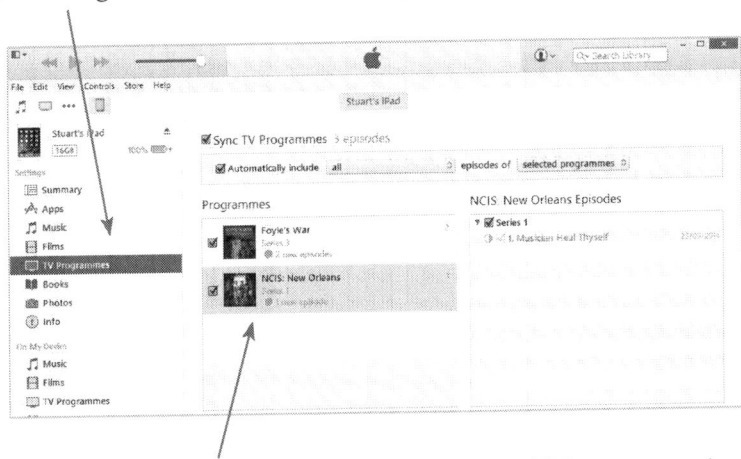

4. In the respective iTunes library, select the film or TV program to be uploaded and tap Apply at the bottom of the screen. The film or TV program will now be uploaded to your iPad

Open your iPad, tap the Videos app, and you will see the film or TV program you have just uploaded.

Uploading Via Wi-Fi
If you don't have any films or TV programs on your computer, you can get them directly from the iTunes Store. Apart from anything else, this will save you having to mess about with iTunes.

We explain how it's done on the next page.

cont'd

1. On the iPad's Home screen, tap the iTunes Store app

2. When the store opens, tap either Films or TV Programmes on the toolbar at the bottom of the screen

3. Find a film to upload. If you know exactly which film you want, use the search box at the top-right to go straight to it. Otherwise, scroll left and right, and up and down, to see what's available

4. When you have made your choice, tap on the image to see the film's details. This gives you a summary of the plot, the cast, and info such as the producing studio, date of release, running time, etc

5. Other options include Reviews, which lets you know how others have rated the film, and Related, which gives you a list of similar films

6. At the right of the screen, you will see HD and SD buttons. If you want the film in high-definition, tap HD – SD will give you standard-definition quality. Note that the film will cost less in SD

7. When you are ready to buy, tap the Buy button. For a lower charge you can opt to rent the film by tapping the Rent button

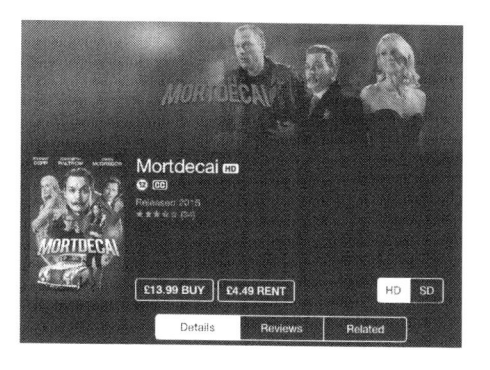

After payment has been taken, the film is downloaded to your iPad where you will find it in the Video app.

Video Storage Space

Of all the various types of data that can be used on your iPad, video demands the most storage space. For example, a two hour film will require approximately 4.0 GB of storage space.

Now, if your particular model has a storage capacity of between 32 GB and 128 GB, this probably won't be an issue for you. But if, like most iPad owners, you are using a 16 GB model, you definitely need to keep an eye on what you are uploading to the device. Otherwise, you may be in the middle of an upload only to see a message pop up stating you are about to run out of storage space.

The first thing to establish is how much free space you currently have:

1. Tap the Settings app on the Home screen
2. Go to General > Usage

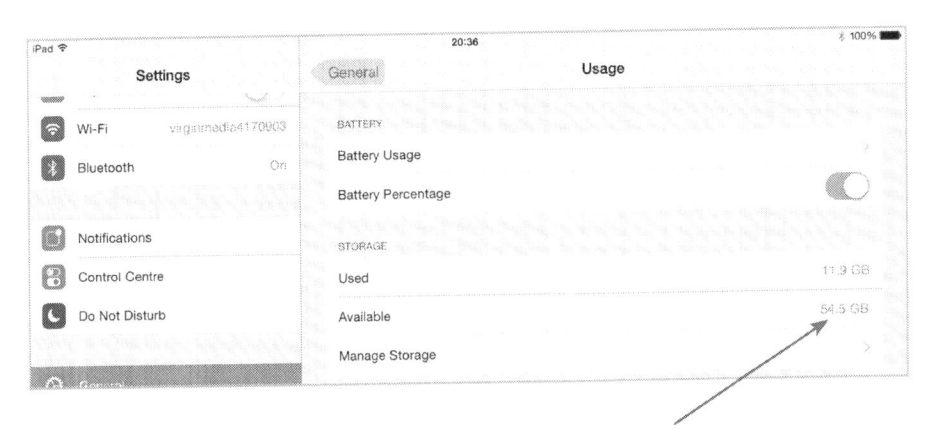

3. In the Storage section, you will see the amount of space currently in use and, more importantly, the amount available (54.5 GB above)

Make a note of the amount of storage you have available. The next time you decide to upload a film, take a look at its file size.

You will find this in the film's details. In the example above, the HD version is 4.31 GB, while the SD version is 1.89 GB. Our example iPad has 54.5 GB of free space so there is plenty of space for either version of the film.

Uploading Video to Facebook

A very popular activity these days, the making and sharing of videos with all and sundry is very easy to do with the iPad:

1. Open the Photos app on the Home screen
2. Go to the Camera Roll and locate the video to be uploaded
3. Tap the video and then tap the Actions button at the bottom-left of the screen

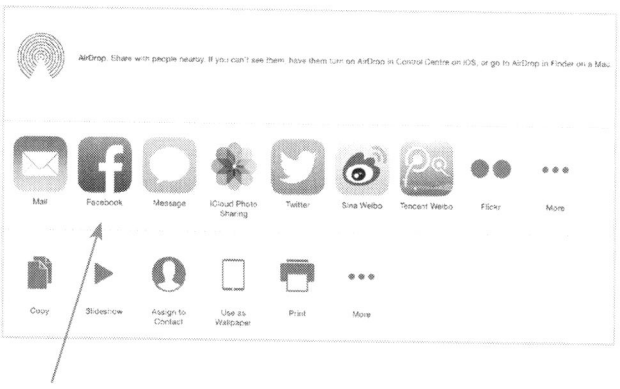

4. In the Actions screen, tap Facebook
5. If you haven't already set up Facebook on your iPad, you will now be prompted to do so. Tap the Settings button to set up an account and then tap Sign In
6. Now go back to the Photos app and tap the Facebook button again

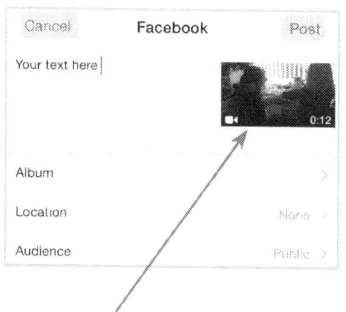

You will see a thumbnail of the video at the top-right. To the left of this, you can type in a message if you want to.

Tapping Details allows you to choose the video size (small, medium or large). You can also add your current location, and specify who can view the video, by tapping Location and Audience respectively.

FaceTime Video Calls

FaceTime is an iPad feature that lets you make video calls to users of other Apple devices (iPad, iPhone, iPod Touch, Mac computers). During these video calls, both parties can see the other.

As the calls are made over Wi-Fi or cellular connections, they are absolutely free (do keep an eye on your data allowance though).

Setting Up FaceTime
Before you can make a video call, you need to set up FaceTime as we explain below:

1. Tap the FaceTime app on the Home screen
2. Enter your Apple ID (your email address) and password
3. Tap Sign In
4. Specify the email address you want other people to use when they call you

Making a FaceTime Call
Initiating a FaceTime video call can be done in the following ways:

1. Open the FaceTime app and enter the name, number or email address of the person you want to contact. Or, if you have recently spoken to the person, their number may be in the list below – select it from there.

   Then tap the FaceTime button – the number will now ring

2. Open the Contacts app on the Home screen and select the required contact. Then tap FaceTime

While the call is in progress, you'll see three icons on the screen. Tapping the camera icon at the left switches to the rear camera, thus letting you show the other person what's in front of you. The red phone icon in the middle lets you end the call, while the microphone icon at the right lets you mute the sound at your end (you will still be able to hear the other person though)

Receiving a FaceTime Call
When someone makes a FaceTime call to you, your iPad will ring and the FaceTime app will open automatically. You will be presented with two on-screen options – Accept or Decline. Make your choice and proceed from there.

cont'd

Disabling FaceTime

Inevitably, there will be times where you don't want to have a face-to-face conversation with someone; there are any number of reasons why this might be so. Or, you may not want to use the feature at all.

In either case, you can disable FaceTime:

1. Tap the Settings app on the Home screen

2. On the left-hand side, scroll down to and tap FaceTime

3. On the right, tap the FaceTime switch to the Off position

Now, people calling you via FaceTime will see a message stating that you are not available.

Play iPad Video on a TV

You don't have to watch your iPad's video content on the device itself – if you prefer, you can watch it on a TV set. This is made possible by the use of Apple's AirPlay feature, which can stream video from an iPad to a suitably equipped device.

To do it, you will need either of the following:

1. An Apple TV that supports AirPlay

2. A Lightening Digital AV Adaptor that lets you use a non-AirPlay television

The Lightening adaptor will connect to an HDMI port on the TV. However, if you have an old TV that only provides a VGA port, you can buy a Lightening to VGA adaptor instead. Either will allow you to stream video to a non-AirPlay TV.

To set up AirPlay streaming:

1. Make sure your iPad and the TV are connected to the same Wi-Fi network

2. Tap the video to be streamed

3. Tap the AirPlay icon

4. Select your AirPlay TV in the pop-up menu as shown on the right

AirPlay	
iPad	
CEN-MEETING RM C	
Apple TV	✓
TuckwoodHay	

With AirPlay Mirroring you can send everything on your iPad's display to an Apple TV, wirelessly.

cont'd

5. After a short period, the video will start playing on the TV

Peer-to-Peer AirPlay

Things are even better for those of you who possess one of the 3rd generation Apple TV models running the latest 7.x firmware, and an iPad that runs iOS 8.

For anyone that does, peer-to-peer AirPlay enables the iPad to be connected to an Apple TV without both devices having to be connected to the same Wi-Fi network. Effectively, the iPad acts as an ad-hoc Wi-Fi hotspot to which the Apple TV can connect directly.

As a result, instead of being limited to places where Wi-Fi is available, not to mention the need to enter Wi-Fi passwords, you can use AirPlay to stream video wherever you happen to be – a network is not required at all – the iPad and the TV are connected directly.

Mirror the iPad's Screen on a TV

Another feature of Apple's AirPlay technology is its ability to mirror the iPad's screen on a TV. This is great for viewing pictures, websites, apps and playing games, etc.

To set this up:

1. Swipe upwards from the bottom of the screen to launch the Control Centre
2. Tap Airplay
3. Select the Apple TV you want to mirror on by tapping its name
4. Tap the Mirroring option to On

From this point on, everything on the iPad's screen will be replicated, or mirrored, on the TV set. To turn mirroring off, tap the mirroring switch to the Off position.

The minimum requirements for mirroring are:

- Apple TV – 2nd or 3rd generation
- iPad 2 or newer

CHAPTER 11

Audio

The ability to store and play music is another of the iPad's great features. Not only can you upload music you already own, you can also buy and download a huge range of music from the iTunes Store.

When doing just about anything connected with music on the iPad, you will be doing it with the Music app. One of its many features is Playlists, which allow you to create lists of just the tracks you want to hear.

Smart Playlists go a step further by automatically updating themselves according to the criteria set. Read on to find out more!

Getting Music on to the iPad 158

Playing Music 160

Playlists 161

Creating a Standard Playlist in iTunes 161

Creating a Smart Playlist in iTunes 162

Creating a Genius Playlist in iTunes 164

Using Playlists 165

Creating Playlists on the iPad 166

Audio Settings 169

Controlling Your Music With Siri 170

Getting Music on to the iPad

Uploading From a Computer

One of the first things many iPad users want to do is get their computer-based music collection on to the device. To do this, it is necessary to first place the required music in the iTunes music library:

1. On the computer, open iTunes

2. At the top-left, click File and then click 'Add Folder to Library'

3. Browse to the folder that contains your music collection

4. Select the folder and then click Select Folder at the bottom

Your music collection will now be added to the iTunes music library. The next stage is to transfer it to the iPad:

1. Connect the iPad to the computer and open iTunes

2. In iTunes, click the iPad button under the menu bar at the top-left

3. In the Settings section on the sidebar, click Music

4. On the right-hand side of the screen, check the Sync Music checkbox

5. You now have a choice to make: transfer your entire music collection or just part of it. If it's the former, select 'Entire Music Library' and if it's the latter, select 'Selected playlists, artists, albums and genres'

6. Beneath these two options, you'll see further options to 'Include Music Videos' and 'Include Voice Memos', both of which are self-explanatory. If you select the 'Automatically fill free space with songs' option, this will fill any remaining space on the iPad with a selection of similar music from the library

cont'd

7. If you've elected to transfer the entire collection, all you have to do now is click the Sync button at the bottom-right of the screen

8. If you want to transfer just some of the tracks in the collection, however, go to the Artists section on the right of the screen and select the ones you want. Having done so, then click the Sync button

Downloading from the iTunes Store

The easiest way to get music on the iPad is to download it directly to the device from the iTunes Store. Just tap on the iTunes Store app and then when it opens, tap Music on the menu bar at the bottom of the screen.

Browsing the store, and buying and downloading music, is much the same procedure as with buying apps and videos, so we won't repeat it.

Downloading Via iCloud

This method only applies to music purchased from the iTunes Store. As we saw above, the easiest way to get music on to the iPad is to open the store on the device and simply download any purchases directly to it.

However, there may be occasions when your iPad is not to hand. In these situations, you can use another iOS device – a Mac, computer, iPhone, or iPod Touch – to buy the music and then have it sent automatically to your iPad. This is known as automatic downloading.

To set it up:

1. Tap the Settings app on the Home screen

2. Tap iTunes & App Store

3. In the Automatic Downloads section, tap the Music switch to the On position

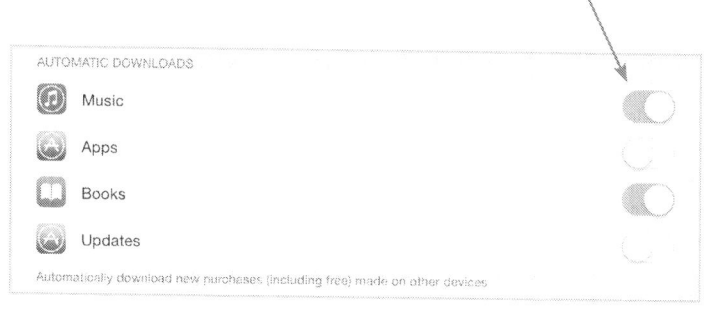

From this point on, every time you purchase music from the iTunes Store with any iOS device, it is sent automatically to your iCloud account, and then from there onwards to all your other devices, including the iPad.

Playing Music

Having got some tracks on to your device, you will now want to play them. On the Home screen, tap the Music app. When it opens, at the bottom of the screen, you will see a number of icons each offering a different view of your music, as shown below:

These give you various options with regard to browsing your music library. For example, tap Artists and you will see an alphabetical list of all the artists, tap Songs for an alphabetical list of all the songs, and tap Genres to see your music sorted by type.

To play a particular track, all you have to do is tap it once – it will start playing immediately. At the top of the screen, you will see the controls.

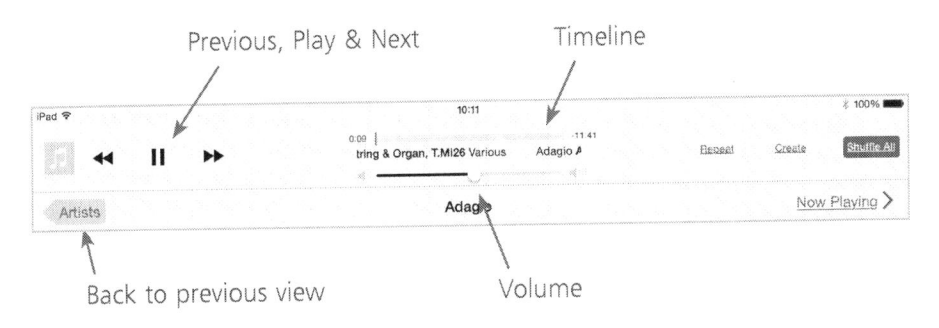

Previous, Play & Next

Timeline

Back to previous view

Volume

When the music starts, the Play button turns into a Pause button – tap it to pause the music – it then reverts to the Play button. Previous and Next take you to the previous and next tracks. The timeline enables you to move about quickly in the track.

At the top-right, you'll see Repeat, Create and Shuffle. The first, Repeat, allows you to either repeat the song or the artist, Create lets you create a Genius Playlist (see page 164), and Shuffle lets you randomly rearrange the order in which tracks are played.

Below Create and Shuffle is a Now Playing link. Tap this to see the above controls in a larger view, as shown on the right.

cont'd

You can also play your music from the Control Centre. Swipe upwards from the bottom of any screen and the Control Centre will slide into view.

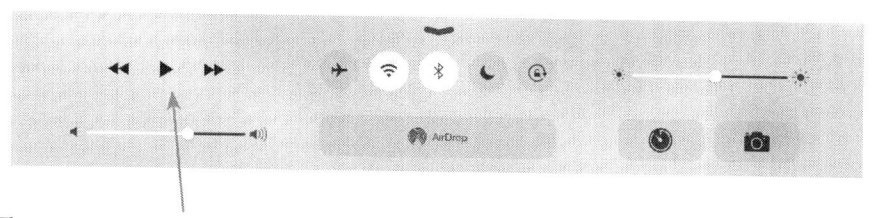

The music controls are on the left and will let you play, pause and stop the last song opened in the Music app. You can also adjust the volume and go to the next or previous track using the Previous and Next buttons. However, you cannot select songs from the Control Centre.

Playlists

Basically, a playlist is a collection of songs that are related in some way or have been specifically selected. They are an important feature not just on the iPad but also in iTunes.

There are three different types of playlist:

- Standard playlist
- Smart playlist
- Genius playlist

We'll begin by taking a look at Standard playlists and how they are used in iTunes.

Creating a Standard Playlist in iTunes

A standard playlist is one in which the contents (songs) are manually controlled as opposed to the Smart and Genius types, both of which are automatic. The steps are:

1. On your computer, open iTunes
2. On the menu bar, click File > New > Playlist
3. In the highlighted box at the top-left, enter a name for the playlist
4. Click once on the screen to save the playlist

cont'd

The playlist is now created. It can be accessed at any time by opening iTunes and clicking the Music button under the menu bar. On the sidebar, at the bottom, you will see the playlist. Click it to open it.

To add music to your playlist:

1. Tap the 'Add To...' button at the top-right of the screen

2. In the window that opens, you will see all the artists in your iTunes music library on the left, and your open playlist on the right

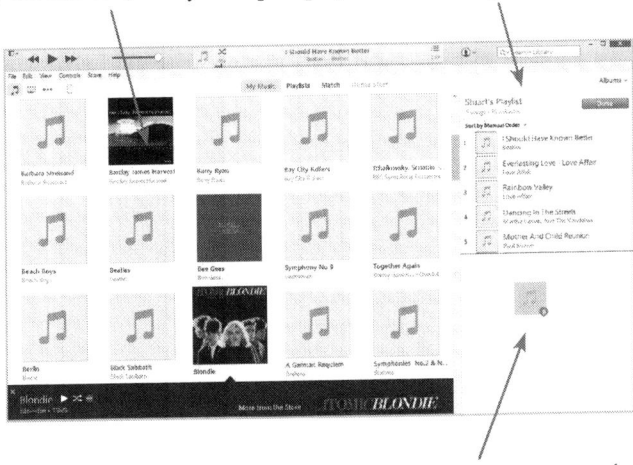

3. Choose a song from the library and simply drag it across to the open playlist and release it

4. If the selected artist has more than one song in the library, click on the artist to open the list of songs. Then drag the ones required over to the playlist

5. When the playlist is complete, click the Done button at the top-right

Creating a Smart Playlist in iTunes
A Standard playlist is built manually and so gives you complete control over its contents.

cont'd

However, this means that updating it also has to be done manually – you cannot just forget about it once created.

With the Smart playlist on the other hand, you can because it updates itself automatically – you don't have to do anything. The playlist is based on specified rules, which update the playlist as your library changes. For example, you could create a smart playlist containing songs by a particular artist. When you add more songs by that artist to your library, they are automatically added to the playlist.

1. On your computer, open iTunes. Then, on the menu bar, click File > New > Smart Playlist

2. The smart playlist options dialogue box opens. This lets you create the rules for your playlist

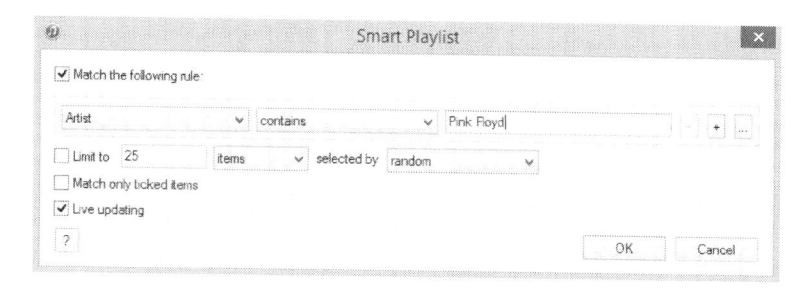

3. The first menu (Artist in our example above), allows you to choose a condition for the rule – there is a huge selection

4. The second menu (contains), lets you choose an operator for the condition – options depend on the field chosen in the first menu

5. What you see in the third field (Pink Floyd) depends on what is selected in the first and second menus. Usually, it is a text field that allows you to enter values manually

6. By clicking the + and ... buttons to open extra lines, you can create as many rules as you need

Other options include 'Limit to', which lets you limit the playlist to a specified number of tracks or length; 'Match only ticked items', which makes sure only tracks whose checkboxes have been ticked are included in the playlist; and 'Live updating', which makes sure the playlist is automatically updated.

Finally, click OK, and then click on the screen once (or tap Enter on the keyboard). The playlist is created and saved in iTunes.

cont'd

Creating a Genius Playlist in iTunes

Genius playlists offer the easiest method of all with which to create a playlist. All you have to do is specify one song and iTunes will then create a playlist containing other songs similar in type.

1. The first step is to turn Genius on. To do this, click Store on the menu bar and then click 'Turn On Genius'

2. In the window that opens, click the 'Turn On Genius' button – the Genius setup routine is initiated

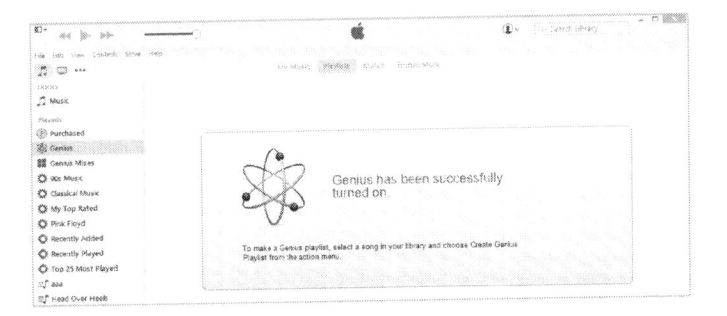

3. When setup is complete, you'll see the screen above

4. On the sidebar, click Music in the Library section

5. Select a song on which to base your Genius playlist

6. Right-click on the song and from the action menu, click 'Create Genius Playlist'

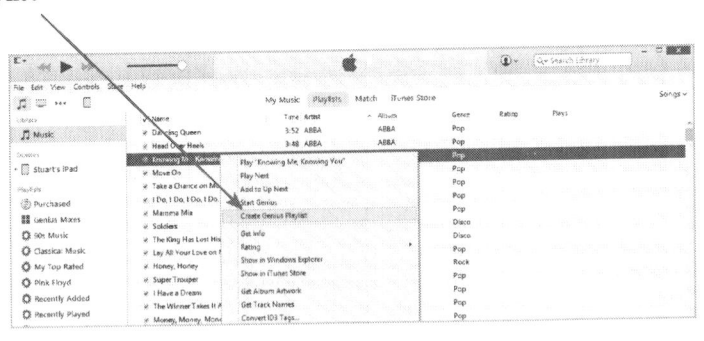

7. The playlist is created and given the name of the song you selected

8. You will now see the new playlist on the sidebar in the Playlists section. If you want to rename it, double-click on the name

Using Playlists

Playlists created in iTunes can be used in two ways:

Playing Music
Having created a playlist of whatever type, you can access it at any time by clicking Playlists at the top of the iTunes window. This opens a sidebar at the left, which shows all your playlists. Note that these include a number of default playlists such as Purchased, 90s Music, Classical Music, My Top Rated, etc.

Click on the desired playlist and a list of all the tracks it contains opens on the right of the window. To play one, select it and then click the Play icon at the top-left of the screen (you can also double-click on it or right-click and select Play from the menu).

You can rearrange the order in which tracks are played by right-clicking on a track and then clicking Play Next – this makes it the next to be played. Subsequent tracks can be queued by right-clicking and clicking 'Add to Up Next'.

To view your Up Next list, click on the three lines at the top of the screen. You'll see how many songs are currently in the queue and what order they'll play in. To clear a list, simply click Clear.

Uploading Music to an iPad
Another very useful way in which playlists can be used is to selectively upload music to your iPad. On pages 158-159, we saw one method of doing this with iTunes. We're now going to show you another way to do it with the aid of a playlist:

1. Connect the iPad to the computer

2. Start iTunes

3. In iTunes, click the iPad button at the top-left of the screen

4. On the sidebar, under Settings, click Music

5. Check the Sync Music box

6. Tick the 'Selected playlists, artists, albums and genres' radio button

7. In the Playlists section on the left, check the playlist to be uploaded

8. Click Apply. iTunes transfers the playlist and its contents to your iPad

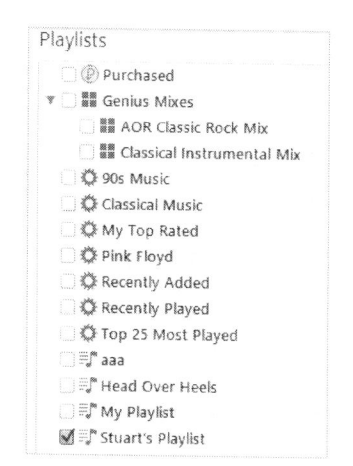

cont'd

9. Now go to the iPad and open the Music app. At the bottom, tap Playlists

10. In the Playlists list, you will see the playlist you've just uploaded. Tap once on it to open it

Creating Playlists on the iPad

So far, we have looked at creating and using playlists in iTunes. However, they can also be created directly on the iPad.

To do it:

1. Tap the Music app on the Home screen

2. Tap Playlists at the bottom-left of the screen

3. The Playlists screen will open and should be empty

4. Place your finger anywhere within the Playlists screen and flick it downwards. Two default playlists will appear – Genius Playlist and New Playlist...

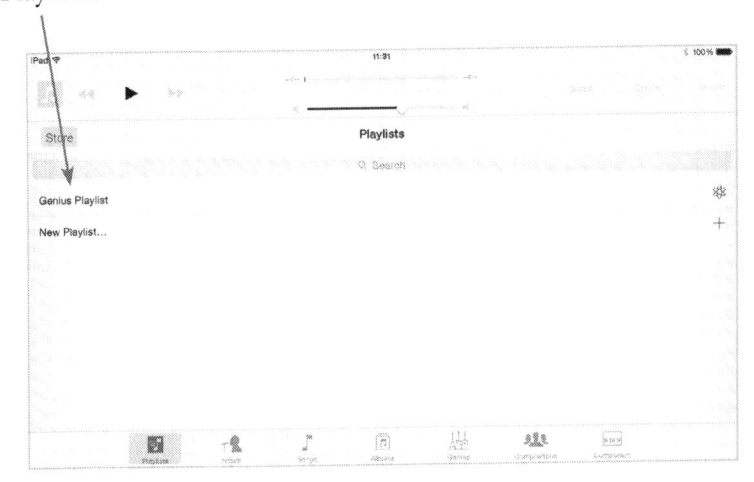

cont'd

5. Tap 'New Playlist...'

6. Enter a name for the playlist and tap Save

7. You will see the renamed playlist in the Playlists screen

To add songs to the new playlist:

1. Tap the playlist to open it. Then tap any of the Songs, Artists or Albums links at the bottom of the screen. In the example below, we have opened the Songs page

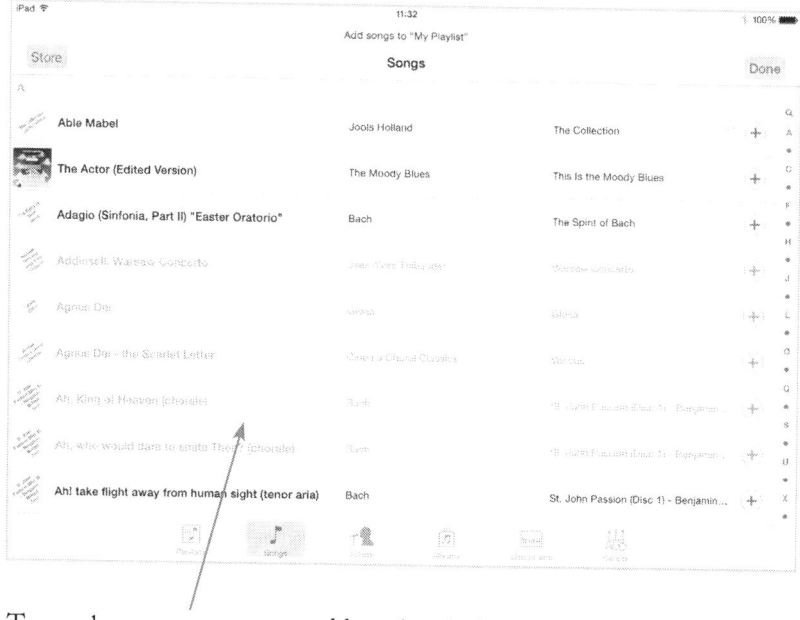

2. Tap each song you want to add to the playlist – they will now be greyed out

3. When you are finished, tap Done at the top-right of the screen

You will now see your playlist and all the songs it contains. To play one, just tap on it.

At the top-right of the playlist window, you will see Delete – tap this to delete the playlist. In the middle, you will see Clear – tap this to remove all songs in the playlist. At the left is Edit – this allows you delete individual songs by tapping the red minus icon to the left of each song; to re-order them by dragging the three-line icon at the far-right up and down; and to add more songs by tapping the + sign.

cont'd

You can also create Genius playlists on the iPad. These work in exactly the same way as Genius playlists created in iTunes:

1. Tap the Music app on the Home screen

2. Tap Playlists at the bottom-left of the screen

3. Place your finger anywhere within the Playlists screen and flick it downwards to reveal the Genius Playlist link

4. Tap Genius Playlist and then in the new window, tap 'Turn On Genius'

5. Read the Terms & Conditions and then tap Accept at the top-right of the screen

6. Genius will now analyse your music library, compare it with those of other Genius users and, finally, deliver its results

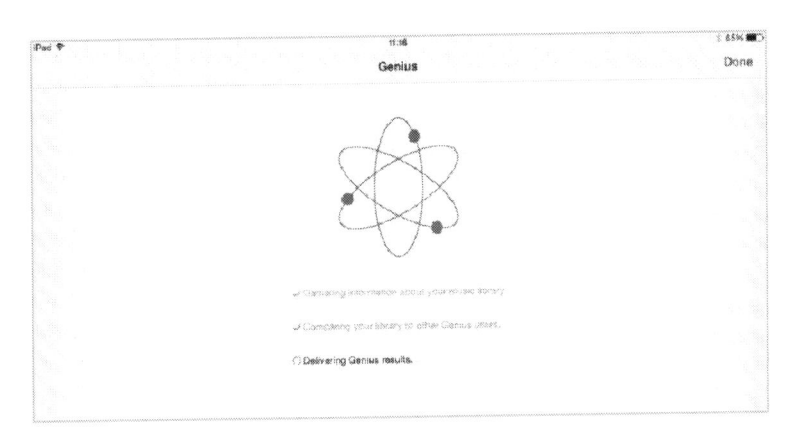

7. Tap Done at the top-right of the screen

8. You are now taken back to the Playlists screen. Tap Genius Playlist again to open it – you will see all the songs it contains

9. Tap a song on which you want to base the playlist. If there aren't enough related songs on the iPad, a menu will pop-up informing you that for this reason a Genius Playlist cannot be created

10. If there are enough related songs however, the playlist is created

An alternative (and quicker) method is to simply play a song on which you want to base the playlist, and then tap Create at the top-right. If there are enough related songs, a Genius Playlist will be created. If not, a pop-up will inform you that one cannot be created.

Audio Settings

Like most aspects of your iPad, there are a number of settings related to audio that you can configure:

1. On the Home screen, tap the Settings app
2. Scroll down on the left-hand side and tap Music

You will then see the following settings:

- **Sound Check** – songs are rarely recorded at the same sound level, so usually their volume is different when played. The Sound Check feature, which is enabled by default, is designed to eliminate this issue by making all tracks play at the same level

- **EQ** – EQ is short for equaliser and it is basically a list of pre-set sound settings that allow you to adjust the sound of the audio by, for example, increasing and reducing bass, boosting the treble, and optimising for speech, etc. There are 23 pre-set options that you can choose from or you can simply turn it off by selecting the Off option

- **Volume Limit** – this is essentially a safety feature that ensures the volume level of the iPad can never be higher than the pre-set level. Turned off by default, you can activate it by tapping the setting and then dragging the slider to the required level

- **Group By Album Artist** – on by default, this setting groups Artists by the value in the Album Artist field instead of the Artist field. With most albums, these two fields are the same but many compilation albums use Various in the Artist field and individual artists in the Album Artist field. By turning this setting off, these compilation albums will be listed under Various in the Artists section

- **Show All Music** – this setting lets you view all your music including music stored in iCloud, or just on the iPad itself

- **Genius** – On by default, this setting allows Apple to analyse the music in the Music app for the purpose of creating Genius playlists

- **Subscribe to iTunes Match** – iTunes Match is a subscription service that enables you to store all your music in iCloud for a yearly fee. Not only can you access the music on the iPad but also on all your other Apple devices as well.

  Apart from ease of access, another big advantage is that your music does not take up any storage space on the iPad. See page 191 for more on iCloud Match

Controlling Your Music With Siri

If you are in a lazy mood, you can get Siri to be your disc jockey. When used for this purpose, the iPad's voice recognition feature is as specific or as general as you like. For example, if you simply say 'play music', it will play a random track from your music library and then, if left, work its way through the entire library.

This may be OK for general background music but for a dedicated 'chilling out' session, more control is required.

So you need to be specific. By so doing, you will be able to play tracks, artists, albums, playlists and genres of your own choosing.

Some typical commands you can use include:

- 'Play music by Pink Floyd'
- 'Play Dark Side of the Moon'
- 'Play jazz'
- 'Play Dave's playlist'

Siri will confirm the command by repeating it back to you and also writing it on the screen.

Other commands include:

- 'Shuffle', which will activate the Music app's Shuffle mode
- 'Shuffle playlist xxx', which will shuffle the tracks in the specified playlist
- 'Play more songs like this'. This command will tell Siri to create a Genius playlist of songs similar to the one currently being played

To control your music, use the following commands:

- Pause or stop
- Play
- Next song (or track)
- Previous song (or track)
- Skip

CHAPTER 12

Reading With the iPad

E-books have arrived and are here to stay. While it is doubtful they will ever completely replace physical books, they do offer certain advantages and features that make them an interesting alternative.

For example: bookmarks mean you will never lose your page; people with poor eyesight can increase text size; you can make notes as you go along; you will never be short of something to read as long as you have a network connection, plus many more.

To find your reading material, you need to access the iBooks Store. We show you how to do this, plus how to review and download your books.

Newspapers & Magazines 172

Books 174

Finding Books 176

Previewing & Downloading Books 177

Syncing Books 178

Controlling Books 179

Working With Text 180

Listen To The iPad 182

Newspapers and Magazines

Your iPad is portable and comes equipped with a high-resolution Retina screen – these two features make it an ideal device on which to read the written word. Yes, you can buy a dedicated Kindle but there is really no need – the iPad is just as good for reading, if not actually better.

To this end, it comes with two reading apps – Newsstand and iBooks. We'll look at the former first.

Newsstand is designed for use with large publications such as newspapers and magazines. Not only does the app enable you to read them, it also helps you to manage them so you can easily see what you have available to read at any time.

1. Tap the Newsstand app to open it
2. Initially, your Newsstand is empty

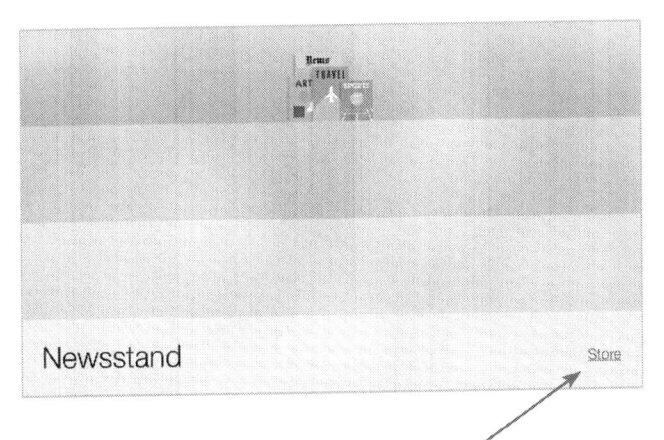

3. Tap Store at the bottom-right of the window

cont'd

4. The store opens with a view of popular publications – scroll to the right and downwards to see what's available

5. Alternatively, tap Categories at the top-left – this opens a scrollable categorised list of newspapers and magazines

6. If you cannot find what you are looking for, try the search box at the top-right

7. Once you have found a publication, you can either download it immediately by tapping the GET button, or preview it by tapping on the publication

8. Downloaded publications are stored in your Newsstand bookcase. To open one, just tap on it

Should you ever wish to delete a downloaded publication, just press and hold on the publication until it starts to jiggle. Then tap the X.

Books

When it comes to reading books on your iPad, the iBooks app is where you need to go. This app enables you to download and store literally hundreds of books across all genres on your iPad. They can then be read whether you're at home, on a plane, on a train, or on a ship – it acts as your own personal library.

Get started by:

1. Tapping the iBooks app on the Home screen
2. The app opens in the All Books view. If you haven't bought any books yet, the view is empty. When you have, they are displayed as shown below:

3. If you see a book with a cloud icon at the top-right corner, it means the book hasn't yet been downloaded to the iPad. To do so, just tap once on the book. Any books without the cloud icon are already on the iPad
4. A blue New banner at the top-right corner of a book indicates that it hasn't been opened yet

At the top and bottom of the screen are a number of icons and links. Working clockwise from top-left, these are:

- ≡ – this option lets you view your library in a number of ways. These include Most Recent, Titles, Authors, and Categories and can be selected from the menu bar at the top of the screen
- **All Books** – this opens a menu that lets you view your books in categories or collections. Default collections are All (everything in the library), Books (just the books), and PDFs (Portable Document Format)

cont'd

- **Select** – tap Select to open the Select Items page. This lets you select books individually, or collectively, by tapping Select All.

  Having done so, you then have two choices: You can tap Move to open the Collections list and select a different collection in which to move the book.

  Or you can tap Delete to delete the book. Note only books that are actually on the iPad can be deleted. If you select a book that is in the cloud, the Delete option will not be available

  Also, deleting a book will not remove it from the collection – it will still be there but will now have the Cloud icon at the top-right corner indicating it is now in the cloud.

  If you don't want to see the book in the collection at all, tap the 'Hide iCloud Books' switch at the bottom of the Collections menu to Off

  Also on the Collections menu is a '+ New Collection' option. This lets you organise your book library by creating any number of collections that can be named appropriately. Having done so, you can move existing books to these collections as described above

At the bottom of the iBooks screen is a toolbar. This offers a number of options:

- **Purchased** – at the far-right of the toolbar, this option shows you two views of your library: the first is All, and the second is 'Not on This iPad', i.e. books that are on the cloud

- **Top Authors** – this opens an alphabetical list of authors, both paid and free. Tap on an author's name to see which of their books are available for download

- **Top Charts** – see what books are currently in the best-seller charts. You can peruse a separate list for both paid and free books

- **Featured** – a scrollable list of selected titles that may appeal to you

- **My Books** – this takes you to your book shelf where your books are listed

Finding Books

To find books to download to your iPad, you need to browse the iBooks Store. To access the store, open the iBooks app and select either 'Top Authors', 'Top Charts', or 'Featured' from the toolbar at the bottom.

All three options show a different view of the store. Below, we see the Featured view:

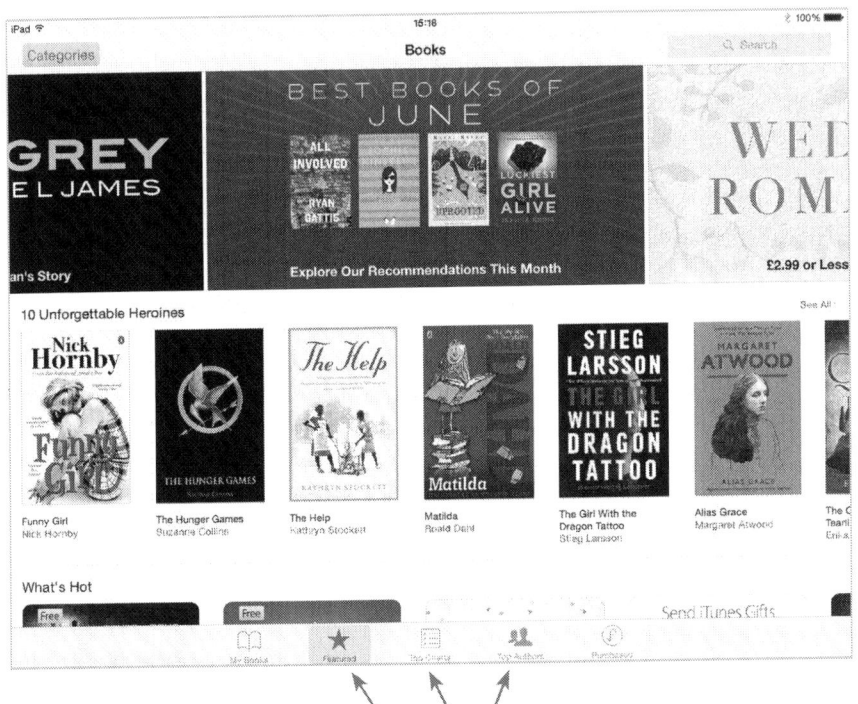

Use these buttons on the toolbar to search for books

If you are looking for something specific, it will probably be quicker to use the search box at the top-right of the screen.

Note that you are not restricted to the iBooks Store for your reading material. The iBooks app supports the EPUB format, which is used by many online book stores. For example, go to www.epubbooks.com and you will find an excellent selection of books that are in the public domain, i.e. are free.

You can also read Kindle books on your iPad. However, this cannot be done with the iBooks app – you will have to download and install the Kindle app. Once done though, your entire Kindle library will be available on it.

The same applies to books purchased from the Barnes & Noble bookstore. Just install the Barnes & Noble app to read them on your iPad.

Previewing & Downloading Books

Having found a book that might be of interest, you now need to look a bit closer before opening your wallet:

1. Tap on the book to open its details page

2. Tap Reviews to see what other readers think of the book

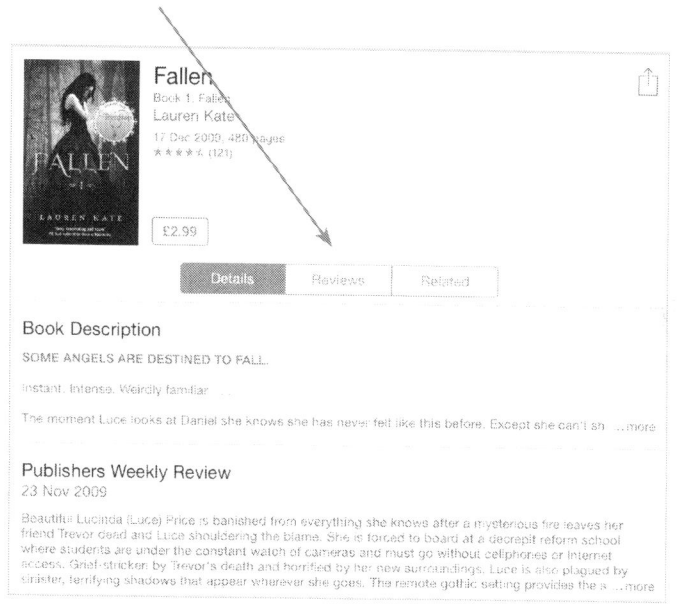

3. If you want to read a sample of the book before committing yourself, tap the SAMPLE button

4. When you are sure you want the book, tap the price button and then the Buy Book button. Enter your password in the iTunes Store login screen and then tap OK

5. The purchase is charged to the credit card registered to your Apple account and the book is then downloaded to your iPad

6. Tap My Books at the bottom-left of the screen and you will see the newly downloaded book at the top-left of your book shelf

Syncing Books

You may already have some e-books on your computer and be looking to get them on to your iPad. This is how to go about it:

1. Connect your iPad to the computer
2. Start iTunes
3. In iTunes, click the iPad button at the top-left of the screen under the menu bar
4. Click Books in the Settings section on the left-hand side
5. Check the box next to Sync Books

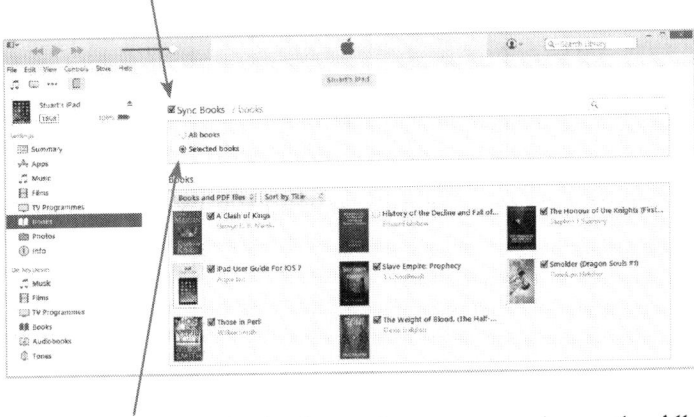

6. If you want to sync all the books on the computer, choose the All Books option
7. If you just want to sync some of them, choose the Selected Books option. Then, in the list of books, check the box next to each book you want to sync
8. Click Apply at the bottom-right of the screen

iTunes will now transfer the selected books to your iPad. Looking ahead, you can configure your iPad to automatically download any books subsequently purchased on another iOS device, e.g. your iPhone.

1. Tap the Settings app
2. On the left-hand side, scroll down to iTunes & App Store
3. In the Automatic Downloads section, tap the Books switch to On

From now on, all e-books purchased on another device will be sent automatically to your iPad.

Controlling Books

Unlike a physical book where what you see is what you get, with e-books there are a number of options that let you control the book, and also tailor the display for a better reading experience.

Open the iBooks app and then select the book you want to read from your library. Then use the following options to read and control the book:

- **View a single page** – hold the iPad in Portrait mode

- **View two pages** – hold the iPad in Landscape mode

- **Turn to the next page** – either tap the right-hand side of the screen or flick to the left of the page with your finger

- **Turn to the previous page** – either tap the left-hand side of the screen or flick to the right of the page with your finger

- **Revealing the controls** – tap anywhere on the screen to reveal the controls – tap on the screen again to conceal them

- **Scroll up and down through the pages** – reveal the controls and tap the Fonts A button at the top-right. Then tap Scrolling View

- **Bookmarks** – to bookmark a page, reveal the controls and tap the Bookmarks button at the top-right

- **Accessing the library** – reveal the controls and tap Library at the top

- **Open the Table of Contents** – tap on the screen to reveal the controls and then tap the Contents button

- **Move about in the book** – tap on the screen to reveal the controls and then, at the bottom of the screen, drag the dot on the slider left or right

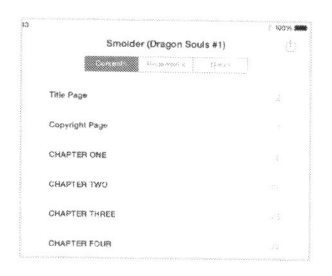

- **Search the book for a specific word or page number** – tap on the screen to reveal the controls and then tap the Search button at the top right of the screen

Working With Text

The iBooks app provides you with a number of ways to view, alter and search the text in any book. You can also look up dictionary definitions and make notes as you go along. Lets take a look at the available options:

Formatting Text

Text in all books uses a specific font – a set of printable or displayable characters in a specific style and size. With a physical book, the font cannot be changed but in an e-book, it can.

One of the most useful changes that can be made is the size of the font. For example, people with poor eyesight can increase it to a level that makes it much easier for them to read. To do this, and more:

1. Open the book and tap on the screen to reveal the controls

2. Tap on the Fonts aA button

3. Tap the small A to reduce the size of the font, and the large A to increase it

4. To change the font itself, tap on the Fonts line. This opens a pop-up giving you seven fonts from which to choose

5. The Fonts menu offers some other options as well. Right at the top is a brilliance control that lets you alter the brightness of the screen

6. Further down is a screen colour control that lets you change the screen colour to White, Sepia or Black. White is the default colour but we recommend using Sepia instead as it is easier on the eye

7. Finally, there is a Auto-Night Theme option. This is designed to reduce excessive glare that can be the cause of eye strain. It uses your location and time to detect when daylight is over and automatically switch to the Night theme – a black background with light grey text

Text Options

When reading an e-book, tapping and holding on a word brings up a toolbar of useful options as shown overleaf:

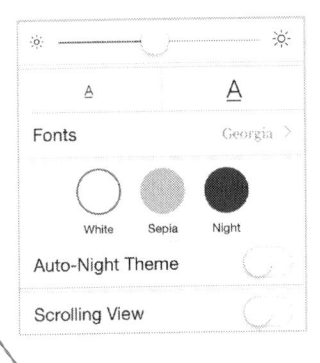

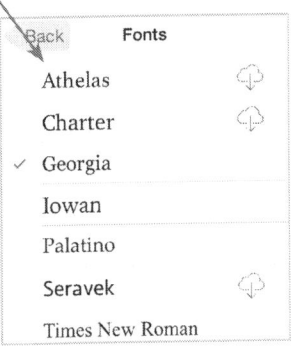

cont'd

These include speaking the word, defining it, highlighting it, searching for other instances, and making notes related to the word. Lets see how these work:

- **Speak...** – if you're not sure how a word is pronounced, tap and hold it to bring up the toolbar. Then tap 'Speak...' (if you don't see it on the toolbar, enable the Speak Selection option – see the screenshot on the next page). The iPad will now speak the word to you

- **Define** – if you aren't sure of the meaning of a word, tap Define. This opens a dictionary definition of the word – you will also see an option for searching the Web.

  If you don't get a definition, it is because there is no dictionary on the iPad. Tap Manage to access a list of dictionaries and tap the one you want – it will now be downloaded

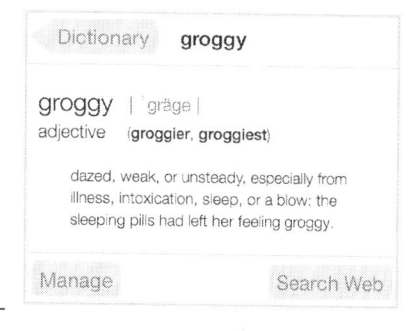

- **Highlight** – you can highlight individual words or phrases. To highlight a specific word, just tap and hold on it. For a phrase, drag the blue dots until the entire phrase is selected. Then tap Highlight on the toolbar – you will see various options such as colour, delete and underline

- **Note** – if you want to make a note at a certain point in a book for later reference, tap and hold on a relevant word to open the toolbar and then tap Note. A blank note will appear along with the keyboard – simply type into it

The word will be highlighted and a yellow square placed in the margin alongside the line containing the note. To read the note, just tap on the square

You can review all your notes and bookmarks by opening the Table of Contents page as described on page 179. On the toolbar at the top, you"ll see Notes and Bookmarks buttons

Listen To The iPad

We saw on the previous page how you can get your iPad to speak words to you. Well, it can actually do a lot more than this – it can read an entire book. The feature that enables this is an accessibility feature called Speech, which we took a brief look at on page 45.

To set this up:

1. Tap the Settings app
2. Go to General > Accessibility > Speech
3. Tap the Speak Screen switch to the On position

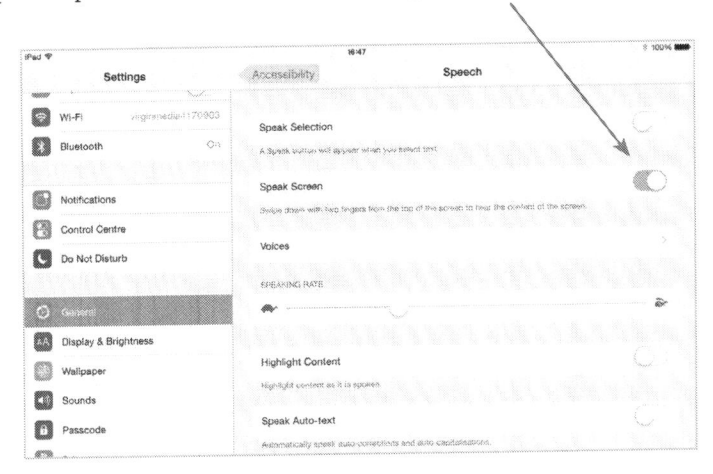

4. Open the book at the page you want to start reading from and drag downwards from the top of the screen with two fingers
5. The iPad now starts reading the book aloud. At the same time, an iBooks toolbar appears on the screen as shown below:

Options on the toolbar include Minimise, Speak Slower, Go back a Page, Pause/Play, Go Forward a Page, Speak Faster, and Close.

While you have the Speech settings screen open, you can set the iPad to speak with a foreign accent by selecting a language – tap Voices to set this. You can also adjust the speed at which it reads by adjusting the Speaking Rate slider.

CHAPTER 13
iCloud & Related Services

So far, we have taken an in-depth look at the main applications provided by the iPad and associated apps – email (Mail app), the Internet (Safari), pictures (Photos app), video (Videos app), music (Music app) and reading (iBooks app).

In this chapter, we will take a closer look at Apple's iCloud feature that allows users to store, share, and access their data in the cloud, i.e. on an Apple server.

We'll also look at various related services offered by Apple that rely on the use of iCloud.

What is Cloud Computing? 184

iCloud Automatic Data Synchronisation 185

iCloud Drive 186

Family Sharing 187

iTunes Match 191

iCloud Keychain 192

iCloud Photo Sharing 193

iCloud Photo Library 194

What is Cloud Computing?

We mention the Cloud and, more specifically, iCloud, quite a few times in this book. What do these two terms means though?

The Cloud

The Cloud or, to give it its full title, Cloud Computing, is a term that describes the storing and access of data on the Internet rather than on your computer's hard drive – the term 'Cloud' is simply a metaphor for the Internet. It originates from the days when, in flowcharts and presentations, the Internet was represented as a fluffy white cumulus cloud.

Cloud computing does not involve the hard drive on your computer in any way. Also, it has nothing to do with having your own dedicated hardware server – storing and accessing data on a home or office network is not classed as using the Cloud. To be classified as cloud computing, data and programs *must* be accessed on the Internet.

Two well known examples of cloud computing include:

- **Google Drive** – provided by Google, this is a service that lets you do your computing almost entirely on the Internet. The programs, or apps, and the data storage are all online – the only thing you need provide is a means of accessing the service. This can be a computer, tablet or smartphone

- **Amazon Cloud Drive** – very similar to Google Drive, Amazon Cloud Drive provides free online storage up to a limit of 5 GB – any more than that and you have to start paying. You also get free mobile apps that allow you to access your data from any device, anywhere

iCloud

A third example of cloud computing, and one of the best known, is Apple's iCloud service. This started out as a simple online storage and data synchronisation service but has rapidly expanded to provide a host of other related services. These include:

- iCloud Automatic Data Synchronisation
- iCloud Drive
- Family Sharing
- iTunes Match
- iCloud Keychain
- iCloud Photo Sharing
- iCloud Photo Library

We'll now take a closer look at these iCloud services and see what they have to offer to iPad users.

iCloud Automatic Data Synchronisation

We've seen several examples of how you can synchronise various types of data, such as your contacts list, between your computer and the iPad. This is done with the iTunes software and saves you having to laboriously enter the data manually on to the iPad. Thankfully, once you've got your data on the device, keeping it updated is just as easy – this is courtesy of iCloud and is known as automatic data synchronisation.

Once you've set up iCloud on your iPad, auto-synchronisation kicks in immediately. It sends your email, along with your contacts, calendars, reminders, notes, and Safari bookmarks, to its central online server. Photo Stream, too, starts automatically uploading any photos you may have taken.

From the server, it is then sent to all your other iOS devices. So if you also have an iPhone, all the data on the iPad will be accessible on the iPhone. The same thing happens to data created on the iPhone – it is sent to the central server and from there is sent to your iPad and other devices. For example, if you make a note with the Note app on your iPad, you can read, edit or delete it with the Note app on your iPhone.

Before you can use iCloud, it must be set up:

1. Tap the Settings app and, on the left-hand side, tap iCloud

2. If you already have an Apple ID, enter the details and tap Sign In

3. If you don't, tap 'Create a New Apple ID' and follow the prompts

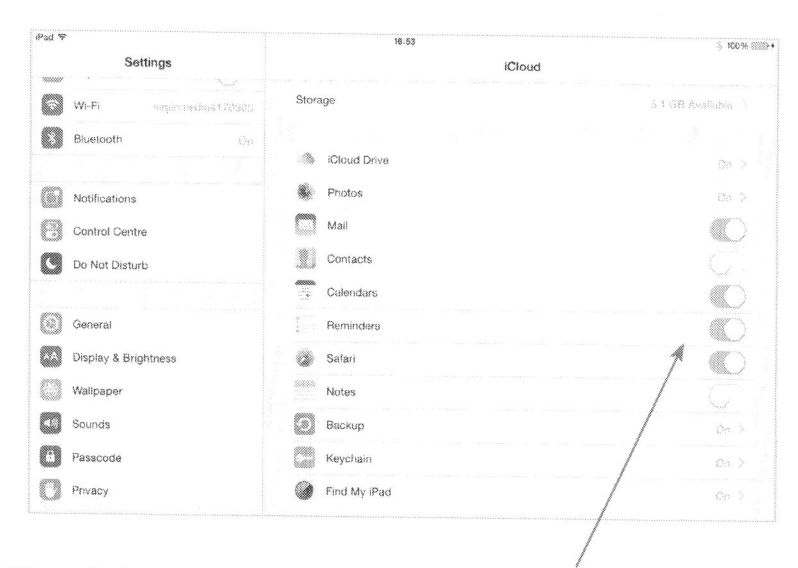

4. If you don't want a particular type of data to be synced, tap the relevant switch to the Off position

iCloud Drive

iCloud Drive is an online storage service that lets you store up to 5 GB of data for free. If you need more than this, paid storage plans are available ranging from 20 GB to 1 TB.

All types of document – presentations, spreadsheets, PDFs, pictures, etc, can be stored on your iCloud Drive. They can be created and accessed on a computer, Mac, iPad, iPhone or iPod Touch.

Things you can do with iCloud Drive include:

- Store and access all your documents in one place from any of your devices
- Keep files and folders up to date across all your devices
- Create new files and folders from iCloud-enabled apps
- Work on the same file across multiple apps. Any changes made to a document on one device automatically appear on all your other devices

If you want to use iCloud Drive with your iPad, you need to switch it on. It can be done by:

1. On the Home screen, tap the Settings app
2. Tap iCloud on the left-hand side
3. Tap iCloud Drive and then tap the iCloud Drive switch to On

Note that any documents that you've already stored in iCloud will now be moved automatically to iCloud Drive. Also, remember to set up iCloud Drive on any other devices you intend to use with it.

To access documents on your iCloud Drive:

1. Using any web browser, go to www.icloud.com and sign in with your Apple ID and password
2. On a Mac running OS X Yosemite, go to iCloud Drive in Finder
3. On a Windows computer running Windows 7 or later, go to File Explorer > iCloud Drive
4. On your iPad, iPhone, or iPod Touch, your documents can be accessed from Apple apps such as Pages, Numbers and Keynote, and any non-Apple apps that support iCloud Drive

Family Sharing

Family Sharing is a feature that makes it possible to share your data with other people – family members being the obvious example. Data that can be shared includes:

- Items purchased from the App Store, such as music, films, books and some types of app
- Pictures and videos
- Your location
- Scheduled events on a family calendar

Setting Up Family Sharing
Before you can use Family Sharing, the feature must be set up and people invited to participate. Do it as described in the following steps:

1. On the Home screen, tap the Settings app

2. Tap iCloud

3. Tap 'Set Up Family Sharing...'

4. Tap Get Started

5. Tap Continue. Note that one person must be in charge of Family Sharing, i.e. organise it, and this will be the person who sets it up. The Family Sharing account will be linked to that persons Apple ID

6. In the next screen, you agree that family members will be able to share iTunes, iBooks and App Store purchases made using your account. If you are happy with this, tap Continue

    If you are not, at the bottom of the screen, you will see an option that allows you to specify a different account from which to share purchases

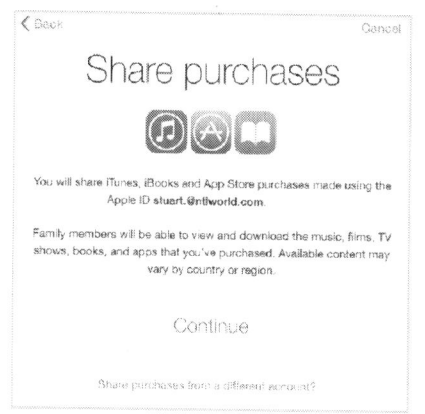

7. You will now see a notice stating that you agree to pay for all purchases initiated by family members with the credit card registered to the specified account. Tap Continue

cont'd

8. You will be asked if you want to share your location with your family. Tap either Share Location or Not Now

9. Family Sharing is now created and you are taken to the Family Members screen in the iCloud section of the Settings App

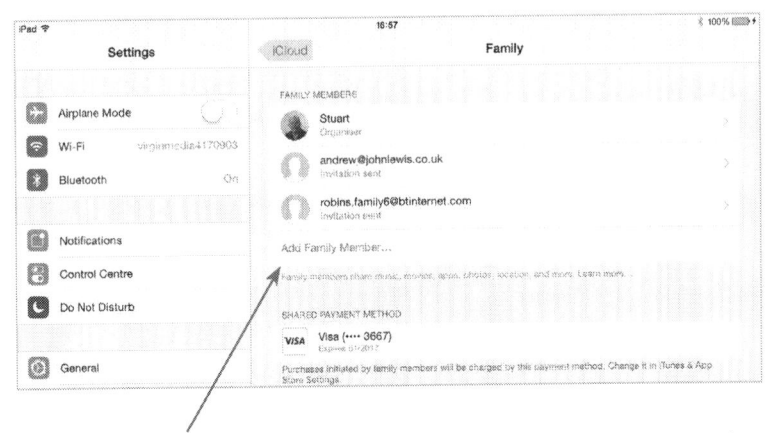

10. Tap 'Add Family Member...'. An email window will open – enter the email address of the person you want to invite and then tap Next to send the invitation. You can invite any number of people in this way

11. You will now see the person you have just invited listed under Family Members. However, he or she will have to accept the invitation before they can take part in Family Sharing

12. Should you ever wish to stop a particular person from participating in Family Sharing, tap their name under Family Members and then tap Remove

Note: to be able to use Family Sharing, invited family members must have an iPad, iPhone or iPod Touch running iOS 8, or a Mac computer running OS X Yosemite.

Sharing Pictures

With Family Sharing set up, you can now start sharing various types of data, one of the most popular of which is pictures. This is easy thanks to the Family photo album that is automatically created within the Photos app when Family Sharing is set up:

1. Open the Photos app

2. Tap the Shared icon at the bottom

3. Tap the Cloud icon to access the Family photo album

cont'd

4. Tap the + button

5. You can now browse through your pictures to select the ones you want to share – just tap each one to be shared. Then tap Done

6. Make sure the Family album is selected as the Shared Album and then tap Post

The selected pictures will now be available for viewing by all members of the Family Sharing group.

Sharing Calendars

When Family Sharing is set up, it also automatically creates a Family calendar that can be used by all members.

1. Tap the Calendar app on the Home screen. Then tap Calendars at the bottom of the screen – you will now see the Family calendar

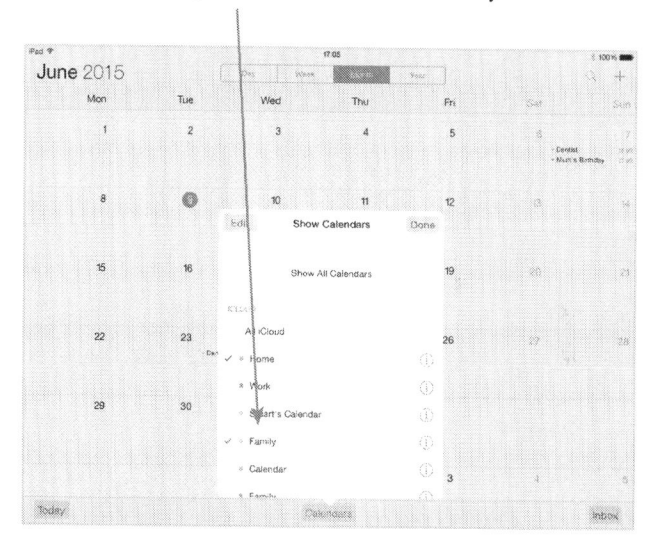

To create an event on the Family calendar:

1. Tap and hold on the desired date

2. Tap Calendar and then select Family Calendar (you may need to hide the keyboard if it is in the way) to make it the active calendar

3. Enter the details for the event

The event will be added to the Family calendar and other members of the Family Sharing group will be sent a notification advising a new event has been posted. It will be visible on the Family calendar on their device.

cont'd

Sharing Music, Books and Films
All members of a Family Sharing group can share purchases from the iTunes Store, the App Store and the iBooks Store:

1. Open the required store – iTunes, App or iBooks

2. Tap the Purchased button at the bottom of the screen

3. Tap My Purchases at the top-left of the screen

4. Tap on a member to see what purchases they have made

5. Tap the buttons at the top of the window to see categorised lists

6. If you want to download an item to your iPad, tap the Cloud icon to the right of it

Sharing Location
Family Sharing also makes it possible to keep track of where your members are. For this to work, however, the other person must have their Apple device switched on and connected to the Internet.

To do it, you need to open the App Store and download the Find My Friends app (just type it into the search box at the top-right). Then open the app and a map will be displayed showing the location of all your family members who happen to be online – very straightforward.

iTunes Match

iTunes Match is a paid subscription service offered by Apple. The basic premise is that it lets you store your entire music collection on the cloud. This includes music you have uploaded to your iPad from your computer and music you have bought from the iTunes Store. As it is located on the cloud, the music can be accessed on all your devices.

How it Works
During the setup procedure, iTunes scans the music tracks on your iPad to see if any of them are available in the iTunes Store. Any tracks that are, i.e. 'match' are automatically uploaded from the store to the cloud. Tracks that aren't in the store are uploaded from the iPad itself. Because the vast majority of your music will be in the store (it contains some 43 million songs), the upload procedure is thus much faster than uploading all the songs from your iPad.

Once uploaded to the cloud, you can listen to your music on an iPhone, iPad, iPod Touch, Mac, PC and Apple TV. There are provisos though:

- iTunes Match is limited to 25,000 songs
- Tracks larger than 200 MB will not be uploaded to iCloud
- Tracks longer than two hours will not be uploaded to iCloud
- Tracks encrypted with Digital Rights Management (DRM) will not be matched or uploaded to iCloud unless your device is authorised for playback of that content

One of the best features of iTunes Match is that the service will automatically upgrade any low-quality music files you have uploadedto a much higher quality level. If you decide to download these high-quality files to your device, they are yours to keep even if you subsequently let your iTunes Match subscription expire.

Setting Up iTunes Match
If you are interested in giving iTunes Match a go on your iPad, you can set it up as detailed below:

1. Tap the Settings app on the Home Screen
2. Scroll down to and tap Music on the left-hand side of the screen
3. Tap 'Subscribe to iTunes Match' on the right
4. You might be asked to validate your billing information. After you've added a valid payment method, tap Subscribe

iCloud Keychain

iCloud Keychain is an Apple password management system. With it, your account names, passwords, and credit card numbers can be safely stored and synced across all your devices. In conjunction with Safari, they can be used to autofill login and credit card number fields.

Setting Up iCloud Keychain
To get started with iCloud Keychain:

1. Open the Settings app

2. Tap iCloud on the left of the screen

3. Tap Keychain on the right and then tap the switch to On

4. You are presented with two options: 'Use 'iCloud Security Code' and 'Create Different Code'. If you select the former, you will be asked to enter the four digit number you use to unlock your iPad.

   If you select the latter, you will be asked to create a different four digit number. In both cases, you will then be asked to specify a phone number that is capable of receiving text messages. Then tap Next – job done

Saving Passwords and Credit Cards
Although it is now activated, you can't use your Keychain yet. You first need to turn on some settings in Safari:

1. Tap the Settings app

2. Scroll down to and tap Safari on the left-hand side of the screen

3. In the General section on the right, tap 'Passwords & Autofill'

4. Tap both 'Names and Passwords' and 'Credit Cards' to On

5. Tap 'Saved Credit Cards' and then enter your iPad passcode when prompted

6. Tap 'Add Credit Card' and then enter the details in the next screen

The next time you go to a password-protected site in Safari and enter the password, you will be offered the option of saving the password so that the next time you visit the site, the password field will be filled in automatically.

The same applies to your credit card – from now on, you will never have to enter the number manually.

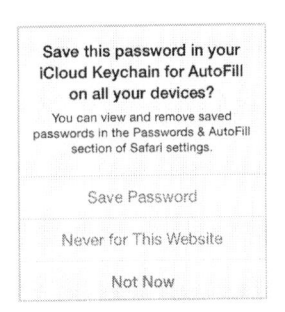

iCloud Photo Sharing

Your iPad's iCloud Photo Sharing feature is designed to not only let you share a designated photo album with your friends, but also to let them add their own pictures to the album.

To set up iCloud Photo Sharing:

1. Tap the Settings app and tap iCloud at the left of the screen

2. Tap Photos on the right and then tap 'iCloud Photo Sharing' to On

3. Close the Settings app and now open the Photos app

4. Tap Shared at the bottom and then tap 'New Shared Album...'

5. Type a name for your shared album and tap Next

6. Enter the email addresses of the people you want to share the album with. If you tap the + button at the right, you can select them from your contacts list

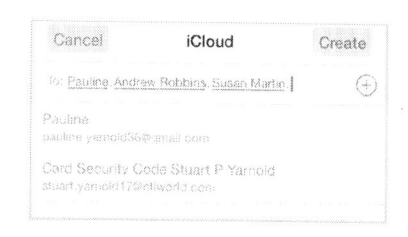

7. Tap Create

8. Open the newly created album and then tap the grey square to open the Moments group in the Photos app

9. Select the pictures and videos you want to share and then tap Done

10. In the pop-up window, type an accompanying note if you want to and then tap Post at the top-right

In the meantime, your invited friends will have received an email containing a 'Subscribe' link. If they click the link, they will be able to view the shared album on their device and add pictures to it themselves.

However, if you'd rather that your friends didn't add their own pictures, you can prevent them from doing so by opening the shared album on your iPad and tapping People at the top-right. This opens an editing screen offering several options.

One of them is 'Subscribers Can Post'. Tap this to Off. Other options let you invite more people to share the album, plus a public website option that lets absolutely anyone view the album.

Pictures and videos stored in Photo Sharing albums do not count with regard to your free 5 GB iCloud data allowance. However, a shared album can hold a maximum of 5000 pictures and videos combined.

iCloud Photo Library

iCloud Photo Library is Apple's latest cloud-based service and its purpose is to move the user's entire photo and video library into the cloud, thus saving space on their iPad and, at the same time, enabling them to seamlessly sync their pictures and videos across all their iOS devices.

When enabled, iCloud Photo Library replaces the Camera Roll and the My Photo Stream album with an All Photos album in the Photos app. It also removes the 30 day restriction on pictures stored in My Photo Stream.

The service uses your free 5 GB iCloud storage space to store the pictures. If your photo collection requires more space than this, you will have to take out a subscription plan.

With this in mind, the iCloud Photo Library service offers a nice feature called Optimise Storage. This helps you make the most of the space on your iPad (or other iOS device) by storing the original high-resolution pictures and videos in iCloud, and keeping optimised low-resolution versions on your device that are also perfectly sized for it.

You can turn on your iCloud Photo Library by:

1. Tapping the Settings app on the Home screen
2. Scrolling down to and tapping Photos & Camera

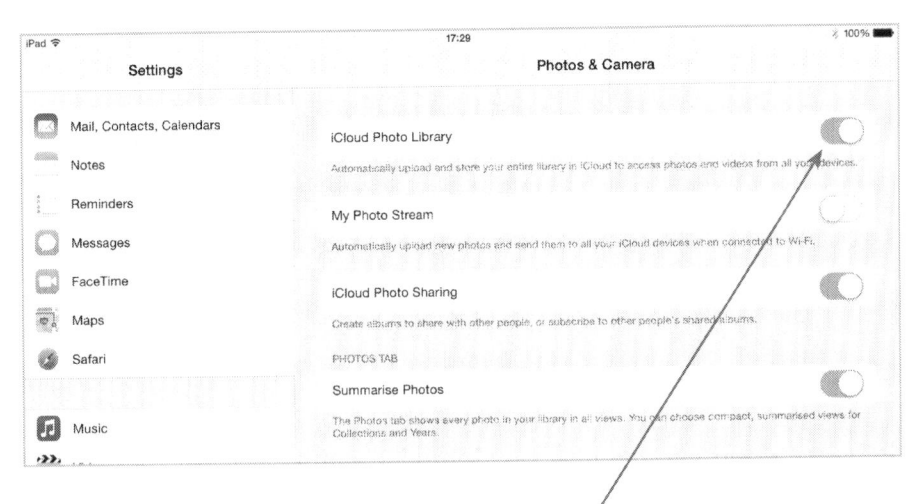

3. Tapping the on/off switch to enable iCloud Photo Library
4. If you want to make use of the Optimise feature to manage your photo library, tap 'Optimise iPad Storage'

CHAPTER 14

Security

If you are like most other users, it won't be long before your iPad is jam-packed with information and data that is either highly personal and thus confidential, or simply too important to lose – indeed, maybe both.

To protect your data, the device provides a number of security features. These include password protection, backing up, and protection controls. In this chapter, we explain how to configure and use these features in order to keep your data safe and secure.

Touch ID & Passcode 196

Content Restriction 198

Backing Up Your iPad 199

Restoring Your iPad 200

Locating & Protecting a Lost iPad 201

Touch ID & Passcode

Your iPad Air 2 comes with fingerprint recognition technology built-in to the Home button. Just touch the button with a finger and your device will be unlocked automatically.

You can also use the feature for making purchases in the App Store, the iTunes Store and the iBooks Store.

Note, however, that a passcode is still required. While Touch ID is designed to minimise the need to use the passcode, it will be required for additional security validation, such as enrolling new fingerprints or making changes in the feature's settings, for example.

Set Up Touch ID
Setting up Touch ID fingerprint recognition is quite a protracted procedure, particularly if you set up more than one finger. To do it:

1. Tap the Settings app

2. On the left-hand side of the screen, tap 'Touch ID & Passcode'

3. On the Enter Passcode screen, specify a four digit number. Confirm the passcode on the next screen

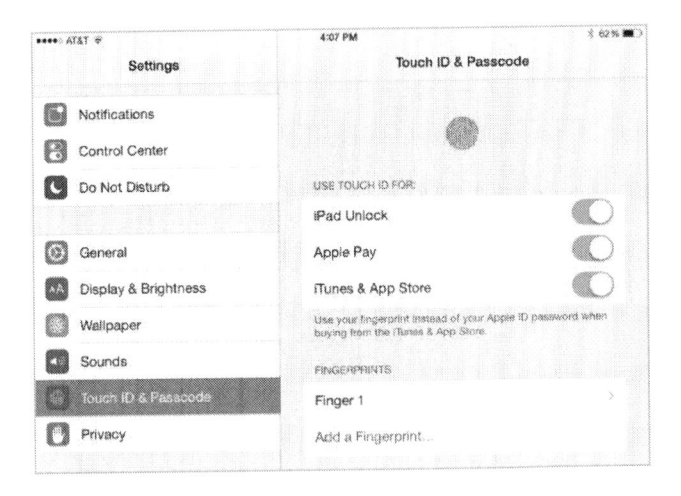

4. Tap 'Add a Fingerprint'

5. Touch the finger you want to use to the Home button and then follow the prompts to scan in your fingerprint

   Repeat this procedure for all fingers you want to use with Touch ID. If other people use it as well and aren't currently available, they can always add their fingerprint later on

cont'd

Using Touch ID to Unlock the iPad

The beauty of Touch ID is that you can unlock your iPad without having to enter a passcode every time. This can be done in two ways:

- Press the Home button to wake your iPad and keep your finger on it

- Press the Sleep/Wake button (at the top-right of the device) to wake your iPad, and then touch the Home button

If Touch ID doesn't recognise your finger, you'll be asked to try again. After five unsuccessful attempts, you'll be asked to enter your passcode. You'll also need to enter your passcode to unlock the iPad in the following situations:

- After restarting the iPad

- When more than 48 hours have elapsed since the last time you unlocked the iPad

- To enter the Touch ID & Passcode settings screen

Using Touch ID for the iTunes, App and iBooks Stores

You can use Touch ID instead of entering your Apple ID password to buy content from the above-mentioned stores.

First though, make sure that iTunes & App Store is turned on in Settings > Touch ID & Passcode. If you can't turn on this setting, you might need to sign in with your Apple ID in Settings > iTunes & App Store.

When done, make purchases with Touch ID by following these steps:

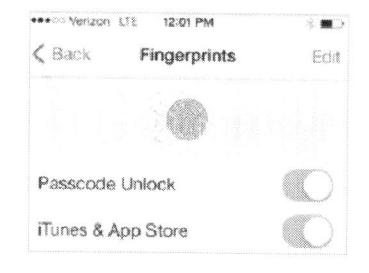

1. Browse to the required item in the store

2. Select the item you wish to purchase. Instead of the Apple ID password prompt, you'll see a Touch ID prompt

3. Touch the Home button with a scanned finger. You'll need to do this for each purchase

If Touch ID doesn't recognize your finger, you'll be asked to try again. After five failed attempts, you'll be given the option to enter your Apple ID password (not the Touch ID passcode, note).

Content Restriction

For many users, it won't really be necessary to lock other people out of their iPad, and so have to go to the bother of setting up Touch ID or using a passcode.

If all you want to do is restrict certain actions and/or access to certain types of data, there is an iPad setting called Restrictions (also known as Parental Controls) that allows you to specify precisely what content can and can't be accessed on your iPad.

It enables you to block apps such as Safari, Camera, and FaceTime, functions such as Siri and AirDrop, and access to the iTunes, iBooks, and App Stores. Content can be blocked by age and rating, as can the ability to make changes to accounts and app settings.

With regard to children, Restrictions provides a way to block access to anything and everything you deem inappropriate for them.

To set up Restrictions:

1. Tap the Settings app and then tap General

2. Scroll down to and tap Restrictions

3. You will notice that the restrictions are greyed-out so they cannot be selected. To make them selectable, tap Enable Restrictions

4. When prompted, enter your passcode and confirm it in the next screen. The restrictions will now be available for selection

The first section, Allow, lets you enable/disable a number of apps by tapping the relevant switch to the On or Off position.

The next section, Allowed Content, lets you specify what types of content can be accessed on the iPad. This includes music, films, and books. You can also set precisely which websites can be accessed.

The 'Privacy' and 'Allow Changes' sections let you prevent unauthorised changes to certain apps and functions.

Backing Up Your iPad

Having configured your iPad to prevent or restrict unauthorised access, you now need to consider the security of your data. This can be compromised in a number of ways – loss of the iPad, accidental deletion, and viruses being typical examples.

The best way of protecting against these scenarios is to make a complete backup of everything on the device. There are two ways to do this: backup to the cloud, i.e. your iCloud account or to your PC. Our recommendation is that you go with the former option as this means you can also restore the backup from the cloud – a connection to a PC is not needed at all.

Backup to the Cloud
This requires you to have an iCloud account. If you don't, set one up as described on page 185. Then:

1. Tap the Settings app and then tap iCloud on the left of the screen

2. Scroll down to and tap Backup

3. Tap the iCloud Backup switch to the On position

4. Enter your enter your Apple password when prompted

5. Tap 'Back Up Now'

Backup to Your Computer
This method requires the use of iTunes which, of course, means you have to connect the iPad to the computer. When you have:

1. Start iTunes

2. At the top-left under the menu bar, click the iPad button

3. On the right, you'll see a Backups section. Here, you'll see options for automatically backing up to iCloud and to This computer

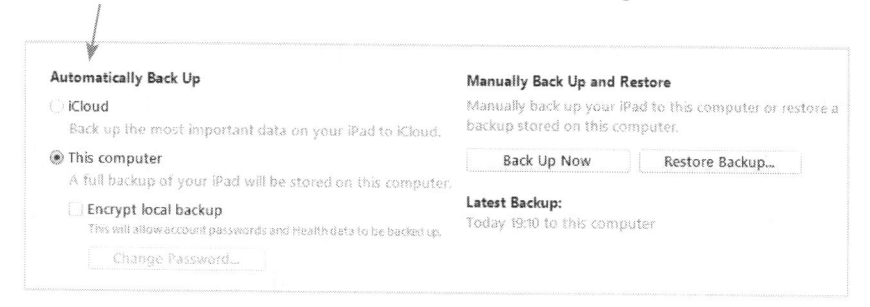

4. Select the This Computer option and then click 'Back Up Now'

Restoring Your iPad

How you go about restoring your iPad from a backup depends on where the backup is located.

Restore From the Cloud
If your backup was done directly from the iPad and saved in the Cloud, the restoration procedure is:

1. Tap the Settings app and then go to General. On the right, scroll down to, and tap, Reset

2. Tap 'Erase All Content And Settings' and then enter your passcode

3. Tap Erase in the pop-up window

4. When the existing data has been deleted, you'll be taken to the setup assistant you saw when first setting up the iPad – tap 'Setup Your Device'

5. Tap 'Restore From a backup'

6. Sign in to iCloud

7. Select the backup you want to use for the restore procedure

Restore From Your Computer
First, connect the iPad to the computer. Having done so, follow the steps below:

1. In iTunes, at the top-left under the menu bar, click the iPad button

2. On the right, you'll see a Backups section. Under 'Manually Backup and Restore', click 'Restore Backup...'

3. In the new window, select a backup to restore from

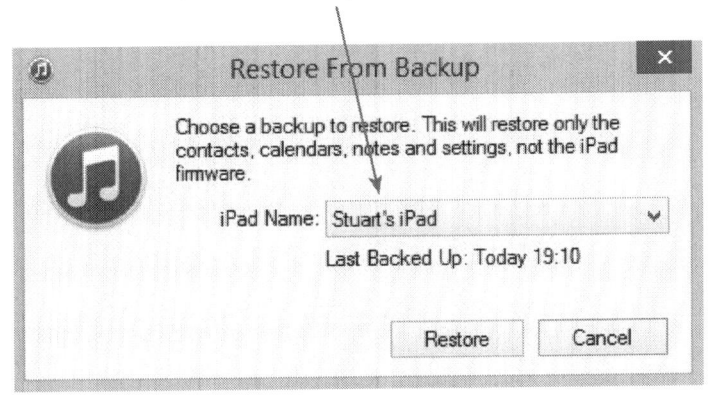

Restore From Backup

Choose a backup to restore. This will restore only the contacts, calendars, notes and settings, not the iPad firmware.

iPad Name: Stuart's iPad

Last Backed Up: Today 19:10

Restore   Cancel

4. Click Restore

Locating & Protecting a Lost iPad

The iPad is a relatively small device and, like all small devices, is easily lost or stolen. As it is quite likely to contain a lot of stuff you'd rather other people didn't see, losing the device can be a bit of a mini crisis.

You may be reassured to know therefore, that should this happen to you there are steps you can take to not only locate the iPad but also to remotely disable it, or even delete everything on it.

The Find My iPhone App

To discover where a missing iPad is located, you need to use an app called Find My iPhone. You will also need the use of an iPhone, a different iPad, or an iPod Touch that has the Find My iPhone app installed on it. If a suitable device isn't available, you can always access the Find My iPhone app on your online iCloud account.

The app works by looking for a signal that the iPad beams out. However, you should be aware that, by default, this signal is turned off. So if you envisage ever having to use Find My iPhone, you must activate the signal on your iPad beforehand:

1. Tap the Settings app

2. On the left of the screen, tap iCloud

3. Tap the 'Find My iPad' switch to the On position

Using the Find My iPhone App to Find a Lost iPad

The steps outlined below will enable you to pinpoint the location of a missing iPad on a map:

1. On another device containing the Find My iPhone app, launch the app – you will be prompted to enter your Apple ID and password

2. The app signs in to your Apple account

3. You'll now see a list of devices the app has found – tap on your missing iPad

4. The app displays the location of your iPad on a map. You can zoom in for a closer look by tapping and spreading your fingers

5. At the bottom of the screen, you'll see see three options: Play Sound, Lost Mode and Erase iPad

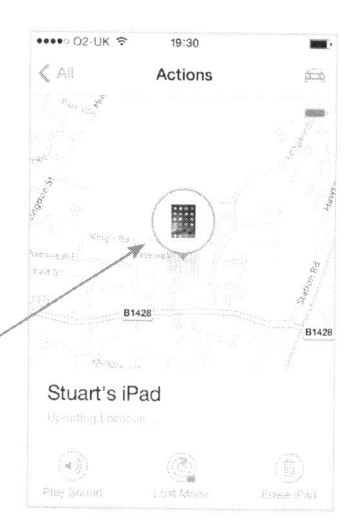

cont'd

- **Play Sound** – if you tap Play Sound, the iPad will play a sound for two minutes, assuming it is switched on and connected to a network. Typically, you'll use this option if you know the device has simply been misplaced

- **Lost Mode** – tap Lost Mode if you want to lock your iPad to prevent unauthorised access. This option also lets you send a phone number where you can be reached to the iPad, plus place a message on it

- **Erase iPad** – the nuclear option to be used when all else has failed. This will remove all data from the iPad

Using the Find My iPhone App on Your iCloud Account

If you don't have another Apple device, you won't be able to use the method outlined above to track and disable your iPad. In this case, you need to go online:

1. Log-in to your iCloud account at www.icloud.com

2. Click Find My iPhone

3. Sign-in with your Apple password

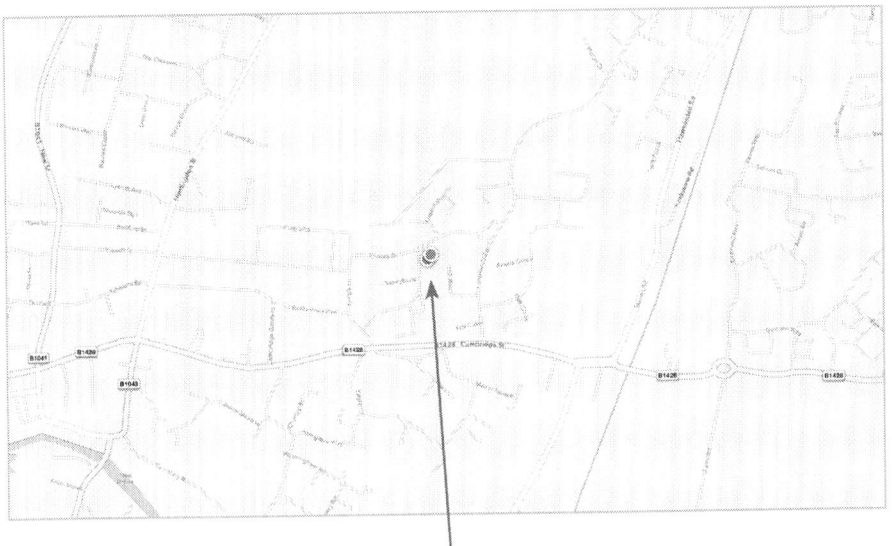

4. A map will open showing the location of your various Apple devices (assuming you have more than one). To see the location of a specific device, select it from the All Devices menu at the top of the screen.

   If you have just one device, that's the one you'll see on the map

CHAPTER 15

Troubleshooting & Maintenance

Your iPad is probably the most reliable computing device you have ever owned. As with all Apple products, it is built to a very high standard. Also, iOS, the operating system that underpins it is a closed platform open only to Apple itself. This means that, unlike Microsoft's Windows and Google's Android operating systems, it is extremely unlikely to be infected with viruses or to suffer problems introduced by poor quality third-party software.

Having said all that, things will go wrong with your iPad occasionally, although they are usually minor issues. In this chapter, we examine problems typically experienced on iPads and also the measures you can take to keep yours running smoothly.

Troubleshooting Techniques 204

Troubleshooting Ancillary Devices 206

Extending Battery Life 207

Updating iOS 8 208

Wi-Fi Connection Issues 209

Managing Storage Space 210

Troubleshooting Techniques

Major problems with iPad's are very rare. Most issues you will have with the device are little more than temporary glitches that can usually be fixed in one of the following ways:

Hard Reset – sometimes an iPad will quite literally 'freeze' and refuse to respond to your touch or to the Home button. This is one of those rare major problems we mentioned above. It's easy enough to resolve, though.

Do it by pressing and holding the Power button and the Home button simultaneously. After about 10 seconds, the screen will go black and then turn white showing the Apple logo – at this point, you can release the buttons. After a few more seconds, the Home screen will appear indicating the reset has been successful.

Reboot the iPad – for the multitude of lesser issues that can occur, absolutely the first thing to try is a reboot, i.e. shut the device down and then restart it. This simple action resets internal mechanisms and settings, and will resolve a whole host of problems.

To do it, press and hold the Power button until you see the 'Slide to Power Off' screen. Drag the slider to commence the shut-down procedure – when it is complete the screen will be completely black. Then restart the iPad by holding the Power button down until you see the Apple logo appear on the screen.

Reset the iPad's Settings – there are hundreds of different settings on your iPad and if any of them become corrupted, a malfunction can occur. Assuming a reboot hasn't fixed the problem, the next thing to try is to reset the iPad to its original settings.

Open the Settings app and tap General on the left of the screen. Then scroll down to, and tap, Reset. Finally, tap 'Reset All Settings'. Be aware that while this should resolve the issue, afterwards you will be faced with the task of setting up your iPad again.

This is one very good reason to make a full backup of your device, which you can subsequently use to restore the settings.

Erase and Restore the iPad – if the problem persists after resetting the settings, things are well and truly snarled up and drastic action is called for. Follow the procedure for resetting the iPad's settings but this time tap 'Erase All Content and Settings'.

This will return the iPad to an 'as new' condition with all your settings, apps and data wiped out – which will not really be what you wanted.

cont'd

However, the problem should also have been wiped out, quite literally, and if you've had the foresight to previously make a backup (as you should always do), then you will then be able to restore your settings, apps and data from the backup.

We explained the procedure for doing this in Chapter 14.

Forcibly Close an App – often the problem will not be the iPad itself but rather one of the apps on it. When an app starts misbehaving, simply shut it down and then restart it. This will usually resolve the issue.

The way to do it is to double-press the Home button to launch the multitasking screen. Here, you'll see large images of all the apps open on the iPad. Locate the one that is misbehaving, place your finger on it and swipe upwards. This action will force it to close. Now restart it.

Delete and Reinstall an App – in the very unlikely event of an app still misbehaving after being shut down and restarted, your only option is to delete and then reinstall it.

To do this, press and hold on the app's icon until it starts to jiggle about. Then tap the X at the top-left of the icon to delete it and tap the Home button to stop the jiggling. Then go the App Store, locate the app and reinstall it.

Update Your iPad & Apps – your iPad's operating system, iOS 8, is prone to unforeseen technical issues – this also applies to the apps that run on the iPad. This is one reason that software manufacturers periodically issue updates – these contain patches to fix problems as and when they come to light.

So, if you are experiencing problems, always check to see if there are any updates available for the iPad, or for a specific app, assuming you suspect that's where the problem lies. We explain how to update your iPad on page 208 and your apps on page 54.

Recharge the iPad – forgive us for stating what will be blindingly obvious to most (but not all!) people – an iPad with a flat battery will not work! If your device shows no signs of life, connect it to the charging dock or a computer.

If it immediately powers up and the Apple logo appears after about 20 seconds or so, then all is well – just leave it to charge up completely – you can still use it in the meantime.

Troubleshooting Ancillary Devices

There is a wide range of ancillary devices that can be connected to an iPad to increase its functionality. These include memory sticks, headsets, adaptors of various kinds, battery chargers, speakers, extension keyboards, plus many more.

Inevitably, there will be occasions when one of these devices doesn't work at all, doesn't work properly, or causes the iPad itself to malfunction. As most of the issues likely to occur have already been experienced by someone else and duly documented, it is quite possible that you will find a solution by doing a Google search.

Or, you try the following:

Connections – yes, we know it sounds obvious, but if a device isn't working at all, absolutely the first thing to check is that it is actually connected. If the problem is intermittent, make sure the connection is sound – try wiggling the cable to see if that makes a difference – if it does, there is a loose connection somewhere.

If other devices are part of the circuit, make sure these are switched on and connected. For example, if you cannot access the Internet on your iPad, check the router and its connections.

Power Cycling – a very well known (and effective) troubleshooting technique, you power-cycle a device by switching it off, waiting about 10 seconds, and then switching it back on again.

This action resets the device and it is very effective at resolving spurious problems. If the device in question doesn't have an on/off switch, unplug it from the power source or remove its batteries.

Duff Batteries – if a battery-powered device hasn't been used for a while and doesn't work, open the battery compartment and check the batteries for leakage. If they have leaked, there is quite likely to be a poor or broken connection to the terminals. It goes without saying, of course, that the batteries won't be any good anyway.

Default Settings – the device may provide a number of configuration settings that allow you to set it up. Check you haven't inadvertently caused the problem yourself through an incorrect setting – do this by using the device's 'Restore default settings' option – most have one.

Firmware – many devices have a tiny internal program that tells the device what to do, and thus controls it. This is known as firmware, and firmware updates are almost always available from the manufacturer. Check to see if one is available; if so, download and install it.

Extending Battery Life

Batteries have their pros and cons – they allow devices to be portable but there are cost and inconvenience factors involved. So it is always worth extending the life of your batteries as much as possible.

With regard to the iPad, these tips will help considerably:

Screen Brightness – your iPad's screen has a voracious appetite for battery power. Reducing its brightness is just about the most effective way to reduce drain on the battery.

Cycling – rechargeable batteries lose their ability to retain a charge over time. A battery that lasts 10 hours when new, may only last 8 hours a year later. You can delay this inevitable decrease in performance by *cycling* the battery periodically. Do it by letting the battery go completely flat and then fully recharging it – this should be done every six weeks or so.

Sleep Mode – if you aren't actually using the iPad, put it to sleep by pressing the Sleep/Wake button. Press the same button again to wake the device.

Networks – Wi-Fi makes regular checks for the presence of Wi-Fi networks. Similarly, if your iPad is equipped with cellular networking, it will constantly be on the look-out for cellular signals.

Bluetooth does the same thing – it is continuously checking for nearby Bluetooth devices. All three types of network place a heavy load on the battery, so turn them off whenever possible.

Mail Check – iPad functions that are constantly active in the background will use battery power constantly. One such function is the Mail app checking the server for new mail. You can restrict the frequency with which it does this by opening the Settings app and tapping Mail, Contacts, Calendars. If you can, deselect the Push option. Also, in the Fetch section, select a longer period or even the Manual option.

Open Apps – the more stuff you have running on your iPad, the more power is needed to keep it all going. Minimise the load placed on the battery by closing all apps that are not being used. Do this by double-tapping the Home button and then swiping upwards on all apps not in use.

Background App Refresh – apps that use Wi-Fi or mobile networks to update their content, make a hit on the battery every time they do so. You can restrict this by going to Settings > General > Background App Refresh. Here, you will see a list of all third-party apps that get their content via a network – turn off as many as you can.

Updating iOS 8

An important part of keeping any computing device in good working order is to check periodically for software updates. This applies particularly to the device's operating system; in the case of the iPad Air 2 – iOS 8.

There are two ways to do this: the first is directly from the iPad and the second is via iTunes. Lets start with the iPad method:

1. Tap the Settings app and go to General > Software Update

2. Tap Software Update and the iPad will check to see if an update is available. If iOS 8 is up to date, you will see a message to this effect

3. If an update is available, you will see a 'Download and Install' link. Tap this and the update will be automatically downloaded and installed

To update your iPad via iTunes:

1. Connect the iPad to your computer and start iTunes

2. In iTunes, click the iPad button at the top-left under the menu bar

3. Click Summary

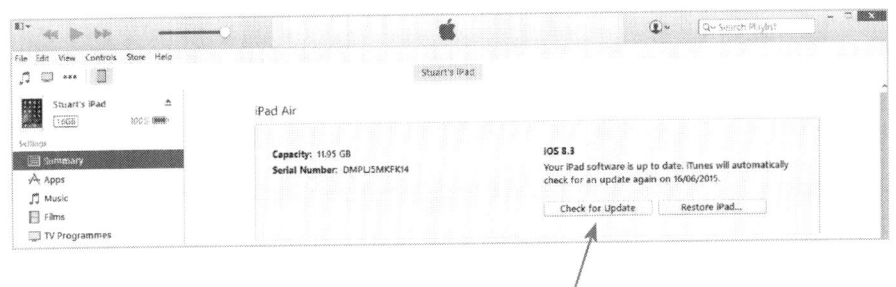

4. On the right of the screen, click 'Check for Update'. iTunes will connect to Apple's servers to see if an update is available; if there is you will see a description of the update

Given that both methods do the job, why would you choose the more long-winded iTunes method? The answer lies with the available amount of storage space on the iPad, and the fact that iOS updates need to be downloaded fully before they can be installed.

This means that if the iPad doesn't have enough storage space for the download, the installation cannot go ahead. Updating via iTunes, however, will download the update to the computer, which will have sufficient storage space thus eliminating this potential problem.

Wi-Fi Connection Issues

Wireless networking is brilliant when it works but when it doesn't, it can be a real head-scratcher trying to work out the cause. This is compounded by the fact the problem might not even be anything to do with the iPad!

Working through the following checklist will usually help:

Check That Wi-Fi is Switched On – there are three settings that can switch your iPad's Wi-Fi off. Access the Control Centre (see page 20) and make sure the Wi-Fi option is on (it is easy to turn this off inadvertently) and that Airplane mode is off.

Then, open the Settings app, tap Wi-Fi on the left of the screen and check that the toggle switch is in the On position.

Connection – is your iPad actually connected to a Wi-Fi network? It is not uncommon for network connections to be dropped for no apparent reason. To check, open the Settings app and at the top-left, you'll see if you are connected or not. If not, tap Wi-Fi and then select a network.

Range – Wi-Fi works over very short distances, typically between 150 and 300 feet depending on the network hardware. If your iPad is further than this from the source of the network, i.e. the router, it won't be able to get a strong enough signal.

The obvious solution is to move closer to the router. For a permanent fix, you can install a Wi-Fi range extender or booster.

Interference – interference from nearby electrical gadgets can cause flaky and unreliable Wi-Fi connections. Check to see if there are any devices operating in close proximity and either turn them off or move them further away.

Router – Wi-Fi signals are produced by routers. There are three issues that can affect these devices: First, the device may be faulty; second, it's firmware may need updating; third, the device may need replacing with a more recent model.

With regard to the latter, the 802.11ac Wi-Fi standard is currently the fastest and offers a speed of up to 1733 Mbps.

Router Lease – when your iPad tries to connect to a Wi-Fi network, the router gives it what's known as a 'DHCP lease' – basically, this allows it to access the network. Spurious connectivity issues can often be resolved by renewing this lease.

Open the Settings app and go to Wi-Fi. Tap the blue Information icon at the right of the network you are using, or attempting to use. Make sure you have selected the DHCP tab and then tap Renew Lease.

Managing Storage Space

One of the iPad's few limitations is the amount of data it can store – this is particularly so with the 16 GB models. However, the limitation is true of all mobile electronic devices, so until data storage technology comes up with a solution, we all just have to make the best of what's available.

To see just how much storage space you have on your iPad:

1. Tap the Settings app

2. Tap General and then tap Usage

3. In the Storage section, you'll see exactly how much of your storage space has been used and how much is still available

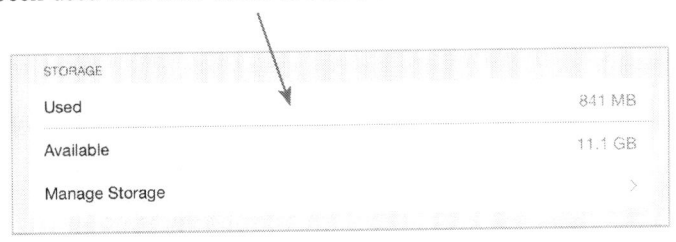

4. Tap Manage Storage to open a list of all the apps installed on the iPad and see how much storage space each is using

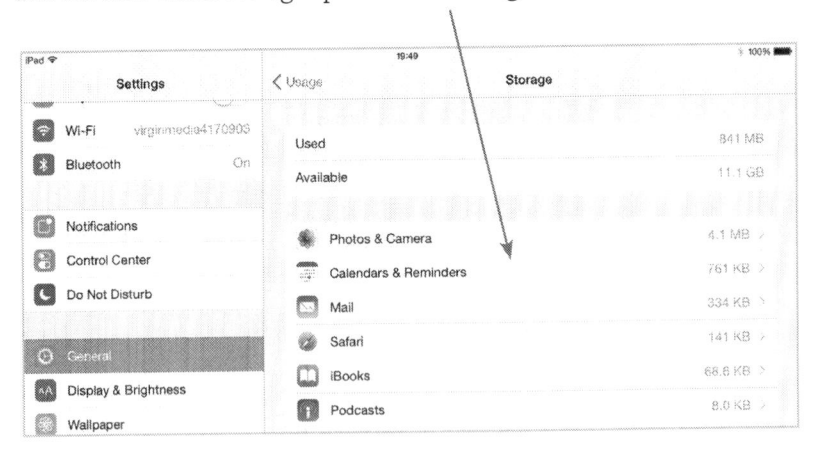

If you need to reclaim some storage space, one option is to delete an app or two. Do it by tapping on the app and then tapping Delete App in the new screen.

If you wish to avoid having to do this, you need to be careful what you put on the iPad. The worst things for using up your storage space are video of any type and high-resolution pictures.

Index

A

Accessibility	44–46
Assistive touch	46
Braille display	44
Hearing aids	45
Invert Colors	44
Larger text	45
Mono audio	45–46
Shortcut	46
Speech	45
Subtitles & captioning	45
Switch control	46
Item scanning	46
Manual selection	46
Point scanning	46
VoiceOver	44
Zoom	44
Ad blocking	86
AirDrop	20, 198
AirPlay	155–156
Peer-to-peer	156
AirPrint	141
Amazon cloud drive	184
Android	14
Apple	
Account	36
Camera connection kit	
SD Card camera reader	133
USB camera adaptor	133
ICloud	184
ID	8
Setting up	37
Logo	9
TV	156
Apps	
Closing completely	19
Definition	48
Deleting	56–57
Managing	55
App Folders	55–56
Moving	55
Opening & closing	56
Pre-installed	48–50
Reinstalling	57
Reviewing & installing	52
Switching between	58
Updating	54
Viewing all open	19
App Store	14, 51, 190, 196
Accessing	51
Browsing	51–52

Audio	
Controlling with Siri	170
Downloading via iCloud	159
Getting on to the iPad	
From the iTunes store	159
Uploading from a PC	158–159
Music app	160
Playing	160–161
Playlists	161–164
Create on the iPad	166–167
Genius Playlist	164
Smart playlist	162–163
Standard playlist	161–162
Using	165–166
Settings	169

B

Baidu	75
Battery	207
Cycling	207
Biometric fingerprint scanner	26
Bluetooth	20, 21, 69–70
Discovering	69–70
Pairing	70
Broadband	60
Browser Apps	
Atomic	86
Dolphin	86
Mercury Browser Pro	86
Opera Mini	86
Puffin	86

C

Calendar	
Accessing	115
Adding events	114
Calendar app	112–113, 115
Creating	115
Default	116
iCloud	115
Multiple	115–116
Setting an alert	117
Viewing	116
Camera	
Camera app	127

211

Controls	127
FaceTime HD	126
Features	128
High dynamic range	127
ISight	126, 144
Video mode features	144
Camera app	142, 145
Time lapse	14
Cellular Data	10
Cellular data plan	63
Charging dock	205
Cloud computing	184
Computer monitor	76
Contacts	106
Adding	106–107
Adding pictures to Contacts app	142
Settings	109–110
Deleting	107–108
Editing	107–108
Finding	108–109
Groups	110–111
Quick access	19
Syncing	110–111
Using	108–109
Using with Siri	111–112
Contacts app	142
Control center	20–21
Accessing	20
Functions	
AirDrop	20
Airplane mode	21
Bluetooth	20
Do not disturb	21
Orientation lock	21
Wi-Fi	20–21
Cursor	33

D

Data roaming	10
Turning off	68
Data roaming charges	10
Data service plan	60
Date & time	
Setting	41
Dictation	32
Digital camera	132
Digital Rights Management (DRM)	191
Downloads manager	86

E

Email	
Apps	
Boxer	104
CloudMagic	104
Dispatch	104
Mail+ for Outlook	104
MyMail	104
Seed Mail	104
Attachment	98
Composing	97
Default account	91
Deleting accounts	92
Disabling accounts	92
Formatting messages	98
Mail app	91, 93, 94, 99, 108–109
Mail server	88
Managing	101
Message folders	101
Thread organization	102
VIPs	101–102
Managing accounts	91–93
Protocols	88
IMAP (Internet Message Access Protocol)	88
POP (Post Office Protocol)	88
Receiving	94–96
Receiving options	
Fetch	96
Manual	96
Push	96
Sending	97–100
Sending attachments	99–100
Sending images	98–99
Services	88
Gmail	88
ICloud	88
Microsoft exchange	88
Yahoo!	88
Setting up an account	89–90
Signatures	100
Switching accounts	93
Syncing an account	90
Using Siri	103
VIP	95
Emoticons	32

F

Facebook	137, 138
FaceTime	13, 36
Family sharing	14
Fast App switcher	12
Favorite apps	17
Find my iPhone	109–110
Flickr	137, 138

G

GameCenter	36
Global Positioning System (GPS)	21, 36
Google	74
Account	86
Google drive	184

H

Handoff	14
HDMI port	155
Headphone	45
Bluetooth	20
Home button	196
Home screen	16–17
Dock bar	17
Navigating between	17
Orientation	17
Landscape mode	17
Portrait mode	17
Resetting	58
Secondary	55
Status bar	17
Activity	17
Battery	17
Network connection	17
Play	17
Rotation lock	17
Time	17
Hotspot	156

I

iBooks app	174–175
Controlling books	179
iBooks Store	
Downloading books	177
Finding Books	176
iCloud	37
Account	202
Automatic data synchronization	185
Drive	14, 186
Family sharing	187–190
Calendars	189
Location	190
Music, books and movies	190
Photo album	188
Photos	188–189
Setting Up	187–188
iTunes Match	169, 191
Keychain	37, 192
My Photo Stream	193
Photo Library	194
Photo sharing	137, 138
Tabs	78
iMessage app	108–109
International data plan	10
Internet	60, 184
Internet Cafe	60
Internet Service Provider (ISP)	62, 89
iPad	
Backing up	38
Cellular data model	60
Controls	
Home button	12
On/off switch	9
Side switch	10
Volume	11
Wake/sleep switch	10
Hardware	
Camera	13
Dual microphones	13
Headphone jack	13
Lightning connector	13
Locking	26
Main screen	17
Managing storage space	210
Naming	38
Setup wizard	8, 36–37
Wi-Fi model	60
iPhone	63
iTunes	90, 132, 136, 148, 158, 173, 190
Store	150, 159

K

Keyboard	29–32
Basics	29–30
Hiding	32
Options	30
Split keyboard	30
Phrase shortcuts	31
Predictive text	14
Third-party	32
Tricks	31–32
Kindle	23, 172, 176

L

Laptop	8
Lightening digital AV adaptor	155
Light sensor	39
Location services	21, 36
Lock screen	20, 22, 25
Auto-lock	25

M

Magnifier	44
Malware	14
Maps	
Current location	124
Getting directions	123
Getting information	124
Live traffic information	124
Tracking	124
Messaging	14
Messaging app	137–138
Microphone	28
Multitasking interface	19, 56
Multi-touch gestures	46
Music app	160, 166
Music controls	12

N

Network	
3G	8, 60, 65
4G	60, 65
HSPA+	65
LTE	65
WiMax	65
Bandwidth	66
Cellular	60
Controlling data usage	67
Setting up	65–66
Tracking data usage	67
Turning off	68
EDGE	65
Local area	36
Speed	66
Wi-Fi	60, 61
Newsstand app	172–173
Notes	121–122
Creating	121
Deleting	122, 124
Editing	121
Formatting	122
Inserting pictures	122
Notes app	121
Notification center	22–24
Notifications	22
Alert	22
Badge	22
Banner	22
Configuring	24
Sound	22

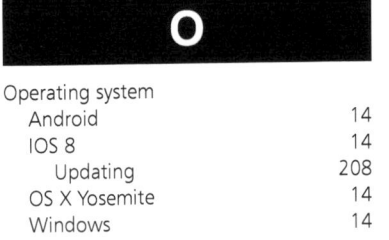

O

Operating system	
Android	14
IOS 8	14
Updating	208
OS X Yosemite	14
Windows	14

P

Parental Controls	198
Passcode	26, 37
Personal hotspot	63
Photos app	14, 129
Camera roll	145, 153
Deleting pictures	136
Editing pictures	139–140
Editing tools	139–140
Moving pictures	135

My Photo Stream	134
Photo albums	131
Sharing pictures	137
Smart groups	129
Uploading photos	132–134
Viewing pictures	130
Printer	
Wireless	84
Printing	141
Privacy	43

R

Radio wave	21
Reminders	118
Deleting	119
Hiding	119
Lists	
Creating	120
Moving/deleting	120
Reminders app	118
Setting a reminder	118
Retina screen	172
Rotor	44
Router	209
Lease	209
Wireless	60, 62

S

Safari	72, 192
Address/search box	73
Autofill	83, 84
Bookmark	
Creating	80
Opening	81
Default search engine	75
Favorites bar	80
Favorites folder	81
History folder	81
History list	83
Navigating	
Links	76
Panning	76
Zooming	76
Navigating a web page	76
Opening a web page	73
Predictive text	73
Private browsing	83

Reader	79
Reading list	82
Searching a web page	74
Searching the Internet	74
Searching with Siri	75
Tabs bar	77
Tabs view	78
Using tabs	77–78
Links	77
Tab button	77
Screen brightness	
Setting	38–39
Screen reader	44
Screen rotation lock	10
Security	
Backing up	
Backup to a PC	199
Backup to the Cloud	199
Backup	
Restoring	200
Content restriction	198
Find My iPhone App	201
Locate a Lost iPad	201–202
Passcode	12
Server	94
Silent mode	10
Siri	12
Activating	28
Skype	60
Sleep mode	10
Sounds	
Alerts/notifications	42
Changing	42
Speaker	
Icon	11
Spotlight search	14, 27
SSID number	62
Standby mode	12

T

Text	
Selecting and moving	33
Selection handle	33
Working with	33
Time zone	41
Touch	85
Touch ID	37
Making purchases with	197
Passcode	196
Setting up	196
Unlocking the iPad	197

Touchscreen	10, 28
Controlling	18
Troubleshooting	
Ancillary devices	206
Techniques	204–205
Erase & Restore	204
Hard Reset	204
Reboot	204
Reset	204
Twitter	137, 138

Commercial	66
Connecting to broadband	62
Connection issues	209
Hotspot	21, 60
Coverage	21
Range extender	209
Set up a connection	61
Set up a tethered connection	63
Turning off	64
Wikipedia	14, 27
Windows	14

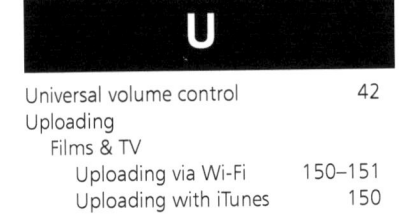

U

Universal volume control	42
Uploading	
Films & TV	
Uploading via Wi-Fi	150–151
Uploading with iTunes	150

Y

Yelp	75

V

VGA port	155
Video	
Editing	147
FaceTime calls	154–155
Format	
H.264	148
Motion JPEG (M-JPEG)	148
MPEG-4	148
Locating	145
Playing	146
Play on a TV	155–156
Recording	145
Uploading to Facebook	153
Virus	14

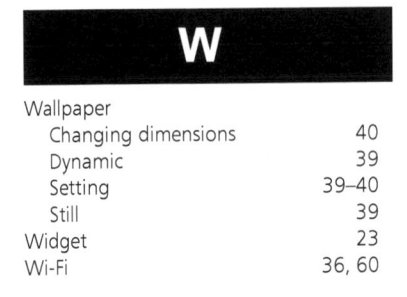

W

Wallpaper	
Changing dimensions	40
Dynamic	39
Setting	39–40
Still	39
Widget	23
Wi-Fi	36, 60

Made in the USA
Lexington, KY
21 November 2015